AMERICAN BUFFET

Favorite Regional Recipes from members of the
General Federation of Women's Clubs
World's largest and oldest women's volunteer service organization

Cover: The historic headquarters of the General Federation of Women's Clubs in Washington, D.C., includes many beautiful antiques, art and serving pieces donated by members from around the country and the world. Some of those objects are pictured throughout this book. Shown on the cover, atop an American Federal mahogany buffet (circa 1850–1860), is a silver epergne, a gift of GFWC Pennsylvania in honor of Louise Brown, GFWC President, 1970–72; a punch bowl and ladle, of Mexican sterling, presented to GFWC by San Antonio, Texas, club members at the 1928 Biennial Convention.

Photo Credits: Richard Rodriguez; Lisa Dugua

This cookbook is a collection of our favorite recipes, which are not necessarily original recipes.

Published by: Favorite Recipes® Press
P.O. Box 305142
Nashville, Tennessee 37230
1-800-358-0560

Library of Congress Number: 93-070636
ISBN: 0-87197-368-5

Printed in the United States of America
First Printing: 1993   50,000 copies

TABLE OF CONTENTS

FOREWORD

American Buffet! What a wonderful title for this cookbook that serves up so tempting a banquet of recipes truly reflecting the delicious diversity of American "home cooking."

American Buffet also is apt because the book has been compiled by an extraordinary group of women, the General Federation of Women's Clubs. For more than 100 years, the Federation's bountiful harvest of members has "cooked up" far more than food to help sustain both the body and soul of America and its richly diverse, ever-changing family structure.

GFWC's menu of long-standing nationwide community service programs and projects dates back to 1890. Very early on it included the foundation and instrumentation of America's Free Library System; and, aptly enough in this instance, at the turn of the century it included crusades that resulted, in 1906, in the passage of the Pure Food and Drugs Act by the U.S. Congress and the subsequent establishment of the U.S. Food and Drug Administration.

American Buffet. How staunchly the title of this book complements and compliments "Unity in Diversity," GFWC's time-honored motto. Both seem to acknowledge with resounding pride America's melting-pot heritage. One invites the world to feast well on American food; the other seems to invite the world to take strength from the history of GFWC, a concept especially heartening as GFWC increasingly expands its principles of community service into new chapters and alliances around the world. Enjoy!

Margaret Adams

Margaret Adams
Senior Editor/National Affairs
Director, The Washington Bureau
Good Housekeeping Magazine

PREFACE

*"The Woman's Club," David Robinson's painting, originally published in **McCall's** magazine to illustrate an article by Dorothy Canfield, hangs in a place of honor at GFWC Headquarters building. Mr. Robinson presented it in honor of the first Nebraska state federation president Flavia Camp Canfield, the writer's mother.*

At the organization meeting of the General Federation of Women's Clubs in 1889, clubwoman Ella Dietz Clymer told the delegates, "We look for unity, but unity in diversity." The aptness of these words that became the Federation's motto is evident in the diverse interests and methods of GFWC members for implementing programs and projects tailored to the needs of their communities. It set the tone for the flexibility that has allowed GFWC to grow and adapt to the lifestyles and concerns of women throughout a century of volunteer work.

State federations began forming almost spontaneously in 1892 and were the first step in securing the kind of local level bond vital to a strong parent organization. With the phenomenal growth of GFWC during its early years, it soon became apparent that another structural change was needed to improve communication between member clubs and the international organization.

Region "councils" or "conferences" were organized over the years that followed—bringing the mission of GFWC

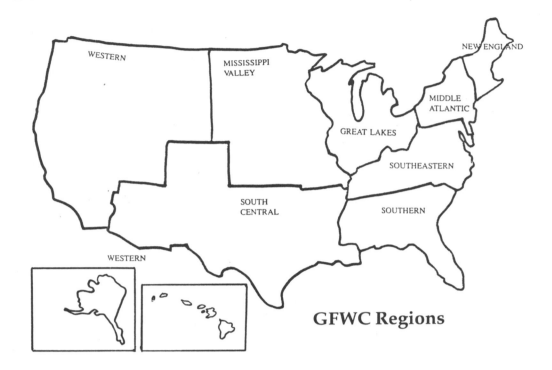

GFWC Regions

even closer to local clubwomen. In 1950, GFWC officially divided the country into four regions and in the ensuing years this number was increased to eight, encompassing all 52 state federations.

GFWC regions hold annual conferences each fall that are attended by GFWC leaders and speakers who promote the Federation's volunteer programs. These meetings not only bridge the gap between local clubs and the national organization, but also allow the individual clubwoman to hone her leadership skills.

Regions tend to be rather informal and relatively autonomous and take enormous pride in the achievements of their member states. Conference attendees welcome the opportunity to share ideas, insights and success stories regarding their community service work and fund-raising projects.

Today, the 350,000 GFWC members who live in the eight regions of our country are business owners, teachers, elected officials, homemakers, corporate executives, college students and retirees—a more diverse group than at any other time in our history. When considering a new GFWC cookbook, this diversity became, by unanimous vote, the obvious theme. Such a book would have something for everyone.

While there are wonderful regional specialties throughout these pages, there also are countless other foods reflecting certain regional variations that are enjoyed nationwide. In reviewing the recipes and making final selections, the cookbook committee discovered that there are many tastes in common in America—no matter where a person is from. In other words, "unity in diversity" is alive and well in the kitchen as well as in the clubhouse.

A BRIEF HISTORY OF THE GENERAL FEDERATION OF WOMEN'S CLUBS

The General Federation of Women's Clubs traces its roots back to Jane Cunningham Croly, an accomplished New York newspaperwoman, who wrote under the pen name of Jennie June. Indignant that she and other women were denied admittance to a banquet honoring Charles Dickens in 1868 at the all-male New York Press Club simply because they were women, she determined to organize a club for women only. The name chosen for this club was Sorosis, a Greek word meaning "an aggregation; a sweet flavor of many fruits." Although its founders originally supposed they were starting a new movement, they became aware over the years of the existence of other women's clubs that had formed independently to meet the needs of women in the expanding country.

As Sorosis approached its 21st year, Mrs. Croly proposed a conference in New York that brought together delegates from 61 women's clubs. On the last day of the conference, the women took action to form a permanent organization. A committee to draft a constitution and plan of organization to be ratified the following year was chosen, with Sorosis President Ella Dietz Clymer as chairman. The constitution was adopted in 1890, and the General Federation of Women's Clubs was born. It was chartered in 1901 by the U.S. Congress.

At first, women's clubs joined the General Federation directly, but they later came into membership through state federations, which began forming in 1892. GFWC also counts international clubs among its members. Although women's clubs were founded primarily as a means of self-education and development for women, gradually the emphasis of most local clubs changed to one of community

Bookmobiles, such as the one above funded by the New Hampshire Federation, were effectively used by women's clubs to promote education in communities around the country. GFWC is credited by the American Library Association with founding seventy-five percent of America's public libraries.

service and improvement. GFWC's programmatic areas of activity include the arts, conservation, education, home life, international affairs, and public affairs, as well as various special projects. The Federation also has a distinguished record of legislative activity on issues of historical importance, beginning with the establishment of a national model for juvenile courts and service in the forefront of the conservation movement resulting in the establishment of the first Forest Reserve in 1899. In the early 1900s, GFWC turned the tide for passage of the Pure Food and Drugs Act, and supported legislation for

Federated clubwomen's "Buy a Bomber" bond campaign during World War II raised over $1 million. Forty-seven state federations sold enough bonds to buy one or more bombers. Many of these planes carried the names of GFWC federations and clubs.

the eight-hour workday and the first child labor law. And, as early as 1944, GFWC endorsed a resolution supporting equal rights and responsibilities for women.

In 1922, the General Federation purchased a five-story brick and stone mansion in Washington, D.C. for its headquarters. Located at 1734 N Street, N.W., the building has an interesting history and retains much of its original character and elegance. Today the building provides office space for a professional staff that works with clubwomen to administer programs and services for the organization, and also is the residence of the GFWC International President during her term of office. The building was named a National Historic Landmark in 1991.

The small banding together of existing clubs which began in 1890 has grown into the largest organization of women volunteers in the world. GFWC now numbers nearly 350,000 members in 8,500 clubs across the United States, with additional millions of members in over 30 countries.

GFWC Headquarters in the nation's capital, a five story stone and brick mansion at 1734 N Street, N.W., was built in 1875 by Rear Admiral William Radford. It was designated a National Historic Landmark by the Secretary of the Interior in 1991. Less than five percent of women's history sites carry National Historic Landmark designation.

APPETIZERS, SOUPS & SALADS

This Chickering walnut baby
grand piano, presented by the
GFWC Music Clubs in 1922, is in
the music room on the second
floor of Headquarters. The
Herschede mahogany grandfather
clock was a gift of the
Connecticut Federation of
Women's Clubs.

FALL APPLE DIP

8 ounces cream cheese, softened
3/4 cup packed brown sugar
1 teaspoon vanilla extract

1 cup chopped salted peanuts
3 golden Delicious apples, sliced
1/2 cup orange juice

- Combine cream cheese, brown sugar and vanilla in bowl; mix until smooth. Sprinkle with peanuts. Dip apple slices in orange juice; arrange around dip.
- Yield: 8 servings.

Approx Per Serving: Cal 318; Prot 6 g; Carbo 38 g; Fiber 3 g; T Fat 17 g; 47% Calories from Fat; Chol 31 mg; Sod 160 mg.

*Cindy Reed, **Southeastern Region***
GFWC—Waynesboro Junior Woman's Club, Waynesboro VA

CHEESY ARTICHOKE AND CHILI DIP

1 14-ounce can artichoke hearts
1 4-ounce can chopped green chilies
1 4-ounce can chopped black olives

1 cup mayonnaise
1 cup grated Parmesan cheese
1 cup shredded Cheddar cheese

- Drain and chop artichokes. Mix with remaining ingredients except Cheddar cheese in bowl. Spoon into 10-inch quiche pan; sprinkle with Cheddar cheese.
- Bake at 350 degrees for 20 minutes. Serve with tortilla chips.
- Yield: 12 servings.

Approx Per Serving: Cal 230; Prot 6 g; Carbo 3 g; Fiber <1 g; T Fat 22 g; 84% Calories from Fat; Chol 26 mg; Sod 509 mg.

*Diane Ebner, **South Central Region***
GFWC—Centennial Woman's Club, Phoenix AZ

BLACK-EYED PEA DIP

2 cups cooked black-eyed peas
1/2 cup melted margarine
1 large jalapeño pepper
1/2 teaspoon jalapeño pepper juice

1 medium onion, chopped
1 clove of garlic
1 cup shredded Cheddar cheese
3/4 to 1 cup milk

- Process peas, margarine, pepper, pepper juice, onion and garlic in blender until smooth. Combine with cheese and 3/4 cup milk in saucepan.
- Heat until cheese melts, adding additional milk as needed for desired consistency. Serve hot or cold with chips or crackers.
- Yield: 16 servings.

Approx Per Serving: Cal 115; Prot 4 g; Carbo 6 g; Fiber 2 g; T Fat 9 g; 67% Calories from Fat; Chol 10 mg; Sod 118 mg.

*Mrs. E. P. Storie, **South Central Region***
GFWC—1933 Study Club, Jefferson TX

CAPONATA

1 medium eggplant, cubed
½ cup olive oil
1 medium onion, chopped
1   16-ounce can tomatoes, crushed
1 cup chopped celery

2 ounces capers, rinsed, drained
¼ cup wine vinegar
2 tablespoons sugar
Salt and pepper to taste

- Sauté eggplant in hot olive oil in skillet for 10 minutes or until very tender; remove with slotted spoon. Add onion to drippings in skillet.
- Sauté for 3 minutes. Add tomatoes and celery. Simmer for 15 minutes. Stir in capers and eggplant.
- Combine vinegar, sugar, salt and pepper in saucepan. Heat until sugar dissolves, stirring constantly. Add to eggplant mixture.
- Simmer, covered, over very low heat for 20 minutes, stirring occasionally. Cool to room temperature. Serve with crackers or bread.
- Yield: 24 servings.

Approx Per Serving: Cal 54; Prot <1 g; Carbo 4 g; Fiber 1 g; T Fat 5 g; 72% Calories from Fat; Chol 0 mg; Sod 36 mg.

Gloria Andriuolo, **Middle Atlantic Region**
GFWC—Contemporary Woman's Club, Westwood NJ

ALASKAN KING CRAB DIP

16 ounces cream cheese
3 tablespoons horseradish
3 tablespoons Worcestershire sauce
3 tablespoons mayonnaise
½ cup finely chopped onion

Salt and pepper to taste
¼ cup (about) evaporated milk
1 cup minced cooked King crab meat
Paprika to taste

- Combine cream cheese, horseradish, Worcestershire sauce, mayonnaise, onion, salt, pepper and evaporated milk in blender container. Process until smooth.
- Combine with crab meat in bowl; mix gently. Spoon into four 4-ounce ovenproof bowls; sprinkle with paprika.
- Bake at 350 degrees for 15 minutes or microwave on High for 6 minutes. Serve with crackers or chips.
- May substitute other seafood for crab meat or omit horseradish. May reheat dip if necessary.
- Yield: 16 servings.

Approx Per Serving: Cal 136; Prot 4 g; Carbo 2 g; Fiber <1 g; T Fat 12 g; 81% Calories from Fat; Chol 42 mg; Sod 156 mg.

Dawn L. Warren, **Western Region**
GFWC—Anchorage Woman's Club, Anchorage AK

MEXICAN GALA LAYERED DIP

1 32-ounce can chili without beans
3 ounces cream cheese
1 16-ounce can refried beans
1 4-ounce can chopped green chilies
2 cups sour cream
1/2 teaspoon each cumin, chili powder
   and minced garlic
2 cups shredded Cheddar cheese

1 8-ounce can sliced black olives,
   drained
1 cup sliced green onions
1 avocado, chopped
1 tablespoon lemon juice
1 tomato, chopped
1 8-ounce package tortilla chips

- Heat chili and cream cheese in saucepan until cream cheese melts, stirring to blend well. Cool to room temperature.
- Layer refried beans, green chilies and chili mixture in 9x13-inch baking dish.
- Blend sour cream, cumin, chili powder and garlic in bowl. Spread half the mixture over layers in dish.
- Sprinkle with half the cheese, olives and green onions.
- Toss avocado with lemon juice in bowl; sprinkle over top.
- Add layers of remaining sour cream mixture, remaining olives, remaining green onions and tomato. Chill overnight.
- Bake at 350 degrees for 30 minutes. Tuck some of the tortilla chips around edge of baking dish; serve remaining chips in basket.
- Yield: 12 servings.

Approx Per Serving: Cal 516; Prot 16 g; Carbo 28 g; Fiber 7 g; T Fat 40 g;
67% Calories from Fat; Chol 45 mg; Sod 1115 mg.

*Jean Gore Barton, **South Central Region***
GFWC—Woman's Club of Colorado Springs, Colorado Springs CO

PUMPKIN DIP

16 ounces cream cheese, softened
4 cups confectioners' sugar
1 30-ounce can pumpkin pie filling

2 teaspoons cinnamon
1 teaspoon ginger

- Beat cream cheese and confectioners' sugar in mixer bowl until light and fluffy.
- Add pumpkin, cinnamon and ginger; mix well. Spoon into serving bowl.
- Chill until serving time. Serve with gingersnaps.
- Yield: 30 servings.

Approx Per Serving: Cal 141; Prot 1 g; Carbo 23 g; Fiber <1 g; T Fat 5 g;
33% Calories from Fat; Chol 17 mg; Sod 53 mg.

*Marie B. Pugh, **Southeastern Region***
GFWC—Randleman Woman's Club, Sophia NC

Scrambled Egg Dip

1 tablespoon margarine
3 tablespoons vinegar
3 tablespoons sugar
3 eggs, beaten

8 ounces cream cheese, chopped
4 green onions, chopped
8 to 10 green olives, sliced

- Melt margarine in skillet. Stir in vinegar and sugar. Add eggs.
- Cook until soft-set, stirring constantly. Stir in cream cheese; remove from heat.
- Add green onions and olives; mix well. Spoon into serving bowl.
- Chill until serving time. Serve with crackers or party rye bread.
- May use egg substitute if preferred.
- Yield: 12 servings.

Approx Per Serving: Cal 111; Prot 3 g; Carbo 4 g; Fiber <1 g; T Fat 9 g;
74% Calories from Fat; Chol 74 mg; Sod 163 mg.

*Mary L. Ungs-Sogaard, **Mississippi Valley Region***
GFWC—Dyersville Federated Woman's Club, Dyersville IA

Casa Pecan Spread

8 ounces cream cheese, softened
2 teaspoons milk
1 2-ounce jar sliced dried beef,
   shredded
2 tablespoons dried onion flakes
1/4 cup chopped green chilies

1/2 teaspoon garlic salt
1/2 teaspoon salt
1/2 teaspoon pepper
1/2 cup sour cream
1/2 cup chopped pecans
1 tablespoon margarine

- Blend cream cheese and milk in mixer bowl. Stir in dried beef, onion flakes, green chilies, garlic salt, salt and pepper. Fold in sour cream.
- Spoon into 8-inch baking dish.
- Sauté pecans in margarine in skillet. Sprinkle over cream cheese mixture.
- Bake at 350 degrees for 20 minutes. Serve hot with crackers.
- May prepare in advance and chill overnight before baking.
- Yield: 8 servings.

Approx Per Serving: Cal 208; Prot 5 g; Carbo 4 g; Fiber 1 g; T Fat 19 g;
83% Calories from Fat; Chol 49 mg; Sod 633 mg.

*Sharlene Glock, **South Central Region***
GFWC—Las Cruces Progress Club, Las Cruces NM

1848—Ladies Physiological Society of Boston formed. It is the oldest continuously active federated woman's club in the United States.

JOSÉ'S SALSA

6 small tomatoes, seeded, chopped
1¹/₂ cups chopped green onions
1 medium green bell pepper, chopped
4 cloves of garlic, chopped

4 hot chili peppers, chopped
1¹/₄ cups chopped cilantro
1 teaspoon cayenne pepper

- Combine all ingredients in blender container.
- Process on low speed until coarsely chopped, stirring occasionally.
- Chill in airtight container overnight.
- Yield: 16 servings.

Approx Per Serving: Cal 18; Prot 1 g; Carbo 4 g; Fiber 1 g; T Fat <1 g;
7% Calories from Fat; Chol 0 mg; Sod 6 mg.

Dorothy Schumacher, **Western Region**
GFWC—We & Our Neighbors Club, San José CA

CALIFORNIA GARDEN

16 ounces cream cheese, softened
¹/₂ cup sour cream
3 tablespoons mayonnaise
¹/₄ cup margarine, softened
¹/₄ cup sugar
2 tablespoons golden raisins
2 tablespoons slivered almonds,
   lightly toasted

¹/₂ teaspoon basil
¹/₄ teaspoon oregano
¹/₄ teaspoon parsley flakes
¹/₈ teaspoon Tabasco sauce
1¹/₂ teaspoons garlic salt
¹/₃ cup grated Parmesan cheese
³/₄ teaspoon onion salt
1 teaspoon Worcestershire sauce

- Combine cream cheese, sour cream and mayonnaise in bowl; mix until smooth.
- **California Raisin Spread:** Combine ²/₃ cup cream cheese mixture with margarine, sugar, raisins and almonds in bowl; mix well. Spoon into new 3-inch clay pot; insert plastic flower in pot. Garnish with additional raisins.
- **Valley Green Spread:** Combine 1 cup cream cheese mixture with basil, oregano, parsley flakes, Tabasco sauce and garlic salt in bowl; mix well. Spoon into clay pot; insert plastic flower. Garnish with salad herbs.
- **Desert Sand Spread:** Combine 1 cup cream cheese mixture with Parmesan cheese, onion salt and Worcestershire sauce in bowl; mix well. Spoon into clay pot; insert plastic flower. Garnish with additional Parmesan cheese.
- Presentation: Arrange pots on serving tray. Arrange assorted crackers around pots. May add cut-outs of cactus, California raisins and "valley girls" if desired.
- May serve spreads individually if preferred. Serve California Raisin Spread with fruit slices and crackers; serve Valley Green Spread with carrot sticks; serve Desert Sand Spread with crackers and wedges of red apple.
- Yield: 12 servings.

Approx Per Serving: Cal 252; Prot 4 g; Carbo 8 g; Fiber <1 g; T Fat 23 g;
81% Calories from Fat; Chol 49 mg; Sod 583 mg.

Merillyn Jacobsen, **Western Region**
GFWC—Westlake Women's Club, Westlake Village CA

MUSHROOM PATÉ

1/3 cup minced onion
1/3 cup finely chopped celery
1/4 cup margarine
2 eggs
8 ounces cream cheese, softened
3/4 cup fine dry Italian bread crumbs

1/2 teaspoon basil
1/4 teaspoon rosemary
1/4 teaspoon oregano
1/8 teaspoon pepper
3 cups chopped mushrooms

- Sauté onion and celery in margarine in skillet until tender.
- Combine eggs and cream cheese in food processor container; process until smooth. Add bread crumbs, sautéed mixture, basil, rosemary, oregano and pepper; process until smooth.
- Add mushrooms; process until smooth. Pack into greased 4x8-inch loaf pan.
- Bake, covered with foil, at 400 degrees for 1 1/2 hours. Cool to lukewarm. Invert onto serving plate. Serve with crackers.
- Yield: 16 servings.

Approx Per Serving: Cal 109; Prot 3 g; Carbo 5 g; Fiber 1 g; T Fat 9 g;
64% Calories from Fat; Chol 42 mg; Sod 88 mg.

Joyce E. Duffy, ***Middle Atlantic Region***
GFWC—Cranberry Women's Club, Mars PA

OYSTER ROLLS

8 ounces cream cheese, softened
3 tablespoons sour cream
1 teaspoon Worcestershire sauce
1/2 teaspoon chili powder
1 teaspoon curry powder
1/2 cup chopped pecans

1 7-ounce can smoked oysters,
    drained, chopped
2 tablespoons chopped parsley
1/2 cup chopped pecans
Paprika to taste

- Combine cream cheese, sour cream, Worcestershire sauce, chili powder and curry powder in bowl; mix well.
- Shape into 2 rectangles on waxed paper.
- Combine 1/2 cup pecans, oysters and parsley in bowl; mix well. Spread over cheese rectangles.
- Roll up cheese to enclose filling. Wrap in waxed paper.
- Chill for 24 hours. Coat with mixture of 1/2 cup pecans and paprika.
- Yield: 8 servings.

Approx Per Serving: Cal 210; Prot 3 g; Carbo 4 g; Fiber 1 g; T Fat 21 g;
87% Calories from Fat; Chol 33 mg; Sod 93 mg.

Lorraine L. Ash, ***Southeastern Region***
GFWC—Ocean Park Woman's Club, Virginia Beach VA

WATERCRESS CHEESE SPREAD

1 bunch fresh watercress
8 ounces cream cheese, softened
1 cup mayonnaise-type salad dressing
2 tablespoons dry onion flakes

1 teaspoon lemon pepper
1/2 teaspoon sugar
Salt to taste

- Chop watercress into 1/2-inch pieces, discarding larger stems.
- Beat cream cheese in mixer bowl until light. Beat in salad dressing, onion flakes, lemon pepper and sugar.
- Stir in watercress and salt.
- Chill until serving time. Serve with pumpernickel bread. May store in refrigerator for up to 1 week.
- Yield: 12 servings.

Approx Per Serving: Cal 145; Prot 2 g; Carbo 6 g; Fiber <1 g; T Fat 13 g;
80% Calories from Fat; Chol 26 mg; Sod 264 mg.

Betty M. Holmes, **Southeastern Region**
GFWC—McLean Women's Club, McLean VA

CHICKEN PUFFS

1/4 cup water
2 tablespoons butter
1/4 cup flour
Salt to taste
1 egg
1/4 cup shredded Swiss cheese

2 cups finely chopped cooked chicken
1/4 cup finely chopped celery
2 tablespoons chopped pimento
2 tablespoons dry white wine
1/4 cup mayonnaise

- Bring water and butter to a boil in saucepan. Stir in flour and salt all at once. Cook until mixture forms ball, stirring constantly. Cool slightly.
- Beat in egg until smooth. Stir in cheese. Drop by level teaspoonfuls onto greased baking sheet.
- Bake at 400 degrees for 20 minutes. Cool on wire rack.
- Combine chicken, celery, pimento, wine and mayonnaise in bowl; mix well.
- Split pastry puffs. Fill with chicken mixture.
- Yield: 8 servings.

Approx Per Serving: Cal 183; Prot 13 g; Carbo 4 g; Fiber <1 g; T Fat 13 g;
64% Calories from Fat; Chol 73 mg; Sod 115 mg.

Muriel Strub Pierce, **Southeastern Region**
GFWC—Woman's Club of Falls Church, Falls Church VA

CLAM CRISPS

3 tablespoons finely chopped onion
1 tablespoon butter
5 teaspoons flour
1 cup minced clams
1/2 cup clam liquid

1/4 teaspoon Worcestershire sauce
1/4 teaspoon garlic powder
12 slices bread, crusts trimmed
3 tablespoons butter, softened
1 tablespoon melted butter

- Sauté onion in 1 tablespoon butter until tender. Stir in flour. Add clams, clam liquid, Worcestershire sauce and garlic powder.
- Cook for 2 minutes or until thickened, stirring constantly. Cool to room temperature.
- Flatten bread with rolling pin. Spread lightly with softened butter. Spread with clam mixture.
- Roll up bread to enclose filling; secure with wooden picks. Brush with melted butter; cut into halves. Place on baking sheet.
- Bake at 425 degrees for 8 to 10 minutes or until golden brown. Serve hot.
- Yield: 24 servings.

Approx Per Serving: Cal 52; Prot 1 g; Carbo 5 g; Fiber <1 g; T Fat 3 g;
51% Calories from Fat; Chol 9 mg; Sod 84 mg.

Gerda I. Naveira, **Middle Atlantic Region**
GFWC—Great Bay Woman's Club, Tuckerton NJ

MINIATURE CRAB CAKES

1 egg, beaten
1 tablespoon mayonnaise
1/2 teaspoon lemon juice
1 tablespoon melted butter
2 slices white bread, crumbled
2 tablespoons finely chopped parsley

1 teaspoon dry mustard
1/2 teaspoon Worcestershire sauce
Salt and pepper to taste
1 pound cooked fresh crab meat
2 tablespoons oil

- Combine first 10 ingredients in bowl; mix well. Add crab meat; mix gently. Shape into 24 small crab cakes.
- Brown in oil in skillet for 5 minutes on each side. Serve with cocktail sauce or tartar sauce.
- Yield: 24 servings.

Approx Per Serving: Cal 48; Prot 4 g; Carbo 1 g; Fiber <1 g; T Fat 3 g;
53% Calories from Fat; Chol 29 mg; Sod 76 mg.

Mearlene White, **Southeastern Region**
GFWC—Woman's Club of Potomac, Darnestown MD

CRAB STRUDELS

½ cup chopped shallots
½ cup butter
1 cup dry vermouth
2 6-ounce cans crab meat, flaked
4 ounces cream cheese, chopped
¼ cup chopped parsley

4 egg yolks
1 teaspoon salt
½ teaspoon pepper
8 frozen phyllo sheets, thawed
½ cup melted butter
1 egg, beaten

▪ Sauté shallots in ½ cup butter in 10-inch skillet for 3 minutes or until golden brown. Stir in vermouth. Bring to a boil. Cook for 3 to 5 minutes or until liquid is reduced by ½; remove from heat. Add crab meat, cream cheese, parsley, egg yolks, salt and pepper, stirring until cream cheese melts; cool.
▪ Layer 4 phyllo sheets on kitchen towel, brushing each sheet with melted butter. Spoon half the crab mixture lengthwise onto sheets, leaving 2-inch edges on long sides. Roll from long side to enclose filling. Place on greased 10x15-inch baking sheet. Repeat with remaining ingredients. Brush with melted butter and beaten egg.
▪ Bake at 350 degrees for 15 minutes. Increase oven temperature to 450 degrees. Bake for 5 to 10 minutes longer or until strudels are crisp and brown.
▪ Cut each strudel crosswise into 12 slices. Serve warm, garnished with parsley sprigs and lemon wedges.
▪ Yield: 24 servings.

Approx Per Serving: Cal 147; Prot 5 g; Carbo 6 g; Fiber <1 g; T Fat 11 g;
69% Calories from Fat; Chol 83 mg; Sod 246 mg.

Mrs. Richard Locaitis, **Middle Atlantic Region**
GFWC—Perry Highland Junior Woman's Club, Pittsburgh PA

MICHIGAN PARTY CHEESE BAKE

4 cups cracker crumbs
1 cup melted butter
½ teaspoon curry powder
2 cups chopped sweet onions
Salt to taste
1½ cups shredded Cheddar cheese

3 cups milk, scalded
3 eggs, slightly beaten
1 teaspoon salt
Red pepper to taste
¾ cup grated Parmesan cheese
1 teaspoon paprika

▪ Mix cracker crumbs with melted butter and curry powder in bowl. Press ¾ of the mixture into 11x16-inch baking pan.
▪ Spread onions over crumb mixture; sprinkle with salt to taste and Cheddar cheese.
▪ Combine milk, eggs, 1 teaspoon salt and red pepper in bowl; mix well. Spoon over cheese. Top with remaining crumb mixture, Parmesan cheese and paprika.
▪ Bake at 375 degrees for 25 minutes. Cut into 2-inch squares.
▪ Yield: 40 servings.

Approx Per Serving: Cal 119; Prot 3 g; Carbo 8 g; Fiber <1 g; T Fat 8 g;
63% Calories from Fat; Chol 39 mg; Sod 268 mg.

Derrielene Day, **Great Lakes Region**
GFWC—Big Rapids Women's Club, Big Rapids, MI

WHITE PIZZA

2 prepared rectangular pizza shells
8 ounces each shredded mozzarella
cheese, white American cheese
and white Cheddar cheese

1 or 2 tablespoons olive oil
1 small onion, thinly sliced into rings
1 tablespoon each rosemary, oregano,
basil and pepper

- Sprinkle 1 pizza shell with mixture of cheeses. Top with remaining pizza shell; brush with olive oil. Arrange onion rings over top; sprinkle with mixture of seasonings.
- Bake at 450 degrees on middle oven rack for 10 minutes or until light brown. Cut into serving pieces.
- Yield: 12 servings.

Approx Per Serving: Cal 333; Prot 16 g; Carbo 24 g; Fiber <1 g; T Fat 19 g;
52% Calories from Fat; Chol 53 mg; Sod 678 mg.

*Judi Stankowich, **Middle Atlantic Region***
GFWC—Women's Club of Laflin, Laflin PA

SWEET AND SOUR KIELBASA

1 pound smoked kielbasa, sliced
diagonally ¼ inch thick

1 envelope Durkee's sweet and sour
mix, prepared

- Steam kielbasa on rack in saucepan over boiling water for 10 minutes.
- Combine sausage and sauce in serving bowl; mix well. Serve on crackers.
- Yield: 4 servings.

Approx Per Serving: Cal 240; Prot 7 g; Carbo 19 g; Fiber <1 g; T Fat 15 g;
55% Calories from Fat; Chol 35 mg; Sod 769 mg.

*Paula Schlice, **Great Lakes Region***
GFWC—Stevens Point Woman's Club, Stevens Point WI

TORTILLA ROLL-UPS

16 ounces cream cheese, softened
1 7-ounce can chopped green chilies
1 12-ounce jar salsa
2 green onions, chopped
1 cup refried beans

1½ cups shredded Cheddar cheese
1 4-ounce can sliced black olives,
drained
12 large flour tortillas

- Mix first 5 ingredients in mixer bowl until smooth. Stir in Cheddar cheese and olives.
- Spread on tortillas; roll tortillas to enclose filling.
- Chill, wrapped, in refrigerator. Cut into 1 to 1½-inch pieces 1 hour before serving.
- Yield: 50 servings.

Approx Per Serving: Cal 99; Prot 3 g; Carbo 10 g; Fiber 1 g; T Fat 6 g;
51% Calories from Fat; Chol 14 mg; Sod 237 mg.

*Sherry Winik, **Western Region***
GFWC—Ebell Club of Irvine, Irvine CA

BEER-CHEESE SOUP

1 cup flour
1/2 cup melted butter
4 cups chicken broth
1 1/2 cups cream
1   16-ounce jar Cheez Whiz

3/4 cup beer
1 tablespoon Worcestershire sauce
1/4 cup chopped chives
1/2 teaspoon yellow food coloring

- Blend flour into melted butter in large heavy saucepan. Cook for 5 minutes, stirring occasionally. Stir in chicken broth and cream.
- Cook until thickened, stirring constantly. Stir in Cheez Whiz until smooth. Add beer, Worcestershire sauce, chives and food coloring; mix well.
- Simmer for 15 minutes, stirring constantly. Garnish servings with popcorn.
- Yield: 8 servings.

Approx Per Serving: Cal 529; Prot 17 g; Carbo 19 g; Fiber 1 g; T Fat 43 g;
73% Calories from Fat; Chol 129 mg; Sod 1194 mg.

*Trudy Johnson, **Great Lakes Region***
GFWC—Centuria Woman's Club, Centuria WI

DRUNKEN PINTO BEAN SOUP

3 to 4 cups dried pinto beans
2 quarts water
2 or 3 slices bacon, chopped
1 medium onion, chopped

3 jalapeño peppers, seeded, chopped
Salt to taste
2   12-ounce cans beer

- Soak beans in water to cover in saucepan overnight; drain and rinse.
- Combine beans with 2 quarts water, bacon and onion in saucepan.
- Cook over medium-low heat for several hours until partially tender. Add peppers and salt. Stir in beer.
- Simmer until beans are tender and soup no longer has aroma of beer, stirring occasionally.
- Serve in Mexican pottery bowls with beef tamales and tortillas.
- May substitute ham bone and chopped ham for bacon.
- Yield: 8 servings.

Approx Per Serving: Cal 365; Prot 23 g; Carbo 60 g; Fiber 21 g; T Fat 2 g;
5% Calories from Fat; Chol 2 mg; Sod 65 mg.

*Gladys Bigelow, **South Central Region***
GFWC—Decora Women's Study Club, Victoria TX

JERSEY BLUEBERRY SOUP

1 envelope unflavored gelatin
1/4 cup sugar
2 1/2 cups water
2 tablespoons lemon juice

1 pint fresh blueberries
1/2 teaspoon cinnamon
2 cups half and half

- Mix unflavored gelatin and sugar with 1 cup water in medium saucepan; let stand for 2 minutes.
- Cook over low heat for 5 minutes or until gelatin dissolves, stirring constantly. Stir in remaining 1 1/2 cups water, lemon juice, blueberries and cinnamon.
- Simmer for 15 minutes or until blueberries are tender, stirring frequently and crushing berries slightly with spoon. Cool completely.
- Stir in half and half. Chill for 4 hours to overnight; soup will thicken as it chills.
- Serve cold. Garnish servings with lemon slices and additional fresh blueberries.
- Yield: 6 servings.

Approx Per Serving: Cal 170; Prot 4 g; Carbo 19 g; Fiber 1 g; T Fat 9 g;
48% Calories from Fat; Chol 30 mg; Sod 37 mg.

Mary Lou Sullivan, **Middle Atlantic Region**
GFWC—Third District Junior Alumni Women's Club, Pennsauken NJ

BUTTERNUT SQUASH SOUP

1   1-pound butternut squash, peeled,
     seeded, chopped
3 medium tart apples, peeled, chopped
1 medium onion, chopped
3   10-ounce cans chicken broth
2 broth cans water
2 slices bread, crumbled

1/4 teaspoon rosemary
1/4 teaspoon marjoram
1 teaspoon salt
Pepper to taste
1/4 cup cream
Parsley to taste

- Combine squash, apples, onion, chicken broth, water, bread crumbs, rosemary, marjoram, salt and pepper in saucepan.
- Bring to a boil; reduce heat. Simmer for 45 minutes. Cool to room temperature.
- Process squash mixture 1/4 at a time in blender until smooth. Combine with cream and parsley in saucepan.
- Cook just until heated through.
- Yield: 10 servings.

Approx Per Serving: Cal 95; Prot 3 g; Carbo 15 g; Fiber 2 g; T Fat 3 g;
28% Calories from Fat; Chol 9 mg; Sod 517 mg.

Helen Vanderbilt, **Middle Atlantic Region**
GFWC—Mountain Lakes Woman's Club, Mountain Lakes NJ

CREAMY CABBAGE SOUP

2 cups chopped cooked ham
10 cups coarsely chopped cabbage
1¹/₂ cups shredded carrots
1 cup chopped celery
¹/₄ cup chopped onion
1 cup cooked wild rice
5 cups water

¹/₄ cup butter
2 teaspoons instant chicken bouillon
¹/₂ teaspoon celery salt
1 5-ounce can evaporated milk
¹/₃ cup flour
³/₄ cup water
Salt and pepper to taste

- Combine ham, cabbage, carrots, celery, onion, wild rice, 5 cups water, butter, chicken bouillon and celery salt in large heavy saucepan; mix well.
- Cook for 10 to 12 minutes or until mixture comes to a boil; reduce heat. Simmer for 35 to 40 minutes or until vegetables are tender-crisp.
- Stir in evaporated milk and mixture of flour and ³/₄ cup water.
- Cook for 10 to 15 minutes or until soup comes to a boil, stirring constantly. Cook for 1 minute longer. Season with salt and pepper to taste.
- Yield: 10 servings.

Approx Per Serving: Cal 165; Prot 11 g; Carbo 15 g; Fiber 3 g; T Fat 8 g; 40% Calories from Fat; Chol 32 mg; Sod 760 mg.

*Tamara J. Phillips, **Great Lakes Region***
GFWC—Colfax Club, Colfax WI

CABBAGE-POTATO-LEEK AND SAUSAGE SOUP AU GRATIN

1 pound smoked sausage, sliced
    ¹/₄ inch thick
¹/₂ cup oil
4 cups thinly sliced leeks
4 cloves of garlic, chopped
6 cups chicken stock

6 cups beef stock
6 cups shredded cabbage
2 pounds red potatoes, coarsely
    chopped
1¹/₂ cups grated Parmesan cheese
24 large croutons

- Cook sausage in hot oil in large stockpot for 2 minutes. Add leeks.
- Sauté for 2 to 3 minutes, stirring constantly. Add garlic.
- Sauté for 30 seconds. Stir in chicken stock, beef stock, cabbage and potatoes.
- Bring to a boil; reduce heat. Simmer for 1 hour.
- Ladle into soup cups. Stir 1 tablespoon cheese into each serving. Top with crouton.
- This recipe is a favorite from Rob Menzer, owner of Glen Brook Inn, Wantage, New Jersey, where we hold our dinner meetings.
- Yield: 24 servings.

Approx Per Serving: Cal 164; Prot 7 g; Carbo 13 g; Fiber 1 g; T Fat 10 g; 52% Calories from Fat; Chol 10 mg; Sod 642 mg.

*Kathleen Hunterton, **Middle Atlantic Region***
The Sussex Woman's Club, Sussex NJ

Chicken and Corn Soup

4 cups chicken stock
4 cups fresh corn kernels
1/2 cup chopped celery
1/4 cup finely chopped onion
2 cups chopped potatoes

Salt to taste
1/4 teaspoon pepper
2 cups chopped cooked chicken
2 hard-boiled eggs, chopped
1 tablespoon chopped parsley

- Bring chicken stock to a boil in large saucepan. Add corn, celery, onion, potatoes, salt and pepper.
- Cook for 20 to 25 minutes or until vegetables are tender. Stir in chicken, eggs and chopped parsley.
- Simmer for 8 minutes.
- May substitute canned corn for fresh corn, adding it with chicken. This is known as Hinkel Welschkarn Suup.
- Yield: 8 servings.

Approx Per Serving: Cal 204; Prot 18 g; Carbo 23 g; Fiber 4 g; T Fat 6 g;
24% Calories from Fat; Chol 85 mg; Sod 455 mg.

Kathy Krantz, **Middle Atlantic Region**
GFWC—Lititz Woman's Club, Lititz PA

Soup du Crocodile

2 tablespoons oil
1 cup brown gravy
1   16-ounce can whole tomatoes
2 cups chopped onions
1 cup chopped celery
2/3 cup chopped green bell pepper
1 lemon, sliced
1/4 cup chopped parsley

3 or 4 basil leaves
1 teaspoon garlic powder
1 tablespoon salt
1 teaspoon red pepper
1 teaspoon black pepper
2 quarts water
2 pounds alligator tail meat, chopped

- Heat oil in stockpot. Stir in gravy, tomatoes, onions, celery, green pepper, lemon, parsley, basil, garlic powder, salt, red pepper and black pepper. Add water.
- Bring to a boil. Add alligator meat.
- Simmer, covered, for 2 1/2 to 3 hours or until meat is tender.
- May add 1 teaspoon sherry to each serving. May substitute mixture of dark and light chicken meat for alligator.
- Yield: 10 servings.

Approx Per Serving: Cal 71; Prot 2 g; Carbo 7 g; Fiber 2 g; T Fat 4 g;
53% Calories from Fat; Chol 0 mg; Sod 864 mg.

Marsha W. Cabuk, **South Central Region**
GFWC—Caddoan Club, Oak Ridge LA

JERSEY CORN AND POTATO CHOWDER

1 cup chopped onion
2 tablespoons butter
2 cups chopped potatoes
2 cups chicken broth
1/2 teaspoon curry powder
1/2 teaspoon salt

1/4 teaspoon pepper
2 cups fresh Jersey corn kernels
1 12-ounce can evaporated milk
1/4 cup flour
1/2 cup water

- Sauté onion in butter in 4-quart stockpot until tender. Add potatoes, chicken broth, curry powder, salt and pepper; mix well.
- Simmer, covered, for 15 minutes or until potatoes are tender; remove from heat.
- Add corn and evaporated milk. Stir in mixture of flour and water.
- Cook over medium heat until soup is thickened and corn is tender, stirring constantly.
- Yield: 6 servings.

Approx Per Serving: Cal 234; Prot 9 g; Carbo 31 g; Fiber 3 g; T Fat 10 g;
35% Calories from Fat; Chol 27 mg; Sod 539 mg.

Joan Packlaian, ***Middle Atlantic Region***
GFWC—Ewing Woman's Club, Trenton NJ

DUTCH HOLLOW HICKORY NUT SOUP

1 1/2 cups hickory nuts
3 medium carrots
3 stalks celery
1 medium onion
2 cloves of garlic, chopped
1/2 cup margarine
5 cups chicken stock

2 tablespoons flour
1/4 teaspoon nutmeg
Cayenne pepper to taste
2 bay leaves
Salt and freshly ground black pepper
    to taste

- Process hickory nuts in food processor until finely chopped. Process carrots, celery and onion until chopped.
- Sauté chopped vegetables, garlic and 3/4 cup hickory nuts in margarine in saucepan until vegetables are tender. Cool to room temperature.
- Combine with a small amount of chicken stock in food processor container; process until smooth. Return to saucepan. Sprinkle with flour; mix well.
- Cook for several minutes or until thickened, stirring constantly. Stir in remaining stock, nutmeg, cayenne pepper and bay leaves. Simmer for 1 hour; discard bay leaves. Add remaining hickory nuts, salt and black pepper.
- Heat soup to serving temperature; do not boil.
- Yield: 6 servings.

Approx Per Serving: Cal 376; Prot 9 g; Carbo 13 g; Fiber 2 g; T Fat 34 g;
78% Calories from Fat; Chol 1 mg; Sod 855 mg.

Natalie Moritz, ***Great Lakes Region***
GFWC—Reedsburg Federated Woman's Club, LaValle WI

PORTUGUESE KALE SOUP

1 pound dried white pea beans
3 small ham soup bones
8 ounces chourico, sliced
1 pound linguica, sliced
2 medium onions, sliced

2 bunches kale
1 tablespoon lemon juice
Salt, cayenne pepper and black
    pepper to taste
5 or 6 potatoes, chopped

- Soak beans in water to cover in large saucepan overnight; drain. Add soup bones and fresh water to cover. Simmer for 1 hour. Add next 4 ingredients.
- Simmer for 1 hour. Add lemon juice, salt, cayenne pepper and black pepper.
- Simmer for 6 to 6½ hours or until of desired consistency, adding water as necessary; do not boil. Add potatoes. Simmer for 30 minutes longer.
- May substitute hot Italian sausage for chourico, mild Italian sausage for linguica, red kidney beans for pea beans and cabbage or frozen kale for fresh kale.
- Yield: 10 servings.

Approx Per Serving: Cal 401; Prot 23 g; Carbo 53 g; Fiber 6 g; T Fat 12 g;
26% Calories from Fat; Chol 35 mg; Sod 515 mg.

Ann L. Holland, GFWC International President, 1992–94, **New England Region**
West Falmouth, MA

BUFFUM'S MEXICAN CHOWDER

1 quart water
1½ beef bouillon cubes
1   2-ounce package *au jus* mix
1 tablespoon minced onion
1 stalk celery, chopped
¾ teaspoon each garlic powder,
    cumin and chili powder
¼ teaspoon oregano
1 bay leaf
8 ounces ground beef
1 small onion, chopped

1 teaspoon garlic powder
1 envelope taco seasoning mix
1 egg, beaten
¾ cup bread crumbs
½ cup cooked rice
1   15-ounce can 3-bean salad, drained,
    rinsed
3 tomatoes, chopped
1 cup canned tomato juice
1 tablespoon lemon juice

- Bring water to a boil in saucepan. Add beef bouillon cubes and *au jus* mix. Bring to a boil. Add next 7 ingredients. Simmer for 10 minutes; set aside.
- Brown ground beef with 1 onion in large saucepan, stirring until ground beef is crumbly; drain. Stir in 1 teaspoon garlic powder and taco seasoning mix.
- Simmer for 15 minutes. Add egg, bread crumbs, rice, bean salad, tomatoes, tomato juice, lemon juice and reserved beef stock. Simmer for 15 minutes. Discard bay leaf.
- May prepare in advance, adding lemon juice after mixture has been brought to a boil and simmered for 15 minutes.
- Yield: 6 servings.

Approx Per Serving: Cal 295; Prot 14 g; Carbo 42 g; Fiber 3 g; T Fat 8 g;
25% Calories from Fat; Chol 62 mg; Sod 2051 mg.

Alice Allen, **Western Region**
GFWC—Norwalk Woman's Club, Whittier CA

HUNTERDON COUNTY SUMMER BOUNTY MINESTRONE

2 mild onions, chopped
3 tablespoons olive oil
3 medium carrots, chopped
2 zucchini, chopped
1 yellow squash, chopped
8 ounces green beans, chopped
4 tomatoes, peeled, chopped

2 stalks celery, chopped
2¹/₂ cups chicken broth
³/₄ cup white wine
1¹/₂ cups water
2 teaspoons minced garlic
¹/₄ cup tomato paste
Salt and pepper to taste

- Sauté onions in olive oil in large stockpot over medium heat for 5 minutes. Add carrots, zucchini, squash, beans, tomatoes and celery.
- Sauté for 10 minutes, stirring occasionally. Stir in chicken broth, wine, water, garlic, tomato paste, salt and pepper. Simmer for 45 minutes, stirring twice.
- Ladle into soup bowls. Garnish servings with Parmesan cheese.
- Yield: 8 servings.

Approx Per Serving: Cal 146; Prot 5 g; Carbo 17 g; Fiber 5 g; T Fat 6 g;
38% Calories from Fat; Chol <1 mg; Sod 277 mg.

Lori Kopf MacWilliam, **Middle Atlantic Region**
GFWC—Junior Woman's Club of North Hunterdon, Inc., Clinton NJ

MULLIGATAWNY SOUP

¹/₂ cup chopped onion
¹/₂ carrot, chopped
2 stalks celery, chopped
¹/₄ cup butter
1¹/₂ tablespoons flour
2 teaspoons curry powder
4 cups chicken broth

1 bay leaf
¹/₄ cup chopped tart apples
¹/₂ cup cooked rice
2 cups chopped cooked chicken
1 teaspoon salt
¹/₄ teaspoon pepper
¹/₂ cup hot cream

- Sauté onion, carrot and celery in butter in large stockpot until tender but not brown. Stir in flour and curry powder.
- Sauté for 3 minutes. Add chicken broth and bay leaf.
- Simmer for 15 minutes. Add apples, rice, chicken, salt and pepper.
- Simmer for 15 minutes. Stir in cream. Heat just to serving temperature; discard bay leaf.
- Serve with salad and fresh homemade bread. May substitute coconut broth for cream or lamb broth and lamb for chicken broth and chicken.
- Yield: 6 servings.

Approx Per Serving: Cal 289; Prot 18 g; Carbo 10 g; Fiber 1 g; T Fat 20 g;
61% Calories from Fat; Chol 90 mg; Sod 999 mg.

Nancy Boyle, **Western Region**
GFWC—Honolulu Women's Club, Honolulu HI

PALM VALLEY CREAM OF PALM SOUP

1 clove of garlic, crushed
1 cup chopped onion
Salt and pepper to taste
1/2 cup butter
1/2 cup flour
2 14-ounce cans chicken broth

1/2 14-ounce can hearts of palm,
   sliced 1/2 inch thick
1 cup half and half
1/2 bunch parsley, finely minced
1 cup shredded Swiss cheese

- Sauté garlic and onion with salt and pepper in butter in large saucepan.
- Stir in flour. Add chicken broth gradually, stirring constantly.
- Simmer for 3 minutes, adding hearts of palm. Stir in half and half.
- Cook just until heated through. Ladle into heated soup cups. Top with parsley and cheese.
- Yield: 4 servings.

Approx Per Serving: Cal 510; Prot 18 g; Carbo 21 g; Fiber 2 g; T Fat 40 g;
70% Calories from Fat; Chol 111 mg; Sod 1182 mg.

Gwen Holborn, *Southern Region*
GFWC—Ponte Vedra Woman's Club, Ponte Vedra Beach FL

SUPER PUMPKIN SOUP

3 10-ounce cans cream of chicken
   soup
3 cups canned pumpkin
3 cups half and half
2 cups chicken broth
2 tablespoons minced parsley

1 1/2 teaspoons sugar
1 1/2 teaspoons sweet basil
1 1/2 teaspoons nutmeg
3/4 teaspoon salt
Pepper to taste

- Combine soup, pumpkin, half and half, chicken broth, parsley, sugar, basil, nutmeg, salt and pepper in saucepan; mix well.
- Simmer for 30 minutes, adjusting seasonings or liquid as needed.
- May substitute milk for half and half.
- Yield: 8 servings.

Approx Per Serving: Cal 261; Prot 8 g; Carbo 20 g; Fiber 2 g; T Fat 17 g;
58% Calories from Fat; Chol 42 mg; Sod 1271 mg.

Pat Conlon, *New England Region*
GFWC—Wilton Woman's Club, Wilton CT

1868—Sorosis, GFWC's "mother club," was founded by Jane Cunningham ("Jennie June") Croly in New York City.

SOUTH JERSEY FRESH TOMATO SOUP

1 medium yellow onion, finely chopped
2 tablespoons oil
5 medium tomatoes, sliced
1/2 teaspoon minced garlic
2 tablespoons tomato paste
2 tablespoons flour

2 tablespoons oil
2 cups chicken broth
3/4 cup half and half
1 medium tomato, peeled, julienned
Salt and white pepper to taste
2 tablespoons minced fresh parsley

- Sauté onion in 2 tablespoons oil in heavy 4-quart saucepan for 1 minute. Add sliced tomatoes and garlic. Sauté for 5 minutes or until tomatoes begin to break up.
- Whisk tomato paste, flour and 2 tablespoons oil together in bowl. Stir into sautéed mixture with chicken broth.
- Bring to a boil over medium heat, stirring constantly; remove from heat.
- Process 1/3 at a time in food processor or blender until smooth. Return to saucepan.
- Simmer for 15 minutes. Stir in half and half, tomato, salt and white pepper.
- Simmer just until heated through. Sprinkle servings with parsley.
- Yield: 5 servings.

Approx Per Serving: Cal 217; Prot 6 g; Carbo 15 g; Fiber 3 g; T Fat 16 g;
64% Calories from Fat; Chol 14 mg; Sod 343 mg.

Joan Gretkowski, ***Middle Atlantic Region***
GFWC—Woman's Club of Pitman, Pitman NJ

SOUTHWESTERN TORTILLA SOUP

2 chicken breasts
1 small onion, chopped
1 clove of garlic, minced
2 tablespoons olive oil
1 4-ounce can chopped green chilies
3 cups tomato juice
3 cups chicken broth
2 cups beef broth
1 14-ounce can chopped tomatoes
1 15-ounce can garbanzo beans, drained

1 tablespoon cumin
1 teaspoon chili powder
1 teaspoon Worcestershire sauce
2 tablespoons chopped fresh cilantro
1 10-ounce package frozen chopped
  spinach
Pepper to taste
4 cups tortilla chips
2 cups shredded mozzarella cheese
Juice of 2 limes

- Cut chicken into bite-sized pieces; rinse and pat dry.
- Sauté chicken, onion and garlic in olive oil in large stockpot until chicken is tender. Add next 9 ingredients. Bring to a boil; reduce heat. Simmer for 1 hour. Add cilantro, spinach and pepper. Simmer for 30 minutes.
- Ladle over tortilla chips and cheese in soup bowls. Squeeze lime juice over soup. Garnish with lime slices.
- Yield: 8 servings.

Approx Per Serving: Cal 360; Prot 22 g; Carbo 34 g; Fiber 3 g; T Fat 16 g;
39% Calories from Fat; Chol 41 mg; Sod 1404 mg.

Rachel Houston, ***South Central Region***
GFWC—White Sands Junior Women's Club, Alamogordo NM

ELEGANT WILD RICE SOUP

1/2 cup uncooked wild rice
2 cups chicken broth
1 tablespoon minced onion
6 tablespoons margarine
1/2 cup flour
1 cup chicken broth

1/3 cup chopped cooked ham
1/3 cup finely grated carrot
3 tablespoons chopped slivered
   almonds
1/2 teaspoon salt
1 cup half and half

- Rinse rice. Simmer rice in 2 cups chicken broth in saucepan for 45 to 60 minutes or until liquid is absorbed and rice is tender; set aside.
- Sauté onion in margarine in 2-quart saucepan until tender. Stir in flour. Add 1 cup broth gradually.
- Bring to a boil, stirring constantly. Cook for 1 minute, stirring constantly. Add rice, ham, carrot, almonds and salt; mix well.
- Simmer for 5 minutes. Stir in half and half.
- Heat to serving temperature. Garnish servings with parsley or chives.
- May substitute milk for half and half.
- Yield: 6 servings.

Approx Per Serving: Cal 283; Prot 9 g; Carbo 21 g; Fiber 1 g; T Fat 18 g;
57% Calories from Fat; Chol 20 mg; Sod 822 mg.

Ione H. Carlson, **Mississippi Valley Region**
GFWC—5th District Officers' Club, Minneapolis MN

MARYLAND CRAB BISQUE

1 teaspoon dried minced onion
1/4 cup flour
1/2 teaspoon salt
1/8 teaspoon pepper

3 tablespoons melted butter
1 cup chicken broth
3 cups milk
1 1/2 cups fresh crab meat

- Stir onion, flour, salt and pepper into butter in large saucepan.
- Cook for several minutes. Stir in chicken broth and milk gradually.
- Cook over low heat until thickened, stirring constantly. Stir in crab meat.
- Simmer, covered, for 5 minutes. Garnish servings with parsley or paprika.
- May substitute lobster or shrimp for crab meat.
- Yield: 6 servings.

Approx Per Serving: Cal 186; Prot 12 g; Carbo 10 g; Fiber <1 g; T Fat 11 g;
52% Calories from Fat; Chol 66 mg; Sod 501 mg.

Dorothy L. Walsh, **Southeastern Region**
GFWC—Woman's Club of Hampstead, Hampstead MD

ALASKAN HALIBUT CHOWDER

16 ounces cream cheese
2¹/₂ cups milk
¹/₄ teaspoon garlic powder
¹/₈ teaspoon black pepper
3 10-ounce cans cream of potato soup
1 10-ounce can cream of mushroom
    soup
1 16-ounce can sliced carrots, drained

1 11-ounce can corn, drained
2 4-ounce cans button mushrooms,
    drained
1 pound bacon, chopped
4 cups (heaping) chopped halibut
8 to 10 green onions with tops, minced
2 cloves of garlic, minced
Cayenne pepper to taste

- Heat first 9 ingredients on High in slow cooker until cream cheese melts.
- Fry bacon in skillet until crisp; drain most of drippings from skillet. Add bacon to slow cooker.
- Sauté halibut, green onions and garlic in drippings in skillet until halibut flakes easily; drain. Add to slow cooker. Add cayenne pepper. Cook until of desired consistency.
- Yield: 12 servings.

Approx Per Serving: Cal 353; Prot 15 g; Carbo 20 g; Fiber 2 g; T Fat 25 g;
61% Calories from Fat; Chol 69 mg; Sod 1314 mg.

*Betty M. Gutoski, **Western Region***
GFWC—College Woman's Club, Fairbanks AK

SURPRISE CLAM CHOWDER

1 quart shucked clams, rinsed
1 gallon water
¹/₃ cup salt
1 2-inch cube salt pork
1 large onion, minced
3 tablespoons flour
2 cups chopped peeled potatoes

3 cups canned tomatoes
¹/₂ cup chopped green bell pepper
¹/₂ bay leaf
3 tablespoons butter
Tarragon and white pepper to taste
1 pound bay scallops, sautéed

- Combine clams with 1 gallon water and salt in large bowl. Let stand in refrigerator for 3 to 12 hours; drain, reserving liquid.
- Cut hard parts of clams from soft parts, reserving both parts; chop clams.
- Render salt pork in saucepan; remove with slotted spoon. Add onion and hard parts of clams to drippings. Sauté for 5 minutes. Stir in flour. Cook for several minutes. Stir in reserved liquid and next 4 ingredients.
- Simmer, covered, until potatoes are tender. Add salt pork, soft parts of clams and butter. Simmer for 5 minutes or until clams are cooked through. Season with tarragon and white pepper. Cool to room temperature. Chill overnight.
- Cook chowder until heated through. Add scallops. Heat to serving temperature; discard bay leaf. Serve with oyster crackers.
- Yield: 8 servings.

Approx Per Serving: Cal 242; Prot 25 g; Carbo 18 g; Fiber 2 g; T Fat 8 g;
30% Calories from Fat; Chol 64 mg; Sod 4649 mg.

*Mary Ann Barile, **Middle Atlantic Region***
GFWC—Country Shore Women's Club, Marmora NJ

OYSTER CHOWDER

1 pint oysters
1 large onion, chopped
1/2 cup butter
1/2 cup water
2 potatoes, peeled, chopped
2 stalks celery, chopped

1 carrot, chopped
1/4 cup flour
3 cups milk
1 1/2 teaspoons salt
1/2 teaspoon white pepper

- Drain oysters, reserving liquid. Chop oysters.
- Sauté onion in butter in heavy saucepan. Add water, potatoes, celery and carrot.
- Simmer, covered, until vegetables are tender. Stir in flour. Add milk, liquid from oysters, salt and white pepper.
- Cook over low heat until mixture thickens, stirring constantly. Add oysters.
- Cook for 2 to 3 minutes or just until oysters are cooked through; do not overcook. Garnish servings with parsley. Serve immediately; do not reheat.
- Yield: 4 servings.

Approx Per Serving: Cal 564; Prot 23 g; Carbo 36 g; Fiber 11 g; T Fat 139 g;
84% Calories from Fat; Chol 620 mg; Sod 1323 mg.

Linnea Lightner, **Southeastern Region**
GFWC—Tri Club Woman's Club, Richmond VA

NO-ROUX GUMBO

4 or 5 onions, chopped
1 large clove of garlic, chopped
12 ounces okra, sliced
6 tablespoons olive oil
3 cups peeled shrimp
1 1/2 pounds tomatoes, peeled, chopped
3 cups chicken stock

Tabasco sauce to taste
2 cups chopped cooked ham
4 teaspoons filé
1 green bell pepper, chopped
1 pound light fish, chopped
8 ounces sea scallops

- Sauté onions, garlic and okra in 2 tablespoons olive oil in large saucepan for 10 minutes. Add shrimp.
- Cook just until shrimp turn pink; remove shrimp with slotted spoon. Chill until needed. Add tomatoes, chicken stock and Tabasco sauce to saucepan.
- Simmer for 15 minutes. Add ham and 2 teaspoons filé. Simmer for 45 minutes.
- Sauté green pepper in 2 tablespoons olive oil in skillet for 15 minutes. Add to saucepan. Add fish, scallops and remaining 2 tablespoons olive oil to skillet. Sauté for 15 minutes. Add fish mixture, shrimp and remaining 2 teaspoons filé to saucepan.
- Simmer, covered, for 30 minutes, stirring occasionally. Serve over steamed rice with additional filé and Tabasco sauce.
- Yield: 8 servings.

Approx Per Serving: Cal 366; Prot 43 g; Carbo 16 g; Fiber 3 g; T Fat 15 g;
36% Calories from Fat; Chol 179 mg; Sod 993 mg.

Nancy L. Martin, **Southern Region**
GFWC—Women's Club of Pensacola, Inc., Pensacola FL

SEAFOOD GUMBO

1 tablespoon crab boil seasoning
1 cup flour
1½ cups oil
1 cup chopped onion
½ clove of garlic, finely chopped
1 6-ounce can tomato paste
4 quarts water
2 32-ounce cans tomatoes
½ bunch celery, chopped
2 large green bell peppers, chopped

2 cups chopped onions
1 tablespoon Worcestershire sauce
1 teaspoon parsley flakes
1 teaspoon oregano
2 bay leaves
1 tablespoon salt
1 tablespoon pepper
2 cups crab meat
2 pounds peeled shrimp
2 cups sliced okra

- Tie crab boil seasoning in cheesecloth bag.
- Blend flour into oil in saucepan. Cook until medium-dark brown, stirring constantly; remove from heat. Add 1 cup onion, garlic and tomato paste; mix well.
- Combine water, tomatoes, crab boil seasoning, celery, green peppers, 2 cups onions, Worcestershire sauce, parsley flakes, oregano, bay leaves, salt and pepper in large saucepan. Stir in roux.
- Simmer for 2 hours or until vegetables are tender. Add crab meat, shrimp and okra. Simmer for 1 hour, adding water as needed for desired consistency. Remove crab boil bag and bay leaves. Adjust seasonings.
- Serve over rice with corn bread or crackers.
- Yield: 16 servings.

Approx Per Serving: Cal 326; Prot 16 g; Carbo 18 g; Fiber 3 g; T Fat 22 g;
59% Calories from Fat; Chol 105 mg; Sod 759 mg.

*Dixie S. Johnson, **Southern Region***
GFWC—Quest Woman's Club, Enterprise AL

CORN AND SHRIMP SOUP

3 cups chopped onions
1 cup chopped celery
3 cloves of garlic, chopped
2 tablespoons oil
1 16-ounce can tomatoes
4 11-ounce cans Shoe-Peg corn

1½ pounds peeled shrimp, deveined
1 pound cooked ham, chopped
2 8-ounce cans tomato sauce
5 cups water
Salt and pepper to taste

- Sauté onions, celery and garlic in oil in large saucepan. Add tomatoes.
- Cook over medium heat for 5 minutes. Add corn, shrimp and ham.
- Cook until shrimp turn pink. Add tomato sauce and water.
- Bring to a boil; reduce heat. Simmer for 40 minutes. Stir in salt and pepper.
- Yield: 10 servings.

Approx Per Serving: Cal 268; Prot 27 g; Carbo 28 g; Fiber 3 g; T Fat 7 g;
22% Calories from Fat; Chol 131 mg; Sod 1399 mg.

*Cherie Zeringue, **South Central Region***
GFWC—Bayou Junior Woman's Club, Thibodaux LA

CHILI SAUCE RING

2¹/₂ envelopes unflavored gelatin
¹/₄ cup cold water
1 cup chili sauce
1 cup low-fat cottage cheese
1 cup mayonnaise

¹/₄ cup chopped celery
¹/₄ cup chopped green pepper
2 tablespoons chopped green onions
¹/₂ cup sliced stuffed green olives

- Soften gelatin in cold water in small bowl.
- Bring chili sauce to a boil in saucepan. Stir in gelatin until dissolved. Cool to room temperature.
- Add cottage cheese, mayonnaise, celery, green pepper, green onions and olives to cooled mixture; mix well. Spoon into 2-quart ring mold.
- Chill for 4 hours to overnight. Unmold onto serving plate.
- Yield: 8 servings.

Approx Per Serving: Cal 280; Prot 7 g; Carbo 11 g; Fiber 1 g; T Fat 24 g;
75% Calories from Fat; Chol 19 mg; Sod 988 mg.

*Kay Robbins, **Western Region***
GFWC—Van Nuys Club, North Hollywood CA

CORN BREAD SALAD

2 cups self-rising white cornmeal
¹/₈ teaspoon baking soda
2 eggs
2 cups buttermilk
1 tablespoon shortening
1 large green bell pepper, finely
  chopped

1 cup finely chopped celery
2 tomatoes, chopped
1 20-ounce can whole kernel corn,
   drained
6 to 8 green onions, finely chopped
1 cup mayonnaise
Salt and pepper to taste

- Combine cornmeal, baking soda, eggs and buttermilk in bowl; beat 100 strokes.
- Heat shortening in 12-inch cast-iron skillet in preheated 400-degree oven. Add corn bread batter.
- Bake for 30 minutes or until golden brown. Invert corn bread onto plate to cool. Cut into cubes.
- Combine with remaining ingredients in serving bowl; toss lightly to mix.
- Yield: 12 servings.

Approx Per Serving: Cal 316; Prot 7 g; Carbo 34 g; Fiber 1 g; T Fat 18 g;
50% Calories from Fat; Chol 48 mg; Sod 668 mg.

*Glenna Ragan, **South Central Region***
GFWC—20th Century Club, Harrison AR

CHUCK WAGON SALAD

1 16-ounce can French-style green beans	¹/₂ cup each vinegar and oil
1 11-ounce can Shoe-Peg corn	¹/₂ cup sugar
1 16-ounce can small green peas	¹/₂ teaspoon garlic powder
1 2-ounce jar chopped pimento	1 teaspoon salt
1 medium onion, chopped	¹/₂ teaspoon pepper

- Drain canned vegetables. Mix with onion and mixture of remaining ingredients in serving bowl.
- Marinate in refrigerator overnight. Drain before serving.
- Yield: 12 servings.

Approx Per Serving: Cal 174; Prot 3 g; Carbo 21 g; Fiber 3 g; T Fat 10 g;
47% Calories from Fat; Chol 0 mg; Sod 416 mg.
Nutritional information includes entire amount of marinade.

*Vivienne Lindsay, **Western Region***
GFWC—Lancaster Woman's Club, Lancaster CA

MUSHROOMS IN LEMON DRESSING

2 pounds fresh mushrooms, sliced	³/₄ cup oil
2 green onions, thinly sliced	¹/₄ cup red wine vinegar
1 ¹/₂x1¹/₂-inch piece of gingerroot, peeled, minced	2 tablespoons lemon juice
	1 tablespoon soy sauce

- Combine all ingredients in 9x13-inch dish; mix well. Chill, covered, for 4 hours to overnight, stirring occasionally. Drain before serving. Garnish with lemon slices.
- Yield: 8 servings.

Approx Per Serving: Cal 215; Prot 3 g; Carbo 7 g; Fiber 2 g; T Fat 21 g;
83% Calories from Fat; Chol 0 mg; Sod 134 mg.

*Denise B. MacGregor, **Middle Atlantic Region***
GFWC—The Civic League of Mechanicsburg, Mechanicsburg PA

BLACK-EYED PEA SALAD

2 15-ounce cans black-eyed peas	¹/₄ cup each vinegar and oil
¹/₂ cup red onion rings	1 teaspoon sugar
¹/₂ cup chopped green bell pepper	Hot pepper sauce to taste
1 small clove of garlic, minced	Salt and pepper to taste

- Drain peas. Combine peas, onion rings, green pepper and garlic in salad bowl. Add mixture of remaining ingredients; mix gently. Chill, covered, for 12 hours or longer.
- Yield: 8 servings.

Approx Per Serving: Cal 149; Prot 5 g; Carbo 16 g; Fiber 8 g; T Fat 7 g;
44% Calories from Fat; Chol 0 mg; Sod 319 mg.

*Mary McGee, **Southeastern Region***
GFWC—Woman's Club of Hamlet, Inc., Hamlet NC

POPCORN SALAD

1 pound bacon, crisp-fried, crumbled
1 cup shredded Cheddar cheese
1 cup chopped celery
1/2 cup chopped onion

1 cup sliced water chestnuts
2 teaspoons chopped red bell pepper
1 cup mayonnaise
6 cups popped popcorn

- Combine bacon, cheese, celery, onion, water chestnuts, bell pepper and mayonnaise in bowl; mix well. Chill in refrigerator.
- Add popcorn; toss lightly. Serve immediately.
- May chill bacon mixture in refrigerator overnight to enhance flavor, adding popcorn at serving time.
- Yield: 12 servings.

Approx Per Serving: Cal 259; Prot 7 g; Carbo 6 g; Fiber 1 g; T Fat 24 g; 81% Calories from Fat; Chol 30 mg; Sod 354 mg.

Shirley Omlid, **Mississippi Valley Region**
GFWC—Mathein Study Club, Crookston MN

IDAHO POTATO SALAD

6 to 8 very large Idaho potatoes
1 cup (about) French salad dressing
1 cup sliced black olives
1 cup sliced stuffed Manzanillo olives
1 cup chopped dill pickles

6 hard-boiled eggs, cut into quarters
Salt to taste
1 teaspoon coarsely ground pepper
1 to 1 1/2 cups mayonnaise

- Cook potatoes in water in saucepan just until tender. Drain and cool to room temperature. Peel potatoes and cut into bite-sized pieces.
- Combine potatoes with French salad dressing in bowl; toss to coat well. Chill for several hours to overnight.
- Add olives, pickles, eggs, salt and pepper to potatoes; toss to mix well. Add mayonnaise; mix gently.
- Chill for 1 hour or longer. Garnish with additional sliced hard-boiled eggs, parsley and paprika.
- Yield: 12 servings.

Approx Per Serving: Cal 467; Prot 6 g; Carbo 22 g; Fiber 3 g; T Fat 42 g; 78% Calories from Fat; Chol 123 mg; Sod 1100 mg.

Carma H. Smith, **Western Region**
GFWC—Twentieth Century Club, Twin Falls ID

1890—*GFWC was founded to bring together women's clubs throughout the country.*

RHUBARB SALAD

2 cups chopped rhubarb
½ cup sugar
2 cups water
2 3-ounce packages strawberry
   gelatin

2 apples, finely chopped
2 bananas, finely chopped
1 cup crushed pineapple
½ cup chopped pecans

- Combine rhubarb with sugar and water in saucepan.
- Cook until rhubarb is tender. Stir in gelatin until dissolved.
- Chill until partially set. Add apples, bananas, pineapple and pecans; mix gently.
- Chill until set.
- Yield: 6 servings.

Approx Per Serving: Cal 339; Prot 4 g; Carbo 70 g; Fiber 4 g; T Fat 7 g;
18% Calories from Fat; Chol 0 mg; Sod 93 mg.

Mabel Triemer, **Mississippi Valley Region**
GFWC—Philamathian Club, Council Grove KS

SPAGHETTI SQUASH SALAD

1 2½-pound spaghetti squash
8 cherry tomatoes, cut into quarters
1 green bell pepper, chopped
4 scallions, sliced
2 cloves of garlic, minced

1 tablespoon capers
2 tablespoons olive oil
2 tablespoons red wine vinegar
Salt and pepper to taste

- Pierce squash with fork. Place in baking dish.
- Bake at 350 degrees for 45 to 60 minutes or until tender.
- Cut baked squash into halves; discard seed. Remove spaghetti-like strands gently with fork.
- Combine squash with next 5 ingredients in serving bowl. Add olive oil and vinegar; toss to coat well. Season with salt and pepper. Serve immediately.
- Yield: 4 servings.

Approx Per Serving: Cal 161; Prot 3 g; Carbo 23 g; Fiber 9 g; T Fat 8 g;
80% Calories from Fat; Chol 0 mg; Sod 56 mg.

Deborah Lancucki, **Southeastern Region**
GFWC—Junior Women's Club of West Point, West Point VA

1893—*GFWC was among the first women's organizations which participated in the World's Columbian Exposition, the world's fair commemorating the 400th anniversary of Columbus's landing in America.*

SUGARED ALMOND AND ORANGE SALAD

1 egg white, at room temperature
1/4 cup sugar
1 cup sliced almonds
2 tablespoons melted butter
1/2 cup canola oil
1/4 cup sugar
1/4 cup malt vinegar
1/2 teaspoon almond extract

2 tablespoons orange juice
1 teaspoon grated orange rind
1 head red leaf lettuce, torn
1 head green leaf lettuce, torn
1 11-ounce can mandarin oranges, drained
10 fresh strawberries, sliced

- Beat egg white at high speed in mixer bowl until foamy. Add 1/4 cup sugar 1 tablespoon at a time, beating until stiff peaks form. Fold in almonds. Spread in melted butter in 8x8-inch baking pan.
- Bake at 325 degrees for 20 to 25 minutes or until golden brown, stirring every 5 minutes. Cool to room temperature.
- Combine next 6 ingredients in covered jar; shake to dissolve sugar. Chill dressing for 30 minutes.
- Combine dressing with lettuce, oranges and strawberries in salad bowl; toss to coat well. Sprinkle servings with sugared almonds.
- Yield: 6 servings.

Approx Per Serving: Cal 408; Prot 5 g; Carbo 34 g; Fiber 3 g; T Fat 31 g;
64% Calories from Fat; Chol 10 mg; Sod 53 mg.

*Jeanne Sandidge, **Southeastern Region***
GFWC—Southampton Woman's Club, Midlothian VA

JERSEY TOMATO AND ZUCCHINI SALAD

4 cups sliced zucchini
1 cup white wine vinegar
3/4 cup olive oil
2 tablespoons sugar
1 clove of garlic, minced

1 teaspoon each basil and salt
Pepper to taste
1 large onion, sliced
2 Jersey tomatoes, sliced

- Cook zucchini in a small amount of water in saucepan until tender-crisp; drain.
- Combine next 7 ingredients in covered jar; shake to mix well.
- Combine zucchini with marinade in bowl; toss to coat well. Chill overnight. Drain, reserving marinade.
- Arrange zucchini with sliced onion and tomatoes on serving plates; drizzle with reserved marinade.
- Yield: 4 servings.

Approx Per Serving: Cal 435; Prot 3 g; Carbo 19 g; Fiber 3 g; T Fat 41 g;
81% Calories from Fat; Chol 0 mg; Sod 543 mg.

*Diane Senerth, **Middle Atlantic Region***
GFWC—The Contemporary Club, Lawrenceville NJ

RO-TEL TOMATO SALAD

2 3-ounce packages lemon gelatin
2 cups boiling water
1 cup finely chopped celery

2 10-ounce cans Ro-Tel tomatoes
    with green chilies
1/2 teaspoon salt

- Dissolve gelatin in boiling water in bowl. Chill until partially set.
- Add remaining ingredients; mix well. Chill until set. May add pecans if desired.
- Yield: 8 servings.

Approx Per Serving: Cal 92; Prot 3 g; Carbo 22 g; Fiber <1 g; T Fat <1 g;
1% Calories from Fat; Chol 0 mg; Sod 498 mg.

*Marie Ward, **South Central Region***
GFWC—The Phoenix Club, Aspermont TX

SWEET AND SOUR TOMATOES

6 medium home-grown tomatoes,
   peeled, chopped
1/4 cup chopped onions
1 stalk celery, chopped

1/4 cup sugar
1/4 cup vinegar
Pepper to taste

- Combine tomatoes, onions and celery in bowl. Blend sugar and vinegar in small bowl. Stir in pepper.
- Add dressing to tomato mixture. Chill for 3 hours.
- Yield: 8 servings.

Approx Per Serving: Cal 46; Prot 1 g; Carbo 11 g; Fiber 2 g; T Fat <1 g;
4% Calories from Fat; Chol 0 mg; Sod 12 mg.

*Dolores A. Derr, **Middle Atlantic Region***
GFWC—Woman's Club of West Lawn, Sinking Spring PA

TURNIP SLAW

1/4 cup chopped red bell pepper
1/4 cup thinly sliced green onions
1/4 cup mayonnaise
1 tablespoon vinegar

2 tablespoons sugar
1/4 teaspoon salt
1/4 teaspoon pepper
4 cups shredded peeled turnips

- Combine bell pepper, green onions, mayonnaise, vinegar, sugar, salt and pepper in bowl; mix well. Add turnips; toss to coat well.
- Chill for several hours.
- Yield: 6 servings.

Approx Per Serving: Cal 131; Prot 2 g; Carbo 16 g; Fiber 4 g; T Fat 7 g;
49% Calories from Fat; Chol 5 mg; Sod 259 mg.

*Mrs. Vernon Weakley, **Mississippi Valley Region***
GFWC—Moline Musical & Literary Club, Howard KS

PAPAYA SEED DRESSING FOR SLAW

1 cup sugar
1 tablespoon English-style dry mustard
1 cup tarragon vinegar
1¹/₂ teaspoons salt

1 cup oil
¹/₄ cup minced red onion
3 tablespoons fresh papaya seed

- Process sugar, dry mustard, vinegar and salt in blender or food processor until smooth.
- Add oil in fine stream, processing until smooth. Add onion and papaya seed; process until seed are of the consistency of ground pepper.
- Store in refrigerator for up to 3 weeks. Use as dressing for cabbage slaw or with other vegetable salads.
- Yield: 40 (1-tablespoon) servings.

Approx Per Serving: Cal 70; Prot <1 g; Carbo 5 g; Fiber <1 g; T Fat 6 g;
69% Calories from Fat; Chol 0 mg; Sod 80 mg.

Sheryl Sizelove, **Western Region**
GFWC—Menifee Valley Woman's Club, Laguna Niguel CA

CURRIED CHICKEN-STUFFED SHELLS

¹/₂ cup plain yogurt
¹/₃ cup mayonnaise
2 tablespoons lemon juice
2 cloves of garlic, crushed
2 teaspoons prepared mustard
1 tablespoon curry powder

2 cups cooked chicken strips
1¹/₂ cups chopped red bell peppers
1 cup chopped celery
¹/₂ cup unsalted sunflower seed
¹/₂ cup sliced scallions
32 cooked jumbo pasta shells

- Combine yogurt, mayonnaise, lemon juice, garlic, mustard and curry powder in bowl; mix well.
- Add next 5 ingredients; mix gently. Spoon into pasta shells.
- Arrange shells on lettuce-lined plate. Chill until serving time.
- Yield: 8 servings.

Approx Per Serving: Cal 343; Prot 18 g; Carbo 34 g; Fiber 3 g; T Fat 15 g;
40% Calories from Fat; Chol 39 mg; Sod 120 mg.

Barbara Gilligan, **Middle Atlantic Region**
GFWC—Ringwood Woman's Club, Ringwood NJ

1892—*The Chicago Woman's Club assumed the responsibility for the Cook County Jail and for the first time youthful offenders were separated from older prisoners. By 1899 the club had initiated a bill, approved by the Chicago Bar Association, which made the distinction between juveniles and hardened criminals and became the basis for other juvenile court laws to follow.*

SALAD ON THE WILD SIDE

1 cup uncooked wild rice
2 tablespoons salt-free chicken
  bouillon
3 cups boiling water
4 ounces 96% fat-free ham, julienned
3/4 cup each julienned hot pepper
  cheese, broccoli flowerets, red bell
  pepper strips and walnut pieces

1 carrot, thinly sliced
4 green onions, thinly sliced
1/2 cup canola oil
2 tablespoons lemon juice
2 tablespoons white wine vinegar
1/2 teaspoon dry mustard
1/2 teaspoon (or more) curry powder

- Rinse rice with hot water; drain. Simmer rice and bouillon in water in saucepan for 35 to 45 minutes or until rice is tender and liquid is absorbed; cool.
- Combine rice with ham, cheese, broccoli, bell pepper, walnuts, carrot and green onions in serving bowl.
- Combine remaining ingredients in small bowl; beat until smooth.
- Add dressing to salad; toss to mix well. Chill until serving time.
- May substitute turkey ham for ham.
- Yield: 6 servings.

Approx Per Serving: Cal 466; Prot 15 g; Carbo 29 g; Fiber 2 g; T Fat 34 g;
64% Calories from Fat; Chol 23 mg; Sod 343 mg.

*Patricia Kostner, **Great Lakes Region***
GFWC—Bloomer Women's Club, Bloomer WI

ASTA SALAD

1/4 cup mayonnaise
1/4 cup sour cream
4 teaspoons catsup
1 teaspoon brandy
1 teaspoon white wine
1 teaspoon horseradish sauce

Paprika, salt and pepper to taste
1 head Romaine lettuce
Chopped meat of 1 cooked lobster
16 honeydew melon balls
16 cantaloupe balls

- Combine first 9 ingredients in bowl; whisk until smooth. Chill for several hours.
- Line 4 serving plates with lettuce leaves. Chop remaining lettuce.
- Layer chopped lettuce, lobster and melon balls on prepared serving plates. Drizzle with dressing.
- May substitute 8 ounces shrimp for lobster.
- Yield: 4 servings.

Approx Per Serving: Cal 225; Prot 7 g; Carbo 19 g; Fiber 2 g; T Fat 15 g;
63% Calories from Fat; Chol 31 mg; Sod 253 mg.

*Joan M. Prue, **New England Region***
GFWC—Nashaway Woman's Club, Nashua NH

RICE AND SHRIMP SALAD

1 cup uncooked instant rice, prepared
1 cup chopped cauliflower
1/2 cup chopped green bell pepper
1 small onion, chopped
12 stuffed olives, sliced

1   5-ounce can shrimp, drained
1/4 cup mayonnaise
Juice of 1/2 lemon
Tabasco sauce to taste

- Combine all ingredients in bowl; mix well. Chill until serving time.
- Yield: 4 servings.

Approx Per Serving: Cal 264; Prot 11 g; Carbo 25 g; Fiber 2 g; T Fat 14 g; 46% Calories from Fat; Chol 70 mg; Sod 424 mg.

Ethel Reed, **Western Region**
GFWC—St. Helens Woman's Club, St. Helens OR

SEAFOOD PASTA SALAD

1 pound shrimp, peeled, deveined
1 pound scallops
2 pounds uncooked cheese tortellini
1/2 cup olive oil
1/2 cup fresh lemon juice

1 cup fresh basil leaves
1 clove of garlic, minced
1/2 cup grated Parmesan cheese
Pepper to taste

- Cook shrimp and scallops in water to cover in saucepan for 3 to 4 minutes or just until cooked through; drain. Cool. Cook pasta *al dente* using package directions. Cool.
- Process remaining ingredients in food processor or blender container. Combine with seafood and pasta in serving bowl; toss to coat well.
- Chill until serving time. Garnish with additional fresh basil leaves.
- Yield: 12 servings.

Approx Per Serving: Cal 401; Prot 27 g; Carbo 38 g; Fiber <1 g; T Fat 16 g; 36% Calories from Fat; Chol 111 mg; Sod 470 mg.

Ginny Moreno, **New England Region**
GFWC—New Canaan Women's Club, New Canaan CT

SEA ISLAND SALAD

2   7-ounce cans tuna
1   12-ounce can Shoe Peg corn, drained
3 tablespoons sweet pickle relish

2 tablespoons each grated onion and
chopped parsley
1/2 cup mayonnaise

- Combine first 5 ingredients in bowl. Add mayonnaise; toss gently to mix.
- Serve on bed of salad greens. Garnish with green olives and hard-boiled eggs.
- Yield: 4 servings.

Approx Per Serving: Cal 413; Prot 32 g; Carbo 21 g; Fiber 1 g; T Fat 23 g; 50% Calories from Fat; Chol 72 mg; Sod 801 mg.

Pat Guay, **Western Region**
GFWC—Montana, Missoula MT

MEATS

A place setting of Limoge china
in the "Ceralene" pattern and
sterling silver serving pieces and
flatware, along with some lovely
cutwork table linens, all given by
clubwomen, are displayed on the
table in the dining room.

BARBECUED BRISKET

1   5 to 6-pound beef brisket, trimmed
1 tablespoon liquid smoke
2 teaspoons Worcestershire sauce
2 teaspoons each garlic powder, onion
  salt and pepper
1 onion, chopped
1 cup catsup

2 cups water
¼ cup packed brown sugar
¼ cup Worcestershire sauce
¼ cup vinegar
1 tablespoon celery seed
1 teaspoon salt

- Sprinkle brisket with liquid smoke, 2 teaspoons Worcestershire sauce, garlic powder, onion salt and pepper. Place in large roasting pan. Marinate in refrigerator overnight.
- Bake brisket, covered with foil, at 275 degrees for 5 to 6 hours or until very tender; drain. Chill in refrigerator.
- Slice brisket very thin; return to roasting pan.
- Combine remaining ingredients in bowl; mix well. Pour over brisket.
- Bake, uncovered, at 275 degrees for 1½ hours.
- May simmer sauce for 15 minutes before adding to brisket.
- Yield: 10 servings.

Approx Per Serving: Cal 373; Prot 43 g; Carbo 18 g; Fiber 2 g; T Fat 13 g;
31% Calories from Fat; Chol 128 mg; Sod 586 mg.

Lucy C. Meyring, **South Central Region**
GFWC—North Park Woman's Club, Walden CO

BEEF BARBECUE

2 cups chopped onions
1½ cups beef broth
1   12-ounce bottle of catsup
¼ cup vinegar

¼ cup packed brown sugar
1 teaspoon mustard
1   4-to 5-pound beef roast, cooked,
  shredded

- Sauté onions in nonstick saucepan until tender. Add beef broth, catsup, vinegar, brown sugar and mustard; mix well.
- Cook for 5 minutes. Add shredded roast; mix well.
- Simmer for 30 minutes. Serve on hamburger buns.
- Use skimmed pan drippings from cooking roast in beef broth.
- Yield: 16 servings.

Approx Per Serving: Cal 233; Prot 27 g; Carbo 11 g; Fiber 1 g; T Fat 8 g;
33% Calories from Fat; Chol 80 mg; Sod 341 mg.

Cindy Zelinsky, **Middle Atlantic Region**
GFWC—New Brighton Junior Woman's Club, Beaver Falls PA

CHATEAUBRIAND DELUXE

¼ cup chopped green onions
2 tablespoons butter
2 tablespoons soy sauce
1 teaspoon dry Dijon mustard

Freshly ground pepper to taste
¾ cup dry sherry
1   3 to 4-pound beef tenderloin
2 tablespoons butter, softened

▪ Sauté green onions in 2 tablespoons butter in small saucepan until tender but not brown. Stir in soy sauce, dry mustard, pepper and sherry. Heat just to the boiling point.
▪ Spread tenderloin with 2 tablespoons butter. Place on rack in shallow roasting pan.
▪ Roast at 425 degrees for 45 minutes, basting frequently with sauce. Serve with remaining sauce.
▪ Yield: 8 servings.

Approx Per Serving: Cal 379; Prot 43 g; Carbo 1 g; Fiber <1 g; T Fat 19 g;
45% Calories from Fat; Chol 143 mg; Sod 394 mg.

Norma K. Chesney, **Great Lakes Region**
GFWC—Homewood Woman's Club, Homewood IL

FAJITAS

½ cup lime juice
⅓ cup oil
⅓ cup Tequila
4 cloves of garlic, pressed
1½ teaspoons cumin
1 teaspoon oregano

½ teaspoon pepper
3 pounds skirt steak
4 or 5 small unpeeled onions, cut into
   halves lengthwise
20 8-inch flour tortillas

▪ Combine lime juice, oil, Tequila, garlic, cumin, oregano and pepper in bowl; mix well. Trim steaks to fit into 9x13-inch dish. Add marinade. Place onions cut side down in marinade. Chill, covered, for 4 hours to overnight, turning steaks occasionally; drain.
▪ Place onions cut side down on grill.
▪ Grill for 7 minutes. Turn onions over. Add steaks to grill.
▪ Grill for 3 to 5 minutes on each side for rare or until done to taste. Remove steaks and onions to cutting board. Cut steak into thin strips; slice onions.
▪ Allow guests to warm tortillas on grill for 15 to 30 seconds, turning them with tongs. Layer steak strips and onions in tortillas.
▪ Provide bowls of warmed frijoles, salsa, guacamole and sour cream for topping fajitas.
▪ Fajitas were probably first made by Mexican ranch hands who cooked the inexpensive cut of beef over mesquite coals. Skirt steaks come from the diaphragm inside the rib cage. Flank steak may be substituted for skirt steak.
▪ Yield: 10 servings.

Approx Per Serving: Cal 511; Prot 31 g; Carbo 48 g; Fiber 3 g; T Fat 21 g;
37% Calories from Fat; Chol 77 mg; Sod 312 mg.
Nutritional information does not include toppings.

Bobbi Caley, **South Central Region**
GFWC—Las Noches Woman's Club, Tempe AZ

FINNISH PASTIES

1 pound round steak, cut into small
    cubes
6 medium potatoes, chopped
3 or 4 carrots, chopped
1 large onion, chopped
Salt and pepper to taste

1/2 cup shortening
2 cups flour
1 teaspoon salt
1/4 cup water
6 tablespoons butter

- Combine steak, potatoes, carrots, onion, salt and pepper in bowl; mix well.
- Cut shortening into flour and 1 teaspoon salt in bowl. Add water. Mix to form dough.
- Divide dough into 6 equal parts. Roll into 6 plate-sized circles on floured surface.
- Spoon filling onto 1 side of circles; dot with butter. Fold circles over to enclose filling; press edges to seal. Cut vents in tops. Place on baking sheet.
- Bake at 350 degrees for 1 to 1 1/4 hours or until golden brown.
- May substitute 1 rutabaga for 2 of the carrots.
- Yield: 6 servings.

Approx Per Serving: Cal 678; Prot 23 g; Carbo 72 g; Fiber 5 g; T Fat 34 g;
44% Calories from Fat; Chol 74 mg; Sod 501 mg.

*Marge Christensen, **Great Lakes Region***
GFWC—Edmore Woman's Club, Edmore MI

GREEN CHILI STEW

1 pound round steak, cubed
1/2 teaspoon minced garlic
2 teaspoons salt

1 cup canned tomatoes
1 cup water
1 29-ounce can chopped green chilies

- Brown steak in nonstick saucepan sprayed with nonstick cooking spray. Add garlic and salt.
- Sauté until garlic is light brown. Add tomatoes and water.
- Simmer until beef is tender. Stir in green chilies.
- Cook for 5 minutes longer.
- Yield: 4 servings.

Approx Per Serving: Cal 213; Prot 24 g; Carbo 15 g; Fiber 1 g; T Fat 7 g;
28% Calories from Fat; Chol 64 mg; Sod 2658 mg.

*Julie Melick, **South Central Region***
GFWC—Cosmopolitan Women's Club of Albuquerque, Placitas NM

1923—*The Village Improvement Association of Doylestown, Pennsylvania, founded an emergency room which is now the not-for-profit Doylestown Hospital. It is still the only hospital owned and operated by a federated woman's club.*

MACHACA BEEF

1   1½ to 2-pound beef roast
1 large onion, sliced
1   4-ounce can chopped green chilies
2 beef bouillon cubes
1½ teaspoons dry mustard

½ teaspoon garlic powder
1 teaspoon seasoned salt
½ teaspoon pepper
1 cup salsa

- Combine roast with next 7 ingredients in slow cooker. Add enough water to cover.
- Cook on Low overnight or on High until beef is tender. Drain, reserving liquid. Shred beef.
- Combine beef with salsa and enough reserved liquid if necessary to make of desired consistency.
- Use as filling for burritos or tacos.
- Yield: 10 servings.

Approx Per Serving: Cal 139; Prot 18 g; Carbo 4 g; Fiber <1 g; T Fat 5 g; 37% Calories from Fat; Chol 51 mg; Sod 553 mg.

Debbie Grieder, **South Central Region**
GFWC—Paradise Valley Junior Woman's Club, Phoenix AZ

REUBEN CASSEROLE

1   12-ounce package seasoned
    croutons
1   12-ounce can corned beef, crumbled
1   16-ounce can sauerkraut, drained

8 ounces Swiss cheese, sliced
3 eggs
2 cups milk

- Layer half the croutons, corned beef, sauerkraut, remaining croutons and cheese in 7x11-inch baking dish.
- Beat eggs with milk in bowl. Pour over layers.
- Bake at 325 degrees for 25 minutes or until set.
- Yield: 6 servings.

Approx Per Serving: Cal 598; Prot 40 g; Carbo 50 g; Fiber 2 g; T Fat 27 g; 40% Calories from Fat; Chol 201 mg; Sod 1991 mg.

Janice A. Wheeler, **Middle Atlantic Region**
GFWC—Civic League of Mechanicsburg, Mechanicsburg PA

SIRLOIN TIP SUNDAY DINNER

1 pound fresh mushrooms, sliced
3 medium onions, sliced
2 cloves of garlic, minced
1/2 cup butter
2 pounds sirloin, cubed

2 1/2 cups water
1/2 cup red wine
2 bouillon cubes
3 tablespoons soy sauce
3 tablespoons cornstarch

- Sauté mushrooms, onions and garlic in butter in skillet. Remove to 10x10-inch casserole with slotted spoon. Add sirloin cubes to drippings in skillet.
- Sauté beef until brown. Add to casserole. Add remaining ingredients to skillet, stirring to deglaze.
- Cook until thickened, stirring constantly. Add to casserole. Chill overnight.
- Bake, covered, at 325 degrees for 2 hours. Serve over mashed potatoes or noodles.
- Yield: 6 servings.

Approx Per Serving: Cal 416; Prot 32 g; Carbo 15 g; Fiber 3 g; T Fat 25 g;
54% Calories from Fat; Chol 126 mg; Sod 983 mg.

Katy H. Grubbs, **Southeastern Region**
GFWC—Old Town Woman's Club, Winston-Salem NC

BARBECUE CUPS

1 pound ground beef
3/4 cup barbecue sauce
1/2 cup chopped onion

3 tablespoons brown sugar
1   10-count can biscuits
3/4 cup shredded Cheddar cheese

- Brown ground beef in skillet, stirring until crumbly; drain. Add barbecue sauce, onion and brown sugar; mix well.
- Simmer for 20 minutes.
- Separate biscuits and press into greased muffin cups. Spoon meat mixture into cups. Sprinkle with cheese.
- Bake at 375 degrees for 12 minutes or until golden brown.
- Yield: 10 servings.

Approx Per Serving: Cal 221; Prot 12 g; Carbo 16 g; Fiber 1 g; T Fat 12 g;
48% Calories from Fat; Chol 40 mg; Sod 482 mg.

Linda Ellixson, **Southeastern Region**
GFWC—Virgilina Club, Virgilina VA

GOURMET CHILI

2 pounds lean ground beef
2 medium onions, finely chopped
1 cup chopped red and green bell
    pepper
6 cloves of garlic, pressed
2 16-ounce cans whole tomatoes,
    chopped

2 16-ounce cans red kidney beans
1/4 cup chili powder
1 tablespoon cumin seed
1 tablespoon oregano
1 tablespoon salt
1/2 teaspoon cracked pepper

- Brown ground beef in 4-quart saucepan, stirring until crumbly; drain. Add onions, bell pepper and garlic.
- Sauté until vegetables are tender. Add remaining ingredients; mix well.
- Simmer, covered, for 1 to 3 hours or until done to taste, stirring frequently and adding water if needed for desired consistency.
- May substitute lean chili beef if preferred and use longer cooking time.
- Yield: 8 servings.

Approx Per Serving: Cal 376; Prot 29 g; Carbo 28 g; Fiber 12 g; T Fat 17 g;
41% Calories from Fat; Chol 74 mg; Sod 1482 mg.

Margaret Dudley, **South Central Region**
GFWC—Comanche Study Club, Comanche TX

QUICK CHILI

1 1/2 pounds ground beef
Salt and pepper to taste
1 8-ounce can tomato sauce

1 10-ounce can Ro-Tel tomatoes with
    green chilies
1 7-ounce can ranch-style beans

- Brown ground beef with salt and pepper in saucepan, stirring until crumbly; drain. Add remaining ingredients.
- Simmer for 1 to 1 1/2 hours or until done to taste.
- Yield: 4 servings.

Approx Per Serving: Cal 424; Prot 35 g; Carbo 15 g; Fiber 1 g; T Fat 25 g;
53% Calories from Fat; Chol 111 mg; Sod 881 mg.

Linda Turner, **South Central Region**
GFWC—Adelante Club, Borger TX

1925—*The GFWC Weirton Woman's Club of West Virginia established a public library and continues to support the library with financial contributions, a memorial book program, volunteer hours and leadership through the library's Board of Directors.*

MEATBALLS IN SAUERBRATEN SAUCE

1¹/₂ pounds lean ground chuck
1 egg
¹/₄ cup chopped onion
Thyme to taste
1 tablespoon oil
1 cup cold water
1¹/₂ teaspoons cornstarch

2 tablespoons catsup
1 tablespoon cider vinegar
1¹/₂ tablespoons brown sugar
¹/₂ teaspoon each cloves, ginger and
 pepper
1 bay leaf

- Combine ground chuck, egg, onion and thyme in bowl; mix well. Shape into 6 oblong patties.
- Brown patties on both sides in hot oil in skillet; remove patties to paper towel and drain skillet.
- Add mixture of water and cornstarch to skillet. Stir in remaining ingredients.
- Cook until thickened and bubbly, stirring constantly; reduce heat. Add beef patties to skillet.
- Simmer, covered, for 20 minutes. Discard bay leaf.
- Yield: 6 servings.

Approx Per Serving: Cal 287; Prot 22 g; Carbo 6 g; Fiber <1 g; T Fat 19 g;
61% Calories from Fat; Chol 110 mg; Sod 137 mg.

Mary Sullivan, **Great Lakes Region**
GFWC—Mequon-Thiensville Junior Woman's Club, Mequon WI

MEATBALLS WITH KRAUT

1 cup seasoned bread crumbs
2 pounds ground beef
3 eggs
1 envelope onion soup mix
1 12-ounce bottle of chili sauce

1 cup water
1 16-ounce can cranberry sauce
1 cup packed brown sugar
1¹/₂ cups drained sauerkraut

- Process bread crumbs in blender until finely ground. Combine with ground beef, eggs and soup mix in bowl; mix well. Shape into small meatballs.
- Brown in skillet sprayed with nonstick cooking spray; drain. Place meatballs in slow cooker.
- Combine remaining ingredients in bowl; mix well. Spoon over meatballs.
- Cook on High for 2 to 2¹/₂ hours or until done to taste.
- Yield: 8 servings.

Approx Per Serving: Cal 577; Prot 27 g; Carbo 78 g; Fiber 3 g; T Fat 19 g;
29% Calories from Fat; Chol 155 mg; Sod 1155 mg.

Marsha D. Sailor, **Great Lakes Region**
GFWC—Jackson Center Junior American Club, Jackson Center OH

SWEDISH MEATBALLS

2 slices bread, crumbled
1¹/₂ pounds ground round
2 eggs
¹/₂ onion, finely chopped

1 tablespoon brown sugar
¹/₄ teaspoon each allspice and ginger
¹/₈ teaspoon ground cloves
1 teaspoon salt

- Soak bread in water to cover in bowl; drain. Combine bread, ground round, eggs, onion, brown sugar and seasonings in bowl; mix well. Shape into meatballs.
- Brown on all sides in lightly greased skillet over medium heat.
- Yield: 6 servings.

> *Approx Per Serving:* Cal 295; Prot 24 g; Carbo 8 g; Fiber <1 g; T Fat 18 g;
> 56% Calories from Fat; Chol 145 mg; Sod 493 mg.

> *Margaret Swanson,* **Great Lakes Region**
> *GFWC—Culver City Club, Culver IN*

BARBECUED INDIVIDUAL MEAT LOAVES

¹/₄ medium green bell pepper
¹/₂ medium onion
1¹/₂ pounds ground beef
2 slices bread, crumbled
1 egg
¹/₂ teaspoon salt
3 tablespoons catsup
¹/₂ cup milk
¹/₂ teaspoon dry mustard

³/₄ cup catsup
2 tablespoons vinegar
2 tablespoons sugar
1 teaspoon minced onion
¹/₄ cup water
2 teaspoons Worcestershire sauce
¹/₈ teaspoon chili powder
¹/₈ teaspoon cayenne pepper

- Process green pepper and onion in blender until finely chopped. Combine with ground beef, bread crumbs, egg, salt, 3 tablespoons catsup, milk and mustard in bowl. Shape into 6 individual loaves; place in baking dish.
- Combine remaining ingredients in bowl; mix well. Spoon over meat loaves.
- Bake at 350 degrees for 1 hour.
- May bake meat loaves without sauce and freeze until needed. Add sauce and bake for 30 minutes.
- Yield: 6 servings.

> *Approx Per Serving:* Cal 328; Prot 24 g; Carbo 19 g; Fiber 1 g; T Fat 18 g;
> 48% Calories from Fat; Chol 110 mg; Sod 675 mg.

> *Edith Reisler,* **Middle Atlantic Region**
> *GFWC—New Century Club, Coodersport PA*

BEEF SKILLET FIESTA

1 pound ground beef
¼ cup chopped onion
1½ teaspoons chili powder
1 16-ounce can stewed tomatoes
1 beef bouillon cube

1¼ cups boiling water
1 4-ounce can chopped green chilies
1 cup drained whole kernel corn
1⅓ cups uncooked instant rice
1 teaspoon salt

- Brown ground beef with onion in electric skillet or 12-inch skillet, stirring until ground beef is crumbly; drain. Add chili powder and tomatoes.
- Dissolve bouillon cube in boiling water in saucepan. Add to ground beef mixture. Add remaining ingredients; mix well.
- Cook until bubbly; turn off heat or remove from heat. Let stand, covered, for 5 minutes or until rice is tender; mix well.
- Yield: 6 servings.

Approx Per Serving: Cal 286; Prot 17 g; Carbo 30 g; Fiber 1 g; T Fat 11 g; 34% Calories from Fat; Chol 49 mg; Sod 984 mg.

*Kathleen Hall, **South Central Region***
GFWC—Delphian Study Club of Anadarko, Anadarko OK

HAMBURGER STEW

1½ pounds ground beef
1 medium onion, sliced
4 carrots, sliced 1 inch thick
4 potatoes, cut into quarters
Garlic powder, salt and pepper to taste

1 10-ounce can beef broth
½ cup water
1 teaspoon Worcestershire sauce
½ head cabbage, cut into wedges

- Shape ground beef into 6 patties. Brown on both sides in large nonstick skillet or electric skillet; drain.
- Add onion, carrots, potatoes, garlic powder, salt and pepper. Stir in beef broth and water. Sprinkle with Worcestershire sauce.
- Simmer, covered, for 45 minutes or until vegetables are nearly tender. Add cabbage. Simmer for 15 minutes longer.
- Yield: 6 servings.

Approx Per Serving: Cal 346; Prot 24 g; Carbo 26 g; Fiber 4 g; T Fat 16 g; 42% Calories from Fat; Chol 74 mg; Sod 253 mg.

*Roberta A. Dyrsten, GFWC Director of Junior Clubs, 1992–94, **Middle Atlantic Region***
Sparta NJ

MICROWAVE SPAGHETTI PIE

1   7-ounce package spaghetti
2 tablespoons margarine
1/3 cup grated Parmesan cheese
2 eggs, beaten
1 cup cottage cheese

1 pound lean ground chuck, crumbled
1/2 cup chopped onion
1/4 cup chopped green bell pepper
1   16-ounce jar spaghetti sauce
1/2 cup shredded mozzarella cheese

- Cook spaghetti using package directions; drain. Add margarine, Parmesan cheese and eggs; mix well. Shape into shell in 10-inch glass pie plate.
- Microwave on High for 2 minutes. Spread cottage cheese in shell; set aside.
- Microwave ground chuck in microwave-safe colander in glass bowl for 5 minutes, stirring once. Combine with onion and green pepper in glass dish.
- Microwave, covered, on High for 2 to 3 minutes or until onion is tender. Add spaghetti sauce.
- Microwave for 5 to 7 minutes; mix well. Spoon into prepared pie plate.
- Microwave for 6 to 8 minutes, turning plate once. Sprinkle with mozzarella cheese. Microwave for 1 minute or until cheese melts.
- Yield: 4 servings.

Approx Per Serving: Cal 760; Prot 45 g; Carbo 60 g; Fiber 4 g; T Fat 38 g;
45% Calories from Fat; Chol 205 mg; Sod 1122 mg.

*Frances A. Pavcik, **Middle Atlantic Region***
GFWC—Mercer County Federation, Sharpsville PA

PIZZA SPAGHETTI

1   16-ounce package spaghetti
1 cup milk
2 eggs, beaten
1 pound ground beef
1/2 cup chopped onion
1/2 cup chopped green bell pepper

1   32-ounce jar spaghetti sauce
2 cups shredded mozzarella cheese
1 cup sliced mushrooms
1 cup sliced pepperoni
Parsley flakes and Italian seasoning to taste

- Cook spaghetti using package directions; drain. Add mixture of milk and eggs; mix well.
- Brown ground beef with onion and green pepper in skillet, stirring until ground beef is crumbly; drain. Add to spaghetti with spaghetti sauce; mix well. Spoon into 9x13-inch baking dish.
- Top with cheese, mushrooms, pepperoni, parsley flakes and Italian seasoning.
- Bake at 350 degrees for 30 minutes. Let stand for several minutes before serving.
- May vary toppings to suit individual tastes.
- Yield: 8 servings.

Approx Per Serving: Cal 644; Prot 31 g; Carbo 65 g; Fiber 4 g; T Fat 29 g;
40% Calories from Fat; Chol 121 mg; Sod 1022 mg.

*Cheryl M. Gauvey, **Middle Atlantic Region***
GFWC—New Brighton Junior Woman's Club, Beaver PA

PICADILLO

2 pounds ground beef
1 cup chopped onion
2 teaspoons minced garlic
2/3 cup chopped green bell pepper
1 16-ounce can tomatoes, chopped
1/4 cup Worcestershire sauce
1/2 teaspoon each cumin and oregano
1/4 teaspoon each cayenne pepper and
    black pepper

2¼ teaspoons salt
2 10-ounce cans beef broth
2 6-ounce cans tomato paste
1 4-ounce jar chopped pimentos
1 6-ounce can chopped black olives
1 cup slivered almonds
1 cup raisins
1 4-ounce can chopped green chilies

- Brown ground beef in saucepan, stirring until crumbly; drain. Add next 10 ingredients; mix well.
- Cook over medium heat until vegetables are tender. Add beef broth and remaining ingredients; mix well.
- Simmer for 1 hour. Serve over tortilla chips, rice or polenta. May also serve from chafing dish with tortilla chips as appetizer.
- Yield: 8 servings.

Approx Per Serving: Cal 502; Prot 29 g; Carbo 36 g; Fiber 7 g; T Fat 31 g;
51% Calories from Fat; Chol 74 mg; Sod 1355 mg.

Ginger Dudley, **South Central Region**
GFWC—Comanche Study Club, Comanche TX

STUFFED CABBAGE

1½ pounds ground beef
1 pound ground pork
1 cup uncooked rice
1 onion, chopped
1 egg
Garlic powder, salt and pepper to taste

1 head cabbage
1 pound sauerkraut
1 green bell pepper, chopped
1 10-ounce can tomato soup
4 cups whole canned tomatoes
1/4 cup sugar

- Combine ground beef, ground pork and next 6 ingredients in bowl; mix well.
- Cook cabbage in water to cover in saucepan until leaves can be removed. Cut out thick center ribs. Spoon ground beef mixture onto cabbage leaves; roll up leaves to enclose filling.
- Layer half the sauerkraut, half the cabbage rolls, half the green pepper, remaining sauerkraut and remaining cabbage rolls in large saucepan. Pour soup and tomatoes over layers. Top with remaining green pepper; sprinkle with sugar.
- Simmer for 2 to 3 hours or until done to taste, adding water as liquid is absorbed.
- Yield: 8 servings.

Approx Per Serving: Cal 464; Prot 35 g; Carbo 41 g; Fiber 4 g; T Fat 18 g;
35% Calories from Fat; Chol 124 mg; Sod 915 mg.

Debbie Lyons, **Middle Atlantic Region**
GFWC—West Side Junior Women's Club, Luzerne PA

CREAMY TACOS

1½ pounds ground beef
1   10-ounce can Ro-Tel tomatoes with green chilies
2   16-ounce cans pinto beans

1 envelope chili seasoning mix
1 pound Velveeta cheese, cut into cubes
2 cups half and half

- Brown ground beef in 3-quart saucepan, stirring until crumbly; drain. Stir in tomatoes, beans and chili seasoning mix.
- Cook for 5 minutes. Stir in cheese until melted. Add half and half.
- Cook until heated through. Serve over bite-sized tortilla chips. Garnish with lettuce, tomatoes and onions.
- Yield: 8 servings.

> *Approx Per Serving:* Cal 560; Prot 36 g; Carbo 22 g; Fiber <1 g; T Fat 37 g;
> 59% Calories from Fat; Chol 132 mg; Sod 1518 mg.
> Nutritional information does not include tortilla chips or toppings.

> *Becky Meadors,* **South Central Region**
> *GFWC—Women's Community League of Alma, Alma AR*

INDIAN TACOS

2½ cups flour
1 teaspoon salt
1 cup dry milk powder
2 tablespoons baking powder
1 tablespoon oil
1½ cups warm water
1 pound ground beef

½ envelope taco seasoning mix
8 cups oil
3 cups cooked pinto beans
2 tomatoes, chopped
1 small head lettuce, shredded
1 large onion, chopped
3 cups shredded Cheddar cheese

- Mix 2 cups flour, salt, milk, baking powder, 1 tablespoon oil and water in large bowl. Add remaining ½ cup flour; knead until smooth. Let stand for 1 hour.
- Brown ground beef with taco seasoning mix in skillet, stirring until ground beef is crumbly; drain.
- Divide dough into 8 portions. Roll into 6-inch circles on floured surface. Cut small slit in center of each.
- Deep-fry circles in 8 cups 400-degree oil until golden brown; drain.
- Place 1 fry bread on each serving plate. Top with ground beef mixture, beans, tomatoes, lettuce, onion and cheese.
- Yield: 8 servings.

> *Approx Per Serving:* Cal 591; Prot 34 g; Carbo 57 g; Fiber 10 g; T Fat 25 g;
> 38% Calories from Fat; Chol 83 mg; Sod 1080 mg.
> Nutritional information does not include oil for deep frying.

> *Carolyn Riffel,* **South Central Region**
> *GFWC—Philomathic Club, Anadarko OK*

TACO PITAS

1 pound ground beef	1 8-ounce can whole kernel corn,
1 envelope taco seasoning mix	drained
3/4 cup water	5 6-inch pita bread rounds
1 10-ounce can Ro-Tel tomatoes with	1 cup shredded lettuce
green chilies	3/4 cup shredded Cheddar cheese

- Brown ground beef in skillet, stirring until crumbly; drain. Add next 4 ingredients; mix well.
- Simmer for 15 to 20 minutes.
- Cut pita rounds into halves; place on baking sheet.
- Bake at 250 degrees for 10 minutes or until heated through.
- Spoon ground beef into pita pockets. Top with lettuce and cheese.
- Yield: 10 servings.

Approx Per Serving: Cal 248; Prot 15 g; Carbo 25 g; Fiber 1 g; T Fat 10 g; 36% Calories from Fat; Chol 39 mg; Sod 764 mg.

*Judy Weese, **South Central Region***
GFWC—Alma Women's Community League, Alma AR

BEEFY BAKED PASTA FAMILY-STYLE

1 pound coarsely ground lean beef	1/4 cup Parmesan cheese
3 cloves of garlic, pressed	1 teaspoon whole oregano
2 tablespoons olive oil	1/2 teaspoon whole rosemary
1/2 cup half and half	Salt and pepper to taste
3/4 cup spaghetti sauce	12 ounces uncooked penne
3/4 cup brown gravy	1 cup shredded mozzarella cheese

- Brown ground beef and garlic in olive oil in large skillet, stirring until ground beef is crumbly; drain. Add next 8 ingredients; mix well.
- Simmer for several minutes.
- Cook pasta in boiling water in large saucepan just until tender; drain. Add to ground beef mixture; mix well. Spoon into 3-quart baking dish. Top with mozzarella cheese.
- Bake at 350 degrees for 25 minutes or until bubbly.
- Yield: 6 servings.

Approx Per Serving: Cal 544; Prot 28 g; Carbo 51 g; Fiber 3 g; T Fat 25 g; 41% Calories from Fat; Chol 74 mg; Sod 484 mg.

*Jackie Baumler, **Middle Atlantic Region***
GFWC—Cranberry Women's Club, Zelienople PA

BEEF AND BROCCOLI STRUDEL

1 pound ground chuck
1 medium onion, chopped
1 10-ounce package frozen chopped
    broccoli, thawed, drained
8 ounces mozzarella cheese, shredded

1/2 cup sour cream
1/4 cup dry bread crumbs
2 8-count cans crescent rolls
1/4 cup melted butter

- Brown ground chuck with onion in skillet, stirring until ground beef is crumbly; drain. Add next 4 ingredients; mix well.
- Unroll roll dough; do not separate. Place dough side by side on baking sheet; press edges and perforations to seal.
- Spoon ground beef mixture down center of dough. Fold sides over to enclose beef. Press edges to seal. Brush with butter.
- Bake at 350 degrees for 45 minutes or until golden brown.
- Yield: 8 servings.

Approx Per Serving: Cal 505; Prot 21 g; Carbo 29 g; Fiber 1 g; T Fat 34 g;
60% Calories from Fat; Chol 81 mg; Sod 686 mg.

Julie L. Day, **Great Lakes Region**
GFWC—Mattoon Junior Woman's Club, Mattoon IL

BEEF AND TOMATO-STUFFED SHELLS

1 16-ounce can tomatoes, chopped
1/4 cup dry red wine
1 tablespoon cornstarch
2 tablespoons tomato paste
1/2 teaspoon oregano
1/4 teaspoon fennel seed, crushed
12 ounces ground beef

2 cups sliced fresh mushrooms
1/2 cup chopped onion
1/2 cup chopped green bell pepper
1 clove of garlic, minced
1/2 teaspoon salt
8 jumbo pasta shells, cooked
1/4 cup grated Parmesan cheese

- Combine first 6 ingredients in large saucepan; mix well. Cook until thickened, stirring constantly.
- Brown ground beef with mushrooms, onion, green pepper and garlic in skillet, stirring frequently; drain. Add salt and 1/2 cup tomato mixture.
- Spoon ground beef mixture into pasta shells; arrange in 6x10-inch baking dish. Stir any remaining ground beef mixture into tomato mixture. Spoon over shells; top with cheese.
- Bake at 350 degrees for 20 to 25 minutes or until heated through.
- Yield: 4 servings.

Approx Per Serving: Cal 332; Prot 23 g; Carbo 27 g; Fiber 4 g; T Fat 14 g;
39% Calories from Fat; Chol 60 mg; Sod 603 mg.

Beth Clark, **Middle Atlantic Region**
GFWC—Shenango Valley Women's Club, Volant PA

CALIFORNIA FANDANGO

1 pound ground beef
1 medium onion, chopped
1 8-ounce can mushrooms
2 cloves of garlic, minced
1 teaspoon oregano
3 tablespoons butter
Salt and pepper to taste

2 10-ounce packages frozen chopped
   spinach, thawed
1 10-ounce can cream of celery soup
1 cup sour cream
1 tablespoon uncooked rice
6 ounces mozzarella cheese, sliced

- Brown ground beef with onion, mushrooms, garlic and oregano in butter, stirring until ground beef is crumbly; drain. Season with salt and pepper.
- Add spinach, soup, sour cream and rice; mix well. Spoon into 9x13-inch baking dish. Cut cheese into strips; arrange over casserole.
- Bake at 350 degrees for 35 to 40 minutes or until heated through.
- Yield: 6 servings.

Approx Per Serving: Cal 454; Prot 26 g; Carbo 17 g; Fiber 4 g; T Fat 33 g;
64% Calories from Fat; Chol 109 mg; Sod 818 mg.

Dolores E. Myl, **Western Region**
GFWC—Rossmoor Woman's Club, Los Alamitos CA

CHUCK WAGON DINNER-IN-A-DISH

2 medium onions, chopped
1 green bell pepper, chopped
2 tablespoons butter
1 pound ground round
2 eggs, beaten

Salt and pepper to taste
1 20-ounce can whole kernel corn,
   drained
1 20-ounce can stewed tomatoes
½ cup bread crumbs

- Sauté onions and green pepper in butter in skillet. Add ground round, eggs, salt and pepper. Cook until ground beef is brown; drain.
- Layer beef mixture, corn and tomatoes ½ at a time in 1½-quart baking dish. Top with crumbs.
- Bake at 350 degrees for 30 minutes.
- Yield: 6 servings.

Approx Per Serving: Cal 373; Prot 21 g; Carbo 36 g; Fiber 3 g; T Fat 18 g;
41% Calories from Fat; Chol 131 mg; Sod 684 mg.

Christeen Edstrom, **South Central Region**
GFWC—Woman's Club of Colorado Springs, Colorado Springs CO

1930—*At the annual GFWC Convention, the Sakajawea Junior Woman's Club of North Dakota, a Native American junior woman's club, presented an Indian operetta to show cultural diversity in the arts.*

COWBOY HODGEPODGE

2 pounds ground beef
3 10-ounce cans minestrone
2 15-ounce cans ranch-style beans

2 10-ounce cans Ro-Tel tomatoes
   with green chilies

- Brown ground beef in skillet, stirring until crumbly; drain. Add remaining ingredients; mix well. Spoon into baking dish.
- Bake at 300 degrees for 4 hours. Serve with corn bread or crackers.
- Yield: 8 servings.

Approx Per Serving: Cal 422; Prot 30 g; Carbo 30 g; Fiber 1 g; T Fat 21 g; 44% Calories from Fat; Chol 75 mg; Sod 1476 mg.

Jean O'Kief, **South Central Region**
GFWC—Philomathic Study Club, Cleveland OK

ENCHILADA CASSEROLE

1 pound ground beef
1 medium onion, chopped
1 teaspoon oregano
1/2 teaspoon each salt and pepper
1 4-ounce can chopped green chilies

1 8-ounce can tomato sauce
1/2 cup water
6 corn tortillas, torn
2 cups shredded Cheddar cheese

- Brown ground beef with onion, oregano, salt and pepper in skillet, stirring frequently; drain. Stir in green chilies, tomato sauce and water. Cook for several minutes longer.
- Alternate layers of tortillas, ground beef mixture and cheese in 1 1/2-quart baking dish until all ingredients are used.
- Bake at 350 degrees for 20 minutes or until bubbly.
- Yield: 4 servings.

Approx Per Serving: Cal 593; Prot 40 g; Carbo 29 g; Fiber 5 g; T Fat 37 g; 55% Calories from Fat; Chol 134 mg; Sod 1228 mg.

Georgie L. Jones, **South Central Region**
GFWC—Chandler Woman's Club, Chandler AZ

1936—*The Federated Woman's Club of Delta, Colorado, furnished a children's ward at the local hospital.*

TEX-MEX LASAGNA

1 pound ground beef
1/2 cup chopped onion
1 cup tomato paste
1 cup picante sauce
3/4 cup water

1 teaspoon each oregano and basil
1 cup ricotta cheese
2 1/4 cups shredded mozzarella cheese
8 ounces uncooked lasagna noodles

- Brown ground beef with onion in large skillet over medium heat, stirring frequently; drain. Add next 5 ingredients; mix well.
- Combine ricotta cheese and 3/4 cup mozzarella cheese in bowl.
- Spread 1/3 cup ground beef mixture in 8x11-inch baking dish sprayed with nonstick cooking spray. Layer lasagna noodles, cheese mixture and remaining ground beef mixture 1/2 at a time in prepared dish. Top with remaining 1 1/2 cups mozzarella cheese.
- Chill, covered, overnight.
- Bake at 350 degrees for 1 hour or until noodles are tender. Let stand at room temperature for 20 minutes before serving.
- Yield: 6 servings.

Approx Per Serving: Cal 545; Prot 34 g; Carbo 43 g; Fiber 3 g; T Fat 26 g;
43% Calories from Fat; Chol 103 mg; Sod 481 mg.

*Mary Mortimer, **South Central Region***
GFWC—History Club, Fairfield TX

RUNZA CASSEROLE

2 pounds ground beef
1/2 cup chopped onion
Salt to taste
3/4 teaspoon pepper
1/2 head cabbage, finely chopped

1   10-ounce can cream of mushroom
    soup
2   8-count cans crescent rolls
1 cup shredded sharp Cheddar cheese

- Brown ground beef with onion, salt and pepper in large skillet, stirring frequently; drain. Add cabbage.
- Cook until cabbage and onion are tender; remove from heat. Stir in soup.
- Line 9x11-inch baking dish with 1 can roll dough. Layer ground beef mixture and cheese in prepared dish. Top with remaining roll dough; seal edges.
- Bake at 350 degrees for 30 minutes.
- Yield: 8 servings.

Approx Per Serving: Cal 531; Prot 28 g; Carbo 27 g; Fiber 1 g; T Fat 34 g;
59% Calories from Fat; Chol 89 mg; Sod 903 mg.

*Diana Smalley, **Mississippi Valley Region***
GFWC—Papillion Junior Woman's Club, Gretna NE

CALIFORNIA TAMALE PIE

1 large onion, chopped
2 tablespoons oil
2 pounds lean ground beef
1 clove of garlic, finely chopped
1 8-ounce can pitted black olives
1 8-ounce can tomato sauce
1 6-ounce can tomato paste

1 16-ounce can chopped tomatoes
1 16-ounce can corn
1 4-ounce can mushrooms
12 ounces noodles, cooked
1 tablespoon chili powder
4 16-ounce cans tamales

- Sauté onion in oil in Dutch oven. Add ground beef and garlic. Cook until ground beef is brown and crumbly; drain. Stir in undrained olives and next 7 ingredients; mix well.
- Cut tamales into quarters. Fold into ground beef mixture.
- Bake, covered, at 350 degrees until heated through.
- May top with shredded cheese.
- Yield: 12 servings.

Approx Per Serving: Cal 605; Prot 26 g; Carbo 51 g; Fiber 3 g; T Fat 37 g;
51% Calories from Fat; Chol 99 mg; Sod 1356 mg.

Margaret F. Smith, **Western Region**
GFWC—Federated Women's Improvement Club of St. Helena, St. Helena CA

ONE-STEP TAMALE PIE

1 pound ground beef
1 cup chopped onion
2 cloves of garlic, chopped
2 8-ounce cans tomato sauce
1 cup milk
2 eggs, slightly beaten
1/2 cup sliced black olives

1 20-ounce can whole kernel corn, drained
3/4 cup yellow cornmeal
Tabasco sauce to taste
2 1/2 teaspoons chili powder
2 teaspoons salt

- Brown ground beef with onion and garlic in large skillet, stirring frequently; drain. Stir in remaining ingredients. Spoon into 8x12-inch baking dish.
- Bake at 350 degrees for 45 minutes or until knife inserted in center comes out clean. Cut into squares to serve.
- Yield: 8 servings.

Approx Per Serving: Cal 303; Prot 17 g; Carbo 31 g; Fiber 4 g; T Fat 14 g;
39% Calories from Fat; Chol 94 mg; Sod 1191 mg.

Jeanne Virden, **South Central Region**
GFWC—20th Century Club, Big Lake TX

GRILLED KANSAS LAMB CHOPS

2 cups white wine
1 tablespoon each rosemary, garlic
    powder and onion powder

1 teaspoon each salt and pepper
6 lamb chops

- Combine first 6 ingredients in shallow dish; mix well. Add lamb chops.
- Marinate in refrigerator for 6 to 24 hours, turning several times; drain.
- Grill over low coals until done to taste. Serve with minted apple jelly.
- Yield: 6 servings.

Approx Per Serving: Cal 208; Prot 21 g; Carbo <1 g; Fiber 0 g; T Fat 7 g;
29% Calories from Fat; Chol 66 mg; Sod 418 mg.
Nutritional information includes entire amount of marinade.

Rebecca Ninemire, ***Mississippi Valley Region***
GFWC—Tourist Club, Wakeeney KS

BAKED LAMB SHANKS

6 lamb shanks
1 cup flour
2 teaspoons salt
1/2 teaspoon pepper
1/4 cup oil
1 onion, chopped

2 cloves of garlic, pressed
3 cups water
3 beef bouillon cubes
1 bay leaf
1 cup finely chopped carrot
1 cup finely chopped celery

- Coat lamb shanks with mixture of flour, salt and pepper.
- Brown on all sides in oil in skillet; remove to 4-quart baking dish. Drain skillet, reserving 2 tablespoons drippings. Add onion and garlic to drippings in skillet.
- Sauté until onion is tender. Stir in remaining flour mixture and next 3 ingredients.
- Cook until thickened, stirring constantly. Pour over lamb shanks. Sprinkle carrot and celery over lamb.
- Bake, covered, at 375 degrees for 2 hours or until lamb is very tender. Skim fat from surface; adjust seasonings.
- May add brown gravy if desired.
- Yield: 6 servings.

Approx Per Serving: Cal 314; Prot 23 g; Carbo 20 g; Fiber 2 g; T Fat 15 g;
45% Calories from Fat; Chol 63 mg; Sod 1214 mg.

Gerry Clark, ***Southeastern Region***
GFWC—Troy Women's Club, Troy NC

KENTUCKY LAMB IN PEANUT BUTTER SAUCE

2 tablespoons peanut butter
1 teaspoon olive oil
1/2 cup (scant) water

Paprika, nutmeg, salt and freshly
   ground pepper to taste
1/2 cup 1/2-inch pieces cooked lamb

- Stir peanut butter into hot olive oil in skillet. Add remaining ingredients.
- Simmer, covered, for 6 to 7 minutes, stirring occasionally. Adjust seasonings.
- Serve over cooked rice with shredded fresh coconut, hot peppers and mango chutney.
- Yield: 1 serving.

Approx Per Serving: Cal 384; Prot 30 g; Carbo 5 g; Fiber 2 g; T Fat 28 g;
64% Calories from Fat; Chol 66 mg; Sod 189 mg.

Michelle Morrow, ***Southeastern Region***
GFWC—Radcliff Women's Club, Radcliff KY

HAM BALLS

2 cups ground ham
8 ounces sausage
8 ounces ground beef
2 eggs
1 cup tomato juice
1 cup cracker crumbs

1/4 to 1/2 cup minced onion
1/2 cup chopped green bell pepper
1 cup packed brown sugar
1/2 cup vinegar
1/2 cup water
2 teaspoons dry mustard

- Combine ham, sausage and ground beef with next 5 ingredients in bowl; mix well.
  Shape into balls. Place in heavy 9x13-inch baking pan.
- Bake at 350 degrees for 1 hour.
- Combine brown sugar, vinegar, water and dry mustard in bowl; mix well. Pour
  over ham balls.
- Bake for 30 minutes longer.
- May omit ground beef and increase ground ham to 1 1/2 pounds and sausage
  to 1 pound.
- Yield: 12 servings.

Approx Per Serving: Cal 236; Prot 11 g; Carbo 30 g; Fiber 1 g; T Fat 8 g;
31% Calories from Fat; Chol 67 mg; Sod 534 mg.

Karen D. Sisk, ***Mississippi Valley Region***
GFWC—Flint Hills General Federated Women's Club of Manhattan, Manhattan KS

MISSOURI MEAT LOAF

1/2 cup packed brown sugar
1/4 cup vinegar
1/4 cup water
1/2 cup catsup
1/2 teaspoon mustard

1 1/2 pounds ground ham
1 1/2 pounds ground fresh pork
3 eggs
1 1/2 cups graham cracker crumbs
1/2 cup water

- Combine first 5 ingredients in bowl; mix well.
- Combine ham, pork, eggs, cracker crumbs and 1/2 cup water in bowl; mix well. Shape into loaf; place in 9x13-inch baking dish.
- Bake loaf at 400 degrees for 30 minutes, basting frequently with sauce. Decrease oven temperature to 350 degrees.
- Bake for 1 hour longer, basting with sauce.
- Yield: 10 servings.

Approx Per Serving: Cal 391; Prot 37 g; Carbo 31 g; Fiber 1 g; T Fat 13 g;
30% Calories from Fat; Chol 152 mg; Sod 1222 mg.

*Laneve Hendren, **Mississippi Valley Region***
GFWC—20th Century Club, Bethany MO

LETTS-HAM-IT-UP BALLS

2 pounds ground lean ham
2 pounds ground fresh pork
2 cups graham cracker crumbs
2 eggs, beaten
1 1/2 cups milk

1   10-ounce can tomato soup
1/2 cup vinegar
1 1/2 cups packed brown sugar
1 teaspoon dry mustard

- Combine ham and pork with next 4 ingredients in bowl; mix well. Shape by 1/3 cupfuls into balls. Arrange in 9x13-inch baking dish.
- Combine vinegar, brown sugar and dry mustard in saucepan. Heat until brown sugar dissolves, stirring to mix well. Pour over ham balls.
- Bake at 325 degrees for 2 hours, basting twice.
- Yield: 12 servings.

Approx Per Serving: Cal 513; Prot 41 g; Carbo 54 g; Fiber 1 g; T Fat 15 g;
26% Calories from Fat; Chol 137 mg; Sod 1374 mg.

*Corita W. McCormac, **Mississippi Valley Region***
GFWC—Letts Federated Women's Club, Letts IA

ROCKY MOUNTAIN PORK CHOPS

2 16-ounce cans baked beans
6 lean 1/2-inch rib pork chops
11/2 teaspoons prepared mustard
11/2 tablespoons brown sugar

11/2 tablespoons catsup
6 1/4-inch onion slices
6 lemon slices

- Layer baked beans in 9x13-inch baking dish. Arrange pork chops over beans; spread lightly with mustard.
- Sprinkle with brown sugar; drizzle with catsup. Top each pork chop with 1 slice onion and 1 slice lemon, securing with wooden pick.
- Bake at 325 degrees for 11/2 hours.
- Yield: 6 servings.

Approx Per Serving: Cal 398; Prot 40 g; Carbo 38 g; Fiber 5 g; T Fat 11 g; 25% Calories from Fat; Chol 98 mg; Sod 740 mg.

Bobby Bjork, **Western Region**
GFWC—Madison Valley Woman's Club, Ennis MT

STUFFED PORK CHOPS

6 thick pork chops
2 cups soft bread crumbs
1/4 cup melted butter
1 tablespoon onion powder
1/4 teaspoon sage

Salt and pepper to taste
1/2 cup water
6 firm bananas
1/3 cup butter

- Cut pocket in each pork chop, cutting from outer edge to bone. Combine next 6 ingredients in bowl; mix well. Stuff into pockets; secure with wooden picks or small skewers.
- Brown on both sides in skillet over low heat; season with additional salt and pepper. Add water. Simmer, covered, for 1 hour. Discard picks; arrange chops on heated platter.
- Sauté bananas in 1/3 cup butter in skillet over low heat until golden brown. Sprinkle lightly with salt. Arrange around pork chops.
- May thicken pork chops pan juices for gravy if desired.
- Yield: 6 servings.

Approx Per Serving: Cal 532; Prot 34 g; Carbo 34 g; Fiber 3 g; T Fat 29 g; 49% Calories from Fat; Chol 146 mg; Sod 306 mg.

Pat Harper, **Southeastern Region**
GFWC—Clendenin Woman's Club, Clendenin VA

PORK LOIN ROAST WITH APPLE RINGS

Sage, salt and pepper to taste
1 5-pound rolled boneless pork loin
    roast
¼ cup sugar

2 cups water
½ cup red hot cinnamon candies
4 medium tart cooking apples

- Rub sage, salt and pepper over fatty side of roast; place fat side up in roasting pan.
- Roast at 325 degrees for 30 to 35 minutes per pound.
- Cook sugar, water and candies in skillet over medium heat, stirring until candies dissolve. Core apples and cut into ½-inch rings. Add to syrup in skillet.
- Simmer until transparent but not soft, stirring occasionally. Cool in syrup.
- Spoon syrup from apple rings over pork during last 30 minutes of roasting time; baste several times.
- Place roast on serving plate; arrange apple rings around roast. Spoon syrup over top.
- Yield: 15 servings.

Approx Per Serving: Cal 281; Prot 30 g; Carbo 17 g; Fiber 1 g; T Fat 10 g;
32% Calories from Fat; Chol 92 mg; Sod 75 mg.

*Vivian Higdon, **Great Lakes Region***
GFWC—Creve Coeur Woman's Club, Creve Coeur IL

CRANBERRY-GLAZED PORK LOIN

1 8-ounce can whole cranberry sauce
¾ cup barbecue sauce
¾ cup apple juice
1 tablespoon cornstarch

2 tablespoons cold water
1 4 to 5-pound boneless pork loin
    roast
1 teaspoon salt

- Bring cranberry sauce, barbecue sauce and apple juice to a boil in small saucepan. Simmer for 10 minutes. Stir in mixture of cornstarch and cold water. Cook until thickened, stirring constantly.
- Rub roast with salt. Place roast on rack in shallow roasting pan; insert meat thermometer.
- Roast at 325 degrees for 2½ to 3 hours or to 170 degrees on meat thermometer, basting with cranberry mixture during last 45 minutes of roasting time.
- Place roast on serving platter. Skim grease from pan drippings.
- Add remaining drippings to remaining cranberry mixture in saucepan. Heat to serving temperature. Serve with roast.
- Yield: 12 servings.

Approx Per Serving: Cal 318; Prot 38 g; Carbo 11 g; Fiber 1 g; T Fat 13 g;
37% Calories from Fat; Chol 116 mg; Sod 402 mg.

*Ruth DuBois, **New England Region***
GFWC—Dennis Women's Club, Yarmouth Port MA

NORTH COAST PORK ROAST

1 4 to 5-pound boneless pork roast
1/2 teaspoon chili powder
1/2 teaspoon each garlic salt and salt
1/2 cup apple jelly

1/2 cup catsup
1 tablespoon vinegar
1/2 teaspoon chili powder
1 cup crushed corn chips

- Place roast fat side up on rack in shallow roasting pan. Rub with mixture of 1/2 teaspoon chili powder, garlic salt and salt. Insert meat thermometer.
- Roast at 325 degrees for 2 to 2 1/2 hours or to 165 degrees on meat thermometer.
- Combine jelly, catsup, vinegar and 1/2 teaspoon chili powder in small saucepan. Simmer for 2 minutes. Brush over roast; sprinkle with corn chips.
- Roast for 10 to 15 minutes longer or to 170 degrees on meat thermometer. Remove to serving platter; let stand for 10 minutes.
- Add enough water to pan drippings, including corn chips, to measure 1 cup. Bring to a boil in saucepan. Serve with roast.
- Yield: 8 servings.

Approx Per Serving: Cal 512; Prot 57 g; Carbo 21 g; Fiber 1 g; T Fat 21 g; 37% Calories from Fat; Chol 173 mg; Sod 771 mg.

Suzann B. Glenn, **Great Lakes Region**
GFWC—Strongsville Women's League, Strongsville OH

CALIFORNIA SPARE RIBS

1 onion, minced
1 8-ounce can tomato sauce
3/4 cup water
1/2 cup wine vinegar
2 tablespoons Worcestershire sauce
1/4 cup packed brown sugar
1 teaspoon each paprika and chili
   powder

1/4 teaspoon cinnamon
Ground cloves to taste
1 tablespoon salt
1/2 teaspoon pepper
6 pounds pork spare ribs
Wrights barbecue smoke to taste
Seasoned salt to taste

- Simmer first 12 ingredients in large saucepan for several minutes.
- Rub spare ribs with barbecue smoke. Place on rack in broiler pan.
- Broil until brown on both sides; drain. Sprinkle with seasoned salt. Spoon sauce over top.
- Bake, covered, at 350 degrees for 1 1/2 hours, basting several times.
- Yield: 6 servings.

Approx Per Serving: Cal 754; Prot 51 g; Carbo 18 g; Fiber 1 g; T Fat 52 g; 63% Calories from Fat; Chol 208 mg; Sod 1510 mg.

Betty L. Davenport, **Western Region**
GFWC—El Dorado Woman's Club, Long Beach CA

PORK BARBECUE

2 pounds pork shoulder
2 tablespoons oil
1 large onion, chopped
1 large green bell pepper, chopped
2 cloves of garlic, minced
1/4 cup mixed vegetable juice cocktail
2 1/2 ounces cider vinegar
1/2 cup water

1 bay leaf
1/4 cup tomato paste
1/2 teaspoon Tabasco sauce
1/2 ounce oregano
1/2 teaspoon chili powder
1/4 teaspoon crushed red pepper
Salt and black pepper to taste

- Cut pork into 2-inch cubes. Brown in oil in skillet; drain. Add next 7 ingredients; mix well.
- Simmer for 15 to 20 minutes; discard bay leaf.
- Process in food processor until shredded to desired consistency. Combine with tomato paste, Tabasco sauce, oregano, chili powder and red pepper in skillet.
- Simmer for 15 to 20 minutes. Season with salt and black pepper.
- Yield: 8 servings.

Approx Per Serving: Cal 211; Prot 23 g; Carbo 4 g; Fiber 1 g; T Fat 11 g;
47% Calories from Fat; Chol 69 mg; Sod 88 mg.

Terri L. P. Markiewicz, **Southeastern Region**
GFWC—North Mecklenburg Junior Woman's club, Huntersville NC

TAILGATE TENDERLOIN

3 pounds pork tenderloin
2/3 cup soy sauce
2/3 cup packed brown sugar
3 cloves of garlic, minced

2 tablespoons vinegar
2 teaspoons ground ginger
1/3 cup finely chopped crystallized ginger

- Trim tenderloin; place in 9x13-inch baking dish. Combine remaining ingredients in bowl; mix well. Pour over tenderloin.
- Marinate in refrigerator for 6 hours to overnight. Drain, reserving marinade.
- Roast tenderloin at 350 degrees for 30 to 45 minutes or to 170 degrees on meat thermometer. Cool slightly. Cut into 1/4-inch slices.
- Bring reserved marinade to a boil in saucepan. Strain over tenderloin slices in shallow dish. Chill for 4 to 6 hours.
- Yield: 8 servings.

Approx Per Serving: Cal 391; Prot 35 g; Carbo 37 g; Fiber <1 g; T Fat 11 g;
26% Calories from Fat; Chol 104 mg; Sod 1465 mg.

Julia Wheatley, **Southeastern Region**
GFWC—Harrisonburg Junior Woman's Club, Bridgewater VA

PORK AT ITS PEAK

1/2 cup dry white wine
1/4 cup oil
6 tablespoons Dijon mustard
2 tablespoons soy sauce
2 tablespoons fresh lemon juice
2 tablespoons melted butter

1/4 cup chopped mushrooms
2 tablespoons minced onion
1/2 teaspoon celery seed
1/2 teaspoon freshly ground pepper
4 pounds pork tenderloin

- Combine first 10 ingredients in bowl; mix well. Combine with pork in heavy plastic bag; seal tightly.
- Marinate in refrigerator for 24 hours, turning occasionally. Drain, reserving marinade. Place roast in 9x13-inch baking pan.
- Bake roast at 350 degrees for 1 1/4 hours, basting with reserved marinade during last 30 minutes.
- Yield: 10 servings.

Approx Per Serving: Cal 354; Prot 37 g; Carbo 1 g; Fiber <1 g; T Fat 21 g;
55% Calories from Fat; Chol 117 mg; Sod 553 mg.
Nutritional information includes entire amount of marinade.

*Ann H. Jones, **Southeastern Region***
GFWC—Women's Club of Smithfield, Smithfield VA

CALIFORNIA CASSEROLE

1 pound ground pork
1 pound ground veal
1 medium onion, sliced
3 tablespoons oil
2 tablespoons flour
2   8-ounce cans tomato sauce
1/2 cup California Burgundy
2 teaspoons steak sauce

1/2 teaspoon sugar
Minced garlic, basil, rosemary and
   pepper to taste
2 teaspoons salt
1/2 cup grated Parmesan cheese
2 cups cooked rice
1 cup pitted black olives

- Brown pork and veal with onion in oil in skillet, stirring frequently; drain. Stir in flour. Add tomato sauce and wine.
- Cook until thickened, stirring constantly. Stir in next 8 ingredients.
- Simmer until cheese melts, stirring frequently. Add rice and olives. Spoon into 9x13-inch baking dish.
- Bake, covered, at 350 degrees for 30 minutes.
- Bake, uncovered, for 15 minutes longer.
- Yield: 8 servings.

Approx Per Serving: Cal 360; Prot 32 g; Carbo 21 g; Fiber 2 g; T Fat 16 g;
40% Calories from Fat; Chol 104 mg; Sod 1121 mg.

*Theo Vandenberg, **Western Region***
GFWC—Woman's Club of Lodi, Lodi CA

SPAGHETTI CARBONARA

1 pound bacon, chopped
1 onion, chopped
2 cloves of garlic, minced

4 16-ounce cans Italian-style stewed
   tomatoes
1 16-ounce package spaghetti

- Fry bacon in skillet until crisp. Remove bacon with slotted spoon to paper towels to drain, reserving drippings.
- Brown onion and garlic in reserved drippings in skillet. Stir in tomatoes. Simmer until of desired consistency.
- Cook spaghetti using package directions; drain.
- Stir bacon into sauce. Combine with spaghetti in serving bowl; toss to coat well.
- Yield: 6 servings.

Approx Per Serving: Cal 514; Prot 19 g; Carbo 84 g; Fiber 4 g; T Fat 12 g; 21% Calories from Fat; Chol 19 mg; Sod 1336 mg.

*Gloria Malasky, **Middle Atlantic Region***
GFWC—Women's Club of Runnemede, Runnemede NJ

CHILI-EGG PUFF

1 pound sausage
12 eggs
1/2 cup flour
1 teaspoon baking powder
1/2 teaspoon salt

2 cups small curd cottage cheese
1 pound Monterey Jack cheese,
   shredded
1/2 cup melted butter
2 4-ounce cans chopped green chilies

- Brown sausage in skillet, stirring until crumbly; drain.
- Beat eggs in mixer bowl until thick and lemon-colored. Add flour, baking powder, salt, cottage cheese, Monterey Jack cheese and butter; mix well.
- Stir in sausage and green chilies. Spoon into buttered 9x13-inch baking dish.
- Bake at 325 degrees for 40 to 45 minutes or until set. Increase oven temperature to 350 degrees if using metal baking pan.
- Yield: 12 servings.

Approx Per Serving: Cal 414; Prot 24 g; Carbo 7 g; Fiber <1 g; T Fat 32 g; 70% Calories from Fat; Chol 288 mg; Sod 958 mg.

*Viola Good, **Western Region***
GFWC—Riverton Chautauqua, Riverton WY

1938—*GFWC supported the first national child labor law.*

ALL-IN-ONE BRUNCH

1 pound sausage
9 eggs, beaten
3 cups milk
3 slices bread, crumbled
1 4-ounce can mushrooms

1/2 teaspoon dry mustard
1 1/2 teaspoons salt
1 cup shredded American cheese
1/2 cup shredded Cheddar cheese

- Brown sausage in skillet, stirring until crumbly; drain. Add remaining ingredients; mix well.
- Spoon into greased 9x13-inch baking pan. Chill, covered, overnight.
- Bake, uncovered, at 350 degrees for 1 hour. Cut into squares. Serve with muffins.
- Yield: 8 servings.

Approx Per Serving: Cal 357; Prot 21 g; Carbo 11 g; Fiber 1 g; T Fat 25 g; 63% Calories from Fat; Chol 295 mg; Sod 1221 mg.

*June Conaway, **Southeastern Region***
GFWC—West Virginia Federated Women's Clubs, Fairmont WV

KENTUCKY MORNING SAUSAGE BAKE

2 8-count cans crescent rolls
2 pounds sausage
4 eggs, beaten
1 1/2 cups shredded Swiss cheese
1 1/2 cups shredded Cheddar cheese
1/4 cup grated Parmesan cheese

1 teaspoon chopped fresh parsley
1/2 teaspoon dried oregano or 1
   teaspoon fresh oregano
1/4 teaspoon garlic salt
1/2 teaspoon pepper
2 tablespoons evaporated milk

- Line bottom of 9x13-inch baking pan with 1 can roll dough; press edges and perforations to seal.
- Brown sausage in skillet, stirring until crumbly; drain. Spoon into prepared pan.
- Combine next 8 ingredients in mixer bowl; mix well. Pour over sausage. Top with remaining roll dough, sealing edges and perforations. Brush with evaporated milk.
- Bake at 350 degrees for 35 to 40 minutes or until golden brown.
- Yield: 9 servings.

Approx Per Serving: Cal 550; Prot 26 g; Carbo 22 g; Fiber 0 g; T Fat 39 g; 65% Calories from Fat; Chol 173 mg; Sod 1321 mg.

*Betty L. Eggers, **Southeastern Region***
GFWC—Hikes Point Woman's Club, Louisville KY

SOUTHWEST GREEN CHILI

2 pounds sausage
Salt and pepper to taste
3 stalks celery, chopped
2 tomatoes, chopped

½ cup chopped green chilies
2 cloves of garlic, minced
1 cup (or more) salsa

- Brown sausage with salt and pepper in skillet, stirring until crumbly; drain. Add remaining ingredients; mix well.
- Simmer for 30 to 40 minutes or until of desired consistency.
- Serve with buttered flour tortillas or as filling for burritos.
- May substitute ground beef for sausage.
- Yield: 8 servings.

Approx Per Serving: Cal 219; Prot 11 g; Carbo 5 g; Fiber 1 g; T Fat 17 g; 70% Calories from Fat; Chol 43 mg; Sod 943 mg.

Ginger Hunter, **South Central Region**
GFWC—20th Century Research Club, Tonkawa OK

DeFOIS' MICROWAVE RABBIT

3 medium onions, sliced
4 cloves of garlic, minced
1 tablespoon olive oil
1 cup chopped seeded canned
    tomatoes with liquid
½ cup white wine
3 tablespoons flour

1 chicken bouillon cube
½ cup hot water
1 cup mushroom quarters
16 to 18 ounces rabbit, cut up
4 teaspoons chopped parsley
¼ teaspoon each salt and pepper

- Microwave onions and garlic in olive oil on High in 1-quart glass dish for 3 minutes, stirring after 1½ minutes. Add tomatoes, wine, flour and mixture of bouillon cube and hot water; mix well.
- Microwave on High for 5 minutes, stirring after 2½ minutes. Stir in mushrooms.
- Arrange rabbit in dish with thicker portions toward outer edge. Cover with plastic wrap; pierce plastic wrap in 3 or 4 places with fork.
- Microwave on Defrost for 15 minutes or until rabbit is cooked through, turning dish halfway through cooking time. Stir in parsley, salt and pepper. Let stand 5 minutes. Serve over rice with hot sauce.
- May substitute chicken for rabbit.
- Yield: 2 servings.

Approx Per Serving: Cal 519; Prot 43 g; Carbo 36 g; Fiber 6 g; T Fat 17 g; 30% Calories from Fat; Chol 116 mg; Sod 1095 mg.

Athalie Dupre, **South Central Region**
GFWC—Unique Club, Opelousas LA

MAURICE SCHULTE'S VEAL IN WINE

1 pound thin veal cutlets
1/2 cup flour
Italian seasoning, salt and pepper to
taste
2 tablespoons olive oil
2 large onions, chopped
1 green bell pepper, chopped
4 cloves of garlic, minced

4 beef bouillon cubes
1/2 cup hot water
1/2 teaspoon anise
2 tablespoons chopped parsley
Oregano to taste
1/2 cup dry white wine
1/4 to 1/2 cup grated Romano cheese

- Pound veal with meat mallet until very thin. Coat with mixture of flour, Italian seasoning, salt and pepper.
- Brown on both sides in olive oil in skillet; remove veal to 9x13-inch baking dish. Add onions, green pepper and garlic to drippings in skillet.
- Sauté until tender. Stir in bouillon dissolved in hot water. Add anise and parsley.
- Bring to a boil. Stir in oregano. Bring to a simmer. Add wine. Simmer until slightly thickened. Pour over veal.
- Bake, covered, at 300 to 350 degrees for 30 minutes. Sprinkle with cheese.
- Yield: 4 servings.

Approx Per Serving: Cal 346; Prot 30 g; Carbo 21 g; Fiber 2 g; T Fat 13 g;
37% Calories from Fat; Chol 100 mg; Sod 1114 mg.

Sandra Schulte Pollock, **Great Lakes Region**
GFWC—Upper Ohio Valley Junior Women's Club, Richmond OH

BUFFALO MEAT LOAF

2 pounds ground buffalo meat
2 onions, chopped
1 6-ounce can tomato paste
1 16-ounce package crackers, crushed

1 cup milk
2 eggs
Salt and pepper to taste

- Combine all ingredients in large bowl; mix well. Shape into meat loaf; place in baking dish.
- Bake at 350 degrees for 1 hour or until done to taste.
- Yield: 10 servings.

Approx Per Serving: Cal 245; Prot 4 g; Carbo 40 g; Fiber 2 g; T Fat 6 g;
24% Calories from Fat; Chol 61 mg; Sod 622 mg.

Dorothy Boes, **Mississippi Valley Region**
GFWC—Bonesteel Women's Club, Bonesteel SD

VENISON MEATBALLS IN SAUCE

1¹/₂ pounds ground venison
2 cups grated potatoes
²/₃ cup finely chopped onion
¹/₄ cup milk
1 egg
1¹/₂ teaspoons salt

¹/₈ teaspoon pepper
¹/₂ cup butter
¹/₂ cup water
2 tablespoons flour
1¹/₂ cups water
2 cups sour cream

- Combine venison with potatoes, onion, milk, egg, salt and pepper in bowl; mix well. Shape into small meatballs.
- Brown in butter in large skillet over medium heat. Add ¹/₂ cup water. Simmer, covered, for 20 minutes or until cooked through. Remove meatballs with slotted spoon. Stir flour and remaining 1¹/₂ cups water into drippings in skillet.
- Simmer until thickened, stirring constantly. Reduce heat. Stir in sour cream and meatballs; adjust seasonings.
- Simmer until heated through. May add frozen peas if desired.
- Yield: 6 servings.

Approx Per Serving: Cal 536; Prot 31 g; Carbo 25 g; Fiber 2 g; T Fat 35 g;
58% Calories from Fat; Chol 168 mg; Sod 783 mg.

*Kathy Albert, **New England Region***
GFWC—Manchester Juniors Club, Manchester NH

VENISON AND NOODLES

1¹/₂ pounds venison, cubed
¹/₂ cup French salad dressing
1   4-ounce can mushrooms
1 envelope onion soup mix

1 cup water
Garlic salt and pepper to taste
6 ounces uncooked noodles

- Cook venison in salad dressing in electric skillet. Add undrained mushrooms and next 4 ingredients; mix well.
- Simmer until venison is tender, adding additional water if needed for desired consistency.
- Cook noodles using package directions; drain. Serve venison over noodles.
- May thicken venison with flour if desired. May substitute beef or pork for venison.
- Yield: 4 servings.

Approx Per Serving: Cal 527; Prot 45 g; Carbo 34 g; Fiber 1 g; T Fat 23 g;
39% Calories from Fat; Chol 158 mg; Sod 741 mg.

*Betty Haggart, **Great Lakes Region***
GFWC—Clare Study Club, Clare MI

VENISON STEW

3 pounds venison, cubed
3/4 cup flour
2 tablespoons oil
2 tablespoons vinegar
1   16-ounce can cream-style corn
4 medium potatoes, chopped

1 cup chopped onion
2   46-ounce cans tomato juice
1 teaspoon Worcestershire sauce
1 teaspoon sugar
Salt and pepper to taste

- Coat venison with flour. Brown on all sides in oil in large saucepan. Add vinegar and boiling water to cover.
- Simmer for 2 hours. Add remaining ingredients. Simmer for 5 to 6 hours or until done to taste. Flavor improves with reheating.
- Yield: 8 servings.

Approx Per Serving: Cal 386; Prot 36 g; Carbo 49 g; Fiber 6 g; T Fat 6 g;
14% Calories from Fat; Chol 66 mg; Sod 1421 mg.

Mitz Maclay, ***Southeastern Region***
GFWC—Canaan Valley Woman's Club, Davis WV

SWEET AND SOUR VENISON MARINADE

1/2 cup vinegar
1/2 cup soy sauce
1 tablespoon Worcestershire sauce
1/2 cup packed light brown sugar
1/4 cup catsup
2 teaspoons oil

1/2 teaspoon garlic powder
3 pounds venison steak
1 teaspoon cracked pepper
1 teaspoon chopped onion
3/4 cup sour cream
2 teaspoons horseradish

- Combine first 7 ingredients in shallow dish; mix well. Rub venison steak with pepper. Add to marinade. Marinate in refrigerator for 12 hours; drain.
- Grill steak until done to taste.
- Combine onion, sour cream and horseradish in bowl; mix well. Serve with steak for dipping.
- May also be used with pork chops, chicken wings or London broil.
- Yield: 8 servings.

Approx Per Serving: Cal 291; Prot 32 g; Carbo 23 g; Fiber <1 g; T Fat 8 g;
25% Calories from Fat; Chol 76 mg; Sod 1228 mg.

Andrea B. Mallon, ***New England Region***
GFWC—Woman's Club of Norwich, Norwich CT

The English oak slant desk with
its elaborate carving dates from
the first quarter of the 20th
century. It is shown in the
reception room on the first floor,
along with a Lenox "Autumn"
pattern platter, part of GFWC's
china collection.

ALABAMA BRUNSWICK STEW

2 5-pound chickens
5 pounds pork shoulder
8 cups catsup
2 10-ounce bottles of Worcestershire
    sauce
1/2 5-ounce bottle of Tabasco sauce
1 large green bell pepper, chopped

1 large onion, chopped
8 lemons, cut into halves
6 16-ounce cans tomatoes
6 16-ounce cans cream-style corn
2 16-ounce cans green peas
2 16-ounce cans green lima beans

- Rinse chicken well. Combine with water to cover in heavy saucepan.
- Simmer until chicken is tender enough to fall from bones; drain, reserving 1 cup chicken broth.
- Cook pork in water to cover in heavy saucepan until very tender; cool.
- Chop chicken and pork into bite-sized pieces, discarding skin and bones. Combine with reserved broth and next 6 ingredients in heavy saucepan.
- Simmer for 1 hour. Add tomatoes and vegetables. Simmer until heated through. Discard lemons. Serve with corn muffins.
- Yield: 24 servings.

Approx Per Serving: Cal 595; Prot 55 g; Carbo 65 g; Fiber 10 g; T Fat 15 g;
22% Calories from Fat; Chol 142 mg; Sod 2090 mg.

Madelyn Rowell, **Southern Region**
GFWC—Woman's Club of Birmingham, Birmingham AL

SOUTHERN-STYLE BRUNSWICK STEW

5 pounds chicken, cut up
1 meaty ham bone
1/4 cup chopped parsley
1/4 cup chopped chives
Worcestershire sauce and Tabasco
    sauce to taste
Marjoram, salt and pepper to taste
1/2 cup catsup
4 chicken bouillon cubes

2 large onions, chopped
4 16-ounce cans tomatoes
4 16-ounce cans lima beans
12 to 16 potatoes, chopped
1/4 cup packed brown sugar
1/2 cup vinegar
4 to 6 stalks celery, chopped
4 16-ounce cans Shoe Peg corn

- Rinse chicken well. Combine with ham and water to cover in saucepan. Cook until tender. Drain, reserving broth. Cut chicken and ham into bite-sized pieces, discarding bones.
- Combine reserved broth, chicken, ham and remaining ingredients except corn in 12-quart stockpot. Simmer for 2 hours. Stir in corn. May add additional water if needed for desired consistency.
- Yield: 24 servings.

Approx Per Serving: Cal 324; Prot 23 g; Carbo 50 g; Fiber 9 g; T Fat 5 g;
13% Calories from Fat; Chol 44 mg; Sod 964 mg.

Jean Burcher, **Southeastern Region**
GFWC—Woman's Club of Newport News, Hampton VA

WHITE CHILI

1 pound dried Great Northern beans
6 cups (or more) chicken broth
2 cloves of garlic, minced
2 medium onions, chopped
1 tablespoon oil
2 4-ounce cans chopped green chilies
2 teaspoons cumin
1¹/2 teaspoons oregano
¹/4 teaspoon ground cloves

¹/4 teaspoon cayenne pepper
4 cups chopped cooked chicken
3 cups shredded Cheddar cheese
2 cups sour cream
2 4-ounce cans sliced black olives
¹/2 cup chopped green onion with tops
2 cups crushed corn chips
1 8-ounce jar mild salsa
1 8-ounce jar medium salsa

- Soak beans in water to cover in saucepan overnight; drain.
- Bring beans, chicken broth, garlic and half the onions to a boil in large stockpot; reduce heat. Simmer for 3 hours or until beans are tender, adding additional broth if needed for desired consistency.
- Sauté remaining onions in oil in skillet until tender. Add green chilies and seasonings; mix well. Add to beans with chicken.
- Simmer for 1 hour. Serve with bowls of cheese, sour cream, black olives, green onions, corn chips and salsa for topping.
- Yield: 10 servings.

Approx Per Serving: Cal 664; Prot 41 g; Carbo 46 g; Fiber 3 g; T Fat 37 g; 49% Calories from Fat; Chol 107 mg; Sod 1463 mg.

*Lee Jordan, **Western Region***
GFWC—Clayton Woman's Club, Concord CA

CHICKEN CACCIATORE

1 4-pound chicken, cut up
Salt and pepper to taste
¹/2 cup flour
5 tablespoons olive oil
1 clove of garlic, chopped

1 large green bell pepper, sliced
    lengthwise
1 cup canned tomatoes
4 small onions, chopped
1 cup sliced mushrooms

- Rinse chicken and pat dry. Season with salt and pepper; coat with flour.
- Brown in olive oil in skillet for 10 minutes or until brown on both sides. Add garlic, green pepper, tomatoes and onions.
- Simmer, covered, for 40 minutes. Add mushrooms. Simmer for 15 minutes longer or until chicken is tender.
- Yield: 5 servings.

Approx Per Serving: Cal 559; Prot 56 g; Carbo 20 g; Fiber 3 g; T Fat 28 g; 45% Calories from Fat; Chol 162 mg; Sod 237 mg.

*Florence Robbolino, **Middle Atlantic Region***
GFWC—Woman's Club of Saddle Brook, Lodi NJ

CAJUN PLUS QU'UNE POULE

2½ pounds chicken, cut up, skinned
1 pound hot Cajun link sausage, cut
 into 1½-inch pieces
2 cups water
1 to 2 teaspoons Cajun seasoning

1 large onion, coarsely chopped
1 medium green bell pepper, coarsely
 chopped
1 4-ounce can sliced mushrooms
4 cups cooked rice

- Rinse chicken and pat dry. Combine with sausage and water in heavy deep skillet.
- Bring to a boil over high heat; sprinkle with Cajun seasoning. Reduce heat. Simmer, covered, for 15 minutes. Add onion and green pepper.
- Simmer, covered, for 15 minutes. Add mushrooms. Simmer, uncovered, for 15 minutes. Increase heat to high.
- Cook for 10 minutes longer or until thickened to desired consistency, stirring occasionally. Serve over rice
- May serve over wide noodles if preferred.
- Yield: 6 servings.

Approx Per Serving: Cal 476; Prot 38 g; Carbo 37 g; Fiber 2 g; T Fat 18 g;
 36% Calories from Fat; Chol 113 mg; Sod 622 mg.

Johnnie Taylor, **South Central Region**
GFWC—Unique Club and Les Dames d'Etude, Lawtell LA

CAJUN CHICKEN

2 pounds chicken filets
1 large onion, thickly sliced
1 large green bell pepper, thickly
 sliced
2 cloves of garlic, minced

2 tablespoons olive oil
½ cup chopped fresh parsley
1 teaspoon cayenne pepper
1 10-ounce can chicken broth

- Rinse chicken and pat dry; cut into large strips.
- Sauté onion, green pepper and garlic in olive oil in skillet for 5 minutes. Add parsley and chicken; sprinkle with cayenne pepper.
- Cook for 2 to 3 minutes. Stir in chicken broth. Simmer for 20 minutes, adding additional broth if needed.
- Serve over rice.
- Yield: 8 servings.

Approx Per Serving: Cal 187; Prot 28 g; Carbo 3 g; Fiber 1 g; T Fat 7 g;
 33% Calories from Fat; Chol 72 mg; Sod 178 mg.

Rita Peck, **South Central Region**
GFWC—Peoria Woman's Club, Peoria AZ

CHICKEN IN CRANBERRY-CREAM SAUCE

1/2 cup dried cranberries
3 tablespoons Cognac
2 tablespoons Grand Marnier
4 chicken breast filets
1/2 cup flour
2 tablespoons olive oil

2 tablespoons unsalted butter
2/3 cup raspberry vinegar
2 shallots, minced
1 1/2 cups rich chicken stock
1 1/2 cups light cream, at room
  temperature

- Marinate cranberries in Cognac and Grand Marnier in bowl for 30 to 40 minutes.
- Rinse chicken and pat dry. Coat with flour.
- Brown chicken in olive oil and butter in large skillet over medium heat for 5 minutes. Remove chicken to warm serving platter.
- Add vinegar to skillet, stirring over medium-high heat to deglaze. Add shallots and cranberries with marinade.
- Cook for 4 to 5 minutes or until reduced by 1/3. Add chicken stock. Cook for 8 to 10 minutes or until reduced by 1/3. Reduce heat to medium-low. Stir in cream.
- Cook for 4 to 5 minutes or until thickened to desired consistency, stirring constantly. Spoon cream sauce over chicken; spoon cranberries over top. Garnish with parsley.
- Yield: 4 servings.

Approx Per Serving: Cal 576; Prot 34 g; Carbo 41 g; Fiber 3 g; T Fat 27 g;
45% Calories from Fat; Chol 121 mg; Sod 399 mg.

Jane Elizabeth Seaman, **New England Region**
GFWC—Sandwich Junior Women's Club, Sandwich MA

CHICKEN AND DUMPLINGS

1 pound chicken breast filets
2 quarts water
1 stalk celery, cut into quarters
1 onion, sliced
1 carrot, cut into quarters
2 teaspoons salt
Freshly ground pepper to taste

1 cup flour
1 1/2 teaspoons baking powder
1/2 teaspoon salt
1 egg, beaten
1/3 cup milk
2 tablespoons oil

- Rinse chicken well. Combine with next 6 ingredients in 6-quart stockpot.
- Simmer, covered, for 1 to 1 1/2 hours or until chicken is tender. Remove chicken and strain 4 cups or more broth. Cut chicken into bite-sized pieces.
- Sift flour, baking powder and 1/2 teaspoon salt into bowl. Combine egg, milk and oil in small bowl. Add to dry ingredients; mix well.
- Drop by teaspoonfuls into simmering reserved broth in saucepan. Simmer, covered, for 15 minutes. Serve with chicken.
- Yield: 4 servings.

Approx Per Serving: Cal 410; Prot 38 g; Carbo 31 g; Fiber 2 g; T Fat 14 g;
31% Calories from Fat; Chol 129 mg; Sod 2337 mg.

Cheryl Matson, **Southeastern Region**
GFWC—Thomas Jefferson Junior Woman's Club, Richmond VA

CHICKEN PIE DELUXE

8 cups chopped cooked chicken
1/2 cup milk
1/2 cup sour cream
2 10-ounce cans cream of chicken
   soup

1/2 cup cornmeal
1 egg, beaten
3/4 cup milk
1/2 teaspoon salt
2 cups shredded Cheddar cheese

- Combine chicken, 1/2 cup milk, sour cream and soup in saucepan.
- Heat until bubbly, stirring to mix well. Spoon into 9x13-inch baking dish.
- Combine cornmeal, egg, milk and salt in bowl; mix well. Fold in cheese. Spoon over chicken mixture.
- Bake at 375 degrees for 20 to 30 minutes or until topping is golden brown.
- Yield: 8 servings.

Approx Per Serving: Cal 541; Prot 53 g; Carbo 15 g; Fiber 1 g; T Fat 29 g;
49% Calories from Fat; Chol 199 mg; Sod 1018 mg.

*Mary Kay Doppel, **Middle Atlantic Region***
GFWC—Roxbury Women's Club, Succasunna NJ

HUSBAND-LOVING GEORGIA SOUTHERN CHICKEN PIE

1 chicken
4 cups water
1 teaspoon salt
1/2 teaspoon pepper
1/3 cup flour
1/2 teaspoon salt

1/2 teaspoon pepper
1/4 cup melted butter
1/2 cup milk
3 hard-boiled eggs, sliced
1 recipe 2-crust pie pastry
1 tablespoon melted butter

- Rinse chicken well. Combine with water, 1 teaspoon salt and 1/2 teaspoon pepper in large saucepan.
- Simmer for 1 hour or until chicken is tender. Strain and skim broth, reserving 2 cups. Cool chicken and chop into bite-sized pieces, discarding skin and bones.
- Blend flour, 1/2 teaspoon salt and 1/2 teaspoon pepper into 1/4 cup melted butter in large saucepan. Stir in reserved broth and milk. Cook until thickened, stirring constantly. Stir in chicken and eggs.
- Line 2-quart baking dish with half the pastry. Spoon chicken mixture into prepared dish. Top with remaining pastry. Seal edges and cut vents. Brush with 1 tablespoon butter.
- Bake at 400 degrees for 30 to 40 minutes or until pastry is golden brown. Serve with peas and carrots.
- Yield: 6 servings.

Approx Per Serving: Cal 660; Prot 43 g; Carbo 30 g; Fiber 1 g; T Fat 40 g;
55% Calories from Fat; Chol 237 mg; Sod 1378 mg.

*Terry Martin, **Southern Region***
GFWC—Hapeville Woman's Club, Riverdale GA

PENNSYLVANIA DUTCH CHICKEN POTPIE

1 chicken, cut up
1½ teaspoons saffron
1½ teaspoons salt
¼ teaspoon pepper
1½ cups flour
½ teaspoon salt

3 tablespoons melted butter
1 egg
5 tablespoons cold milk
3 to 4 cups water
3 medium potatoes, chopped
Pepper to taste

- Rinse chicken well. Combine with next 3 ingredients to cover in saucepan.
- Cook until chicken is tender. Drain, reserving broth. Cut chicken into bite-sized pieces, discarding skin and bones.
- Combine flour, ½ teaspoon salt, butter and egg in bowl; mix until crumbly. Add milk 1 spoonful at a time, mixing to form soft dough.
- Knead lightly; wrap in waxed paper. Chill for 20 minutes. Roll small portions of the dough at a time very thin on floured surface. Cut into 1½-inch squares.
- Bring reserved chicken broth and 3 to 4 cups water to a boil in large saucepan. Add potatoes. Add dough squares 1 at a time.
- Cook until potatoes are tender. Stir in chicken and pepper to taste.
- Yield: 6 servings.

> *Approx Per Serving:* Cal 459; Prot 39 g; Carbo 38 g; Fiber 2 g; T Fat 16 g;
> 32% Calories from Fat; Chol 154 mg; Sod 877 mg.

> *Faye Z. Dissinger, GFWC First Vice President, 1992–94,* **Middle Atlantic Region**
> *Springfield PA*

WISCONSIN CHICKEN AND CHEDDAR POTPIE

1   10-ounce can cream of chicken soup
½ cup milk
½ cup chopped onion
¼ cup each chopped celery and carrot
3 ounces cream cheese, softened
¼ cup grated Parmesan cheese
1   10-ounce package frozen chopped broccoli

3 cups chopped cooked chicken
1 cup shredded sharp Wisconsin Cheddar cheese
1 cup buttermilk pancake mix
1 egg, slightly beaten
½ cup milk
1 tablespoon oil
¼ cup sliced almonds

- Combine first 7 ingredients in large saucepan; mix well.
- Cook until mixture is bubbly, stirring to mix well. Stir in broccoli and chicken. Cook until heated through. Spoon into 2-quart baking dish.
- Mix Cheddar cheese and pancake mix in medium bowl. Combine egg, ½ cup milk and oil in small bowl; mix well. Add to pancake mixture; mix well.
- Spoon over chicken mixture; top with almonds.
- Bake at 375 degrees for 20 to 25 minutes or until topping is golden brown.
- Yield: 8 servings.

> *Approx Per Serving:* Cal 380; Prot 27 g; Carbo 21 g; Fiber 2 g; T Fat 21 g;
> 49% Calories from Fat; Chol 109 mg; Sod 739 mg.

> *Veronica A. Rychter-Danczyk,* **Great Lakes Region**
> *GFWC—Stevens Point Junior Woman's Club, Stevens Point WI*

GOLDEN GATE CHICKEN

¼ cup soy sauce
1 tablespoon apricot jam
1 tablespoon lemon juice
1 tablespoon chopped onion

8 pieces of chicken
½ cup (or more) flour
¼ cup oil

- Combine first 4 ingredients in bowl; mix well. Rinse chicken and pat dry. Coat with flour.
- Brown chicken in oil in medium skillet. Add soy sauce mixture; mix well.
- Simmer for 30 to 45 minutes or until chicken is tender.
- Serve with rice, potatoes or pasta.
- Yield: 8 servings.

Approx Per Serving: Cal 273; Prot 28 g; Carbo 9 g; Fiber <1 g; T Fat 13 g; 39% Calories from Fat; Chol 81 mg; Sod 593 mg.

Marie H. DuFay, **Western Region**
GFWC—Federated Women's Improvement Club of St. Helena, St. Helena CA

ISLAND-STYLE CHICKEN

1 chicken, cut up
2 tablespoons oil
1 14-ounce can chicken broth
1 20-ounce can pineapple chunks
¼ cup vinegar
2 tablespoons brown sugar

2 teaspoons soy sauce
1 clove of garlic, minced
1 medium green bell pepper, chopped
3 tablespoons cornstarch
¼ cup water

- Rinse chicken and pat dry.
- Brown chicken in oil in electric skillet; drain. Add next 7 ingredients; mix well.
- Simmer for 40 minutes. Stir in mixture of cornstarch and water.
- Cook until thickened, stirring constantly. Serve over parsley rice.
- Yield: 4 servings.

Approx Per Serving: Cal 566; Prot 52 g; Carbo 43 g; Fiber 2 g; T Fat 20 g; 32% Calories from Fat; Chol 152 mg; Sod 638 mg.

Betty Jo Thatcher, **Southern Region**
GFWC—Boynton Beach Sorosis, Inc., Boynton Beach FL

1899—*GFWC established the national model for juvenile courts.*

CHICKEN AND FRUIT KABOBS

6 chicken breast filets
1 small cantaloupe
2 tablespoons olive oil

2 tablespoons honey
2/3 cup lemon juice
1/4 cup chopped fresh mint

- Rinse chicken and pat dry. Cut into 1-inch strips. Cut cantaloupe into balls with melon baller. Combine chicken and cantaloupe in shallow dish.
- Combine remaining ingredients in bowl; mix well. Add half the mixture to chicken; set aside remaining half.
- Marinate in refrigerator for 6 to 8 hours, stirring occasionally.
- Drain, discarding marinade. Thread chicken and cantaloupe alternately on six 12-inch skewers. Place on grill sprayed with oil.
- Grill for 12 minutes, turning and basting with reserved marinade for 12 minutes or until cooked through.
- Yield: 6 servings.

Approx Per Serving: Cal 232; Prot 27 g; Carbo 14 g; Fiber 1 g; T Fat 8 g;
30% Calories from Fat; Chol 72 mg; Sod 70 mg.

Joan M. Geiger, **Middle Atlantic Region**
GFWC—Llanerch Club, Aldan PA

CHICKEN SURABAJA

1/4 cup reduced-sodium soy sauce
2 tablespoons fresh lemon juice
1 clove of garlic, finely chopped
White pepper to taste
3 whole chicken breasts, boned,
    skinned

1/4 cup butter
1/2 cup reduced-sodium soy sauce
2 tablespoons fresh lemon juice
1/2 teaspoon salt
Cayenne pepper to taste

- Combine 1/4 cup soy sauce, 2 tablespoons lemon juice, garlic and white pepper in shallow dish.
- Rinse chicken and pat dry; cut into 1-inch pieces. Add to marinade; mix well.
- Marinate in refrigerator for 1 hour; drain. Thread onto 12 small skewers.
- Combine remaining ingredients in saucepan. Simmer for 2 minutes.
- Grill chicken 6 inches from coals for 6 minutes on each side. Serve chicken with heated sauce.
- Yield: 4 servings.

Approx Per Serving: Cal 335; Prot 40 g; Carbo 6 g; Fiber <1 g; T Fat 16 g;
44% Calories from Fat; Chol 139 mg; Sod 1628 mg.

Jo Sblendorio, **Middle Atlantic Region**
GFWC—Ringwood Woman's Club, Ringwood NJ

CHICKEN LICKEN

4 large chicken breasts
1/4 cup butter
1 large onion, chopped
1 clove of garlic, minced
1 cup chopped fresh or canned
    tomatoes
1 cup chicken broth

1 cup sliced mushrooms
1 teaspoon ginger
1/4 teaspoon chili powder
1 1/2 teaspoons paprika
1 1/2 teaspoons salt
2 tablespoons cornstarch
1 cup whipping cream

- Cut chicken breasts into halves. Rinse and pat dry.
- Brown in butter in heavy saucepan; remove chicken. Add onion and garlic to drippings in saucepan.
- Cook until onion is light brown. Add next 7 ingredients; mix well. Add chicken.
- Simmer, covered, for 40 minutes or until chicken is tender. Remove chicken to warm serving plate. Stir mixture of cornstarch and cream into skillet.
- Cook until thickened, stirring constantly. Spoon over chicken. Serve with noodles or rice.
- Yield: 4 servings.

Approx Per Serving: Cal 499; Prot 30 g; Carbo 11 g; Fiber 2 g; T Fat 37 g; 67% Calories from Fat; Chol 185 mg; Sod 1181 mg.

Joelle Wentz, **Middle Atlantic Region**
GFWC—Woman's League of Mount Holly, Mount Holly NJ

CHICKEN À LA LEMON

1 1/2 pounds chicken breast filets
4 eggs
1/2 cup grated Parmesan cheese
1 cup flour

1/2 cup oil
1/2 cup margarine
1 lemon, sliced
1/2 cup margarine

- Cut chicken into 3-ounce pieces. Rinse and pat dry. Pound thicker pieces with meat mallet to flatten.
- Beat eggs with cheese in bowl. Coat chicken with flour; dip into egg mixture.
- Cook chicken in oil and 1/2 cup margarine in skillet until golden brown on both sides; remove to warm platter. Add lemon slices and 1/2 cup margarine to skillet.
- Sauté lemon slices lightly. Serve lemon-butter with chicken.
- Yield: 4 servings.

Approx Per Serving: Cal 1103; Prot 54 g; Carbo 27 g; Fiber 1 g; T Fat 86 g; 71% Calories from Fat; Chol 329 mg; Sod 888 mg.

Merab Drennen, **Middle Atlantic Region**
GFWC—Woman's Club of Butler, Butler PA

CHICKEN BREASTS MARSALA

4 chicken breast filets
1/2 cup flour
Salt and pepper to taste
2 tablespoons oil
2/3 cup butter

12 ounces mushrooms, sliced
1 cup (about) Marsala
2 teaspoons chopped fresh parsley
1 cup heated beef broth

- Rinse chicken and pat dry. Pound with meat mallet to flatten. Coat with mixture of flour, salt and pepper; shake off excess.
- Sauté in oil in skillet for 2 minutes on each side; remove chicken and drain skillet. Add butter and mushrooms to skillet.
- Sauté mushrooms for 2 minutes. Add chicken and wine.
- Cook until liquid reduced by 1/2. Add parsley, beef broth, salt and pepper. Place chicken on serving plates; spoon sauce over top.
- Yield: 4 servings.

Approx Per Serving: Cal 629; Prot 31 g; Carbo 18 g; Fiber 2 g; T Fat 41 g; 59% Calories from Fat; Chol 155 mg; Sod 526 mg.

*Kellie Deatcher, **Middle Atlantic Region***
GFWC—Newton Junior Woman's Club, Newton NJ

PASTA À LA PASSION

8 ounces chicken breast filets
2 cloves of garlic, minced
1/4 cup extra-virgin olive oil
1 1/2 cups broccoli flowerets
3/4 cup oil-pack dried tomatoes,
    drained, chopped

3/4 cup chicken broth
1 tablespoon butter
1/4 cup white wine
1 teaspoon basil
Red pepper flakes to taste
8 ounces pasta bows, cooked

- Cut chicken into strips; rinse and pat dry.
- Sauté garlic in olive oil in 12-inch skillet for 1 minute. Add chicken. Cook for 2 to 3 minutes or until cooked through. Add broccoli and tomatoes.
- Cook for 1 minute. Stir in remaining ingredients. Simmer for 5 to 7 minutes. Serve with grated cheese.
- Yield: 3 servings.

Approx Per Serving: Cal 632; Prot 30 g; Carbo 62 g; Fiber 5 g; T Fat 28 g; 41% Calories from Fat; Chol 59 mg; Sod 286 mg.

*Joan K. Pascal, **Middle Atlantic Region***
GFWC—Morristown Club, Basking Ridge NJ

PICANTE CHICKEN

4 chicken breast filets
1 cup chopped onion
1 medium green bell pepper, chopped
2 cloves of garlic, minced
1 tablespoon oil
1 15-ounce can stewed tomatoes

2 cups water
1 15-ounce can pinto beans
2/3 to 3/4 cup picante sauce
1 teaspoon cumin
1 teaspoon salt

- Cut chicken into 1-inch pieces. Rinse and pat dry.
- Sauté chicken with onion, green pepper and garlic in oil in heavy saucepan until chicken is white. Add remaining ingredients; mix well.
- Simmer for 20 minutes. Ladle into serving bowls. Garnish with cheese, green onions and/or sour cream.
- May vary amount of water for desired consistency.
- Yield: 6 servings.

Approx Per Serving: Cal 218; Prot 22 g; Carbo 22 g; Fiber 1 g; T Fat 5 g; 20% Calories from Fat; Chol 49 mg; Sod 1081 mg.

Grace New, **South Central Region**
GFWC—Tejas Study Club, Denver City TX

CHICKEN PICCATA

1 pound chicken breast filets
1/2 cup flour
2 tablespoons oil
1/4 cup butter
1/2 cup white wine

1/2 cup chicken stock
1/4 cup butter
1/4 cup water
11/2 tablespoons lemon juice

- Rinse chicken and pat dry. Coat lightly with flour.
- Sauté in oil and 1/4 cup butter in skillet until brown on both sides; remove chicken. Add wine to skillet, stirring to deglaze. Add remaining ingredients; mix well.
- Cook over high heat until sauce is golden brown and reduced by 1/2. Add chicken. Simmer for 20 minutes.
- May substitute additional chicken stock for wine if preferred.
- Yield: 4 servings.

Approx Per Serving: Cal 487; Prot 29 g; Carbo 13 g; Fiber <1 g; T Fat 33 g; 64% Calories from Fat; Chol 134 mg; Sod 355 mg.

Linda Wentzel, **Middle Atlantic Region**
GFWC—Junior Woman's Club, Boyertown PA

SAUTÉED CHICKEN BREASTS WITH HORSERADISH SAUCE

2 pounds chicken breast filets
2 tablespoons flour
1/2 teaspoon salt
1/4 teaspoon pepper
3 tablespoons butter

1 large clove of garlic, pressed
1 cup sliced fresh mushrooms
1/2 5-ounce jar horseradish sauce
1 cup whipping cream

- Rinse chicken and pat dry. Shake with mixture of flour, salt and pepper in bag.
- Brown chicken on both sides in butter in skillet; reduce heat. Cook until tender; remove to heated platter. Add garlic and mushrooms to drippings in skillet.
- Sauté for 1 to 2 minutes. Stir in horseradish sauce and cream.
- Cook until thickened, stirring constantly. Add chicken, turning to coat well. Simmer until heated through. Serve with wild rice.
- Yield: 6 servings.

Approx Per Serving: Cal 434; Prot 37 g; Carbo 6 g; Fiber <1 g; T Fat 29 g; 60% Calories from Fat; Chol 172 mg; Sod 417 mg.

Lois Cerka, *Mississippi Valley Region*
GFWC—World Outlook Club, Colo IA

SAUTÉED CHICKEN BREASTS WITH MUSTARD

4 chicken breast filets
2 tablespoons margarine
1 tablespoon fresh lemon juice
2 to 3 teaspoons cornstarch

1 cup chicken broth
2 to 3 teaspoons Dijon mustard
1 cup sliced mushrooms
4 juice-pack canned pineapple slices

- Rinse chicken and pat dry. Pound between waxed paper to flatten.
- Sauté in margarine in large skillet over medium heat for 5 minutes on each side or until light brown. Sprinkle with lemon juice; remove to warm platter.
- Blend cornstarch with chicken broth in bowl. Add to skillet, stirring to deglaze.
- Bring to a boil and cook for 1 minute, stirring constantly; remove from heat. Whisk in mustard. Add chicken and mushrooms.
- Cook over low heat for 15 to 20 minutes. Place pineapple slice on each filet.
- Place on serving plates; spoon sauce over top. Serve with rice.
- Yield: 4 servings.

Approx Per Serving: Cal 255; Prot 29 g; Carbo 13 g; Fiber 1 g; T Fat 10 g; 35% Calories from Fat; Chol 72 mg; Sod 426 mg.

Lois Turner, *Middle Atlantic Region*
GFWC—Sea Girt Woman's Club, Inc., Sea Girt NJ

SUNFLOWER CHICKEN

1/2 cup cornflake crumbs
1/2 cup chopped sunflower seed
   kernels
2 tablespoons whole sunflower seed
   kernels
2 teaspoons paprika
1 teaspoon each ginger and salt

1/8 teaspoon pepper
1 egg, beaten
2 tablespoons honey
1 tablespoon lemon juice
2 to 3 pounds chicken breast filets
1 teaspoon sunflower oil

- Mix first 7 ingredients in bowl. Beat egg with honey and lemon juice in bowl.
- Rinse chicken and pat dry. Dip in egg mixture; coat with sunflower seed mixture. Arrange in glass dish; drizzle with sunflower oil.
- Microwave, covered with waxed paper, on High for 4 minutes. Turn 1/4 turn. Microwave for 3 to 4 minutes longer or until chicken is cooked through. Let stand for 5 minutes before serving.
- Yield: 6 servings.

Approx Per Serving: Cal 421; Prot 57 g; Carbo 14 g; Fiber 1 g; T Fat 14 g;
31% Calories from Fat; Chol 180 mg; Sod 565 mg.

*Lorraine Reiling, **Mississippi Valley Region***
GFWC—Woman's Literary Club, Winthrop IA

CHICKEN TETRAZZINI

1 large onion, minced
2 stalks celery, chopped
3 tablespoons butter
3 cups chopped cooked chicken
1 cup uncooked spaghetti

1 10-ounce can cream of celery soup
2 1/2 cups chicken broth
1/2 teaspoon salt
1/2 cup grated Parmesan cheese
Paprika to taste

- Sauté onion and celery in butter in skillet until onion is tender. Add next 5 ingredients; mix well.
- Spoon into 3-quart baking dish. Top with cheese and paprika.
- Bake at 350 degrees for 1 hour or until spaghetti is tender.
- May substitute green beans for celery if preferred.
- Yield: 10 servings.

Approx Per Serving: Cal 186; Prot 17 g; Carbo 8 g; Fiber 1 g; T Fat 10 g;
47% Calories from Fat; Chol 53 mg; Sod 663 mg.

*J. Christine Held, **Middle Atlantic Region***
GFWC—Hockessin Community Club, Hockessin DE

TEXAS PANHANDLE CHICKEN TETRAZZINI

1 6-pound chicken
2 teaspoons salt
1/2 teaspoon pepper
2 medium green bell peppers, chopped
1/2 cup butter
1/4 cup flour
2 cups milk
2 10-ounce cans cream of mushroom
   soup
2 2-ounce jars chopped pimento
1 clove of garlic, minced

1 teaspoon Worcestershire sauce
1/2 cup sherry
2 4-ounce cans chopped mushrooms
4 cups shredded American cheese
3/4 cup grated Parmesan cheese
1/4 teaspoon garlic salt
1 16-ounce package spaghetti
2 cups shredded American cheese
1 cup sliced almonds
1 4-ounce can whole mushrooms,
   drained

- Rinse chicken inside and out. Combine with water to cover, salt and pepper in large heavy saucepan. Simmer until chicken is tender; drain, reserving broth. Chop chicken into bite-sized pieces, discarding skin and bones.
- Sauté green peppers in butter in saucepan until tender. Stir in flour. Cook for 1 minute. Stir in milk gradually. Add chicken and next 9 ingredients; mix well. Cook for 10 minutes.
- Add enough water to reserved broth to measure 5 quarts. Bring to a boil in saucepan. Add spaghetti. Cook until tender; drain and rinse.
- Layer spaghetti and chicken mixture 1/2 at a time in 2 greased 9x13-inch baking dishes. Top each with 1 cup shredded American cheese, almonds and whole mushrooms. Bake at 350 degrees for 40 minutes or until bubbly.
- Yield: 20 servings.

Approx Per Serving: Cal 487; Prot 34 g; Carbo 25 g; Fiber 2 g; T Fat 27 g;
51% Calories from Fat; Chol 112 mg; Sod 1195 mg.

Maude W. Yungblut, **South Central Region**
GFWC—Twentieth Century Club, Borger TX

CHICKEN CORDON BLEU

12 chicken breast filets
2 envelopes coating mix for baked
   chicken
12 ounces Swiss cheese, sliced

8 ounces boiled ham, thinly sliced
1 10-ounce can cream of mushroom
   soup
1 cup seasoned bread crumbs

- Rinse chicken and pat dry. Shake 2 pieces at a time in coating mix in plastic bag.
- Layer chicken, cheese and ham 1/2 at a time in lightly greased 10x10-inch baking dish. Spread soup over top; sprinkle with bread crumbs.
- Bake at 325 degrees for 1 hour.
- Yield: 12 servings.

Approx Per Serving: Cal 383; Prot 42 g; Carbo 18 g; Fiber <1 g; T Fat 15 g;
36% Calories from Fat; Chol 109 mg; Sod 934 mg.

Grace I. Kersey, **Middle Atlantic Region**
GFWC—Harrington New Century Club, Harrington DE

HOT BROWN CHICKEN SANDWICH

2 to 3 tablespoons flour
1/4 teaspoon salt
1/8 teaspoon pepper
2 to 3 tablespoons melted butter
1 cup milk

1/4 cup shredded American cheese
4 slices bread, toasted
4 slices baked chicken
8 slices crisp-fried bacon
1/4 cup grated Parmesan cheese

- Blend flour, salt and pepper into butter in saucepan. Cook over low heat until smooth. Stir in milk. Bring to a boil and cook for 1 minute, stirring constantly. Stir in American cheese until melted.
- Arrange toast on rack in broiler pan; arrange chicken on toast. Spoon cheese sauce over chicken; top with bacon and Parmesan cheese. Broil until bubbly.
- Yield: 4 servings.

Approx Per Serving: Cal 386; Prot 21 g; Carbo 21 g; Fiber 1 g; T Fat 24 g; 56% Calories from Fat; Chol 78 mg; Sod 797 mg.

*Martha Berry, **Southeastern Region**
GFWC—Campbellsville Club, Campbellsville KY*

BUFFET CHICKEN

8 chicken breast filets
8 slices boiled ham
1   10-ounce can cream of mushroom
    soup

4 to 6 tablespoons half and half
1/8 teaspoon pepper
1 1/2 cups shredded Cheddar cheese

- Rinse chicken and pat dry. Layer ham and chicken in 2 to 3-quart rectangular baking dish.
- Blend soup, half and half and pepper in bowl. Pour over chicken; sprinkle with Cheddar cheese.
- Bake, covered with foil, at 350 degrees for 1 1/4 hours. Bake, uncovered, for 15 minutes longer.
- May top with mushrooms if desired.
- Yield: 8 servings.

Approx Per Serving: Cal 321; Prot 40 g; Carbo 3 g; Fiber <1 g; T Fat 16 g; 45% Calories from Fat; Chol 115 mg; Sod 862 mg.

*Annette B. Jackson, **Middle Atlantic Region**
GFWC—Wildwood Civic Club, North Wildwood NJ*

1901—*GFWC was chartered by the U.S. Congress.*

CHICKEN GENOA

4 chicken breast filets
1/2 cup grated Parmesan cheese
2 eggs, beaten
1 cup finely crushed crackers
1/2 cup oil

8 ounces Monterey Jack cheese, cut
    into 1/4 inch thick slices
1 pound fresh mushrooms
1/2 cup oil

- Rinse chicken and pat dry. Coat with Parmesan cheese. Dip into eggs; coat with cracker crumbs.
- Brown on both sides in 1/2 cup oil in skillet. Arrange in single layer in baking dish; top with Monterey Jack cheese.
- Sauté mushrooms in 1/2 cup oil and drippings in skillet. Spoon over chicken.
- Bake, covered with foil, at 350 degrees for 45 minutes.
- Yield: 4 servings.

Approx Per Serving: Cal 1035; Prot 51 g; Carbo 22 g; Fiber 3 g; T Fat 83 g;
72% Calories from Fat; Chol 245 mg; Sod 865 mg.

*Janice Bolton, **Middle Atlantic Region***
GFWC—Warrior Run Women's Club, Watsontown PA

CRISP CHEESY CHICKEN BREASTS

6 chicken breast filets
6 slices Swiss cheese
1 10-ounce can cream of chicken soup
1/4 cup water

1/4 cup finely chopped onion
1/2 cup butter
2 cups herb-seasoned stuffing mix

- Rinse chicken and pat dry. Arrange in single layer in buttered rectangular baking pan. Top with cheese; spread mixture of soup and water over top.
- Sauté onion in butter in skillet. Stir in stuffing mix. Sprinkle over casserole.
- Bake, covered with foil, at 325 degrees for 1 hour. Bake, uncovered, for 30 minutes longer or until chicken is tender.
- Yield: 6 servings.

Approx Per Serving: Cal 516; Prot 39 g; Carbo 22 g; Fiber <1 g; T Fat 30 g;
52% Calories from Fat; Chol 143 mg; Sod 948 mg.

*Gail S. Smith, **Middle Atlantic Region***
GFWC—Boyertown Junior Women's Club, Barto PA

1902—*The California Federation of Women's Clubs worked to preserve the mammoth grove of Redwoods at Calveras, California.*

JERSEY SHORE CHICKEN

8 chicken breast filets
Salt and pepper to taste
1/2 cup chopped onion
1/2 cup chopped celery
3 tablespoons butter
3 tablespoons white wine

8 ounces crab meat
1/2 cup herb-seasoned stuffing mix
2 tablespoons flour
1/2 teaspoon paprika
2 tablespoons melted butter

- Rinse chicken and pat dry. Pound with meat mallet to flatten. Season with salt and pepper.
- Sauté onion and celery in 3 tablespoons butter in skillet until tender; remove from heat. Add wine, crab meat and stuffing mix; mix well.
- Spoon crab meat mixture onto chicken filets. Roll chicken to enclose filling; secure with wooden picks. Coat with mixture of flour and paprika. Arrange in baking dish. Drizzle with 2 tablespoons butter.
- Bake at 375 degrees for 1 hour.
- May heat Hollandaise sauce, 1/4 cup wine and 1 cup shredded Swiss cheese in saucepan until smooth to serve over chicken.
- Yield: 8 servings.

Approx Per Serving: Cal 265; Prot 33 g; Carbo 6 g; Fiber <1 g; T Fat 11 g;
39% Calories from Fat; Chol 120 mg; Sod 268 mg.
Nutritional information does not include Hollandaise sauce mixture.

*Sandie Johnston, **Middle Atlantic Region***
GFWC—Women's Club of Clinton, Milford NJ

CHICKEN PARMESAN

1/2 cup grated Parmesan cheese
1 teaspoon basil
Garlic powder, paprika, salt and
pepper to taste

4 chicken breast filets
1/2 cup oil
3/4 cup spaghetti sauce

- Combine first 6 ingredients in bowl; mix well.
- Rinse chicken and pat dry. Coat with 1/4 cup oil. Spread remaining oil in 8x12-inch baking dish. Coat chicken with cheese mixture. Arrange in prepared dish.
- Bake at 350 degrees for 45 minutes. Spread spaghetti sauce over top. Bake for 15 minutes longer.
- Yield: 8 servings.

Approx Per Serving: Cal 239; Prot 16 g; Carbo 4 g; Fiber <1 g; T Fat 18 g;
67% Calories from Fat; Chol 40 mg; Sod 242 mg.

*Althea V. Peters, **Middle Atlantic Region***
GFWC—Senior Women's Club, Clearfield PA

ENCHILADAS VERDES

13 fresh tomatillos, peeled
10 to 12 fresh green chilies, seeded
4 cloves of garlic, chopped
1 large onion, cut into quarters
1 teaspoon salt
1/4 cup chopped cilantro

6 tablespoons oil
3 cups shredded cooked chicken
3 cups shredded Monterey Jack cheese
12 tortillas
1 cup shredded Monterey Jack cheese
2 cups shredded iceberg lettuce

- Cook tomatillos and green chilies in water to cover in medium saucepan over medium heat for 10 minutes; drain.
- Combine tomatillos mixture with next 4 ingredients in blender container; process on High for 1 minute or until smooth.
- Cook blended mixture in 4 tablespoons hot oil in skillet over medium heat for 5 minutes or until thickened, stirring frequently. Add water if needed for desired consistency.
- Mix chicken and 3 cups cheese in medium bowl.
- Soften tortillas in 2 tablespoons hot oil in skillet for 3 to 5 seconds; place on work surface. Spread with chilies mixture; spoon chicken mixture into centers. Roll up tortillas to enclose filling. Place seam side down in baking dish. Sprinkle with 1 cup cheese. Bake at 375 degrees for 5 minutes or until cheese melts. Sprinkle with lettuce. Garnish with radish slices. Serve with sour cream and/or guacamole.
- Yield: 12 servings.

Approx Per Serving: Cal 367; Prot 23 g; Carbo 21 g; Fiber 4 g; T Fat 22 g;
53% Calories from Fat; Chol 66 mg; Sod 419 mg.

Charlotte Varela, **South Central Region**
GFWC—Tempe Junior Woman's Club, Tempe AZ

CHICKEN ENCHILADA CASSEROLE

4 chicken breasts
1 10-ounce can cream of chicken soup
1 10-ounce can cream of mushroom
    soup
1 cup milk

1 medium onion, grated
1 7-ounce can green chili salsa
12 corn tortillas
8 ounces Cheddar cheese, shredded

- Rinse chicken and pat dry. Wrap in foil.
- Bake at 400 degrees for 1 hour; drain, reserving 1 tablespoon cooking liquid. Spread reserved liquid in buttered 9x13-inch baking dish. Chop chicken into bite-sized pieces, discarding skin and bones.
- Combine next 5 ingredients in bowl; mix well. Cut tortillas into 1-inch pieces.
- Layer tortillas, chicken and soup mixture in prepared dish. Top with cheese. Chill, covered, in refrigerator for 24 hours. Bake, covered, at 300 degrees for 1½ hours.
- Yield: 10 servings.

Approx Per Serving: Cal 314; Prot 21 g; Carbo 25 g; Fiber 3 g; T Fat 16 g;
43% Calories from Fat; Chol 59 mg; Sod 768 mg.

Eleanor R. Davis, **South Central Region**
GFWC—Tucson Woman's Club, Tucson AZ

SOUR CREAM-CHICKEN ENCHILADAS

1 pound chicken breast filets, cooked, chopped
2 4-ounce cans mushroom stems and pieces, drained
1 4-ounce can chopped green chilies
1/2 cup dried onion flakes
1 teaspoon chili powder
1/2 teaspoon garlic powder
1/2 teaspoon salt
1/4 teaspoon pepper
12 tortillas
Oil for softening tortillas
31/2 cups sour cream
8 ounces Cheddar cheese, shredded

- Combine chicken with next 7 ingredients in saucepan; mix well.
- Cook over low heat until heated through.
- Soften tortillas in 1/2 inch oil in small skillet over medium-high heat for several seconds on both sides; drain.
- Spoon chicken mixture onto tortillas. Fold tortillas to enclose filling.
- Spread 1 cup sour cream in 9x13-inch baking dish. Arrange tortillas in prepared dish. Top with remaining 21/2 cups sour cream; sprinkle with cheese.
- Yield: 12 servings.

Approx Per Serving: Cal 346; Prot 18 g; Carbo 20 g; Fiber 3 g; T Fat 22 g; 57% Calories from Fat; Chol 74 mg; Sod 412 mg.
Nutritional information does not include oil for softening tortillas.

Susan Chastain, **South Central Region**
GFWC—Santa Fe Junior Women's Club, Santa Fe NM

MEXICAN-STYLE CHICKEN KIEV

8 chicken breast filets
1 7-ounce can chopped green chilies
4 ounces Monterey Jack cheese, cut into 8 strips
1/2 cup fine dry bread crumbs
1/4 cup grated Parmesan cheese
1 tablespoon chili powder
1/4 teaspoon cumin
Salt to taste
1/2 teaspoon pepper
1/2 cup melted butter

- Rinse chicken and pat dry. Pound to 1/4-inch thickness. Spoon green chilies onto filets; top with cheese strips. Roll up to enclose filling; secure with wooden pick.
- Combine next 6 ingredients in bowl. Dip chicken in 6 tablespoons melted butter; coat with bread crumb mixture. Arrange in shallow baking dish. Drizzle with remaining 2 tablespoons butter.
- Chill, covered, for 4 hours to overnight.
- Bake, uncovered, at 400 degrees for 30 minutes or until chicken is tender. Serve with picante sauce.
- Yield: 8 servings.

Approx Per Serving: Cal 340; Prot 32 g; Carbo 7 g; Fiber 1 g; T Fat 20 g; 54% Calories from Fat; Chol 119 mg; Sod 515 mg.

Iris Harlan, **South Central Region**
GFWC—Harden Study Club, Bishop TX

MEXICAN CHICKEN AND RICE

1 chicken
1 onion, chopped
4 cups uncooked instant rice
1 10-ounce can cream of chicken soup
1 10-ounce can cream of mushroom
  soup

1 10-ounce can Ro-Tel tomatoes with
  green chilies
1 1/2 cups shredded sharp Cheddar
  cheese

- Rinse chicken well. Combine with onion and water to cover in saucepan.
- Cook until chicken is tender. Drain, reserving onion and 6 cups broth. Cool chicken and chop into bite-sized pieces, discarding skin and bones.
- Combine reserved onion and broth, rice, soups and tomatoes in bowl; mix well. Stir in chicken. Spoon into buttered 9x13-inch baking dish. Sprinkle with cheese.
- Bake at 350 degrees for 30 minutes or until casserole is bubbly and rice is tender.
- Yield: 8 servings.

Approx Per Serving: Cal 506; Prot 36 g; Carbo 48 g; Fiber 2 g; T Fat 18 g; 33% Calories from Fat; Chol 101 mg; Sod 913 mg.

*Suzette Woods Parker, **South Central Region***
GFWC—Lonoke Century League, Lonoke AR

TEXAS HOSPITALITY CHICKEN

6 chicken breast filets
1 cup plain nonfat yogurt
2 tablespoons chopped green chilies
1/4 teaspoon each cumin and thyme

1/2 teaspoon seasoned salt
3/4 cup cornflake crumbs
2 tablespoons melted margarine

- Rinse chicken and pat dry. Arrange in 9x13-inch baking dish.
- Combine next 5 ingredients in bowl; mix well. Spread over chicken. Top with cornflake crumbs; drizzle with margarine.
- Bake at 350 degrees for 45 minutes or until chicken is cooked and topping is golden brown.
- Yield: 6 servings.

Approx Per Serving: Cal 230; Prot 29 g; Carbo 11 g; Fiber <1 g; T Fat 7 g; 28% Calories from Fat; Chol 73 mg; Sod 351 mg.

*Martha Crump, **South Central Region***
GFWC—Contemporary Study Club, Odessa TX

CHICKEN CASSEROLE

2 cups chopped cooked chicken
2 cups bread cubes
1 cup chopped celery
2 cups chopped onions
1½ cups shredded Cheddar cheese

¼ cup toasted almonds
½ teaspoon salt
⅛ teaspoon pepper
¾ cup mayonnaise-type salad dressing
1 tablespoon lemon juice

- Combine chicken, bread cubes, celery, onions, cheese, almonds, salt and pepper in bowl; mix well.
- Combine salad dressing and lemon juice in small bowl; mix well. Add to chicken mixture; mix gently. Spoon into buttered 9x9-inch baking dish.
- Bake at 350 degrees for 40 to 50 minutes or until bubbly.
- May top with buttered bread crumbs or additional shredded cheese before baking if desired.
- Yield: 6 servings.

Approx Per Serving: Cal 400; Prot 24 g; Carbo 18 g; Fiber 2 g; T Fat 26 g; 59% Calories from Fat; Chol 79 mg; Sod 672 mg.

*Kristine A. Snyder, **Middle Atlantic Region***
GFWC—Women's Club Intermediate League, Butler PA

CHICKEN AND DRESSING CASSEROLE

1   8-ounce package dressing mix
½ cup hot water
¼ cup butter
1   16-ounce can French-style green beans, drained
3 large whole chicken breasts, cooked, chopped

1   8-ounce can sliced mushrooms, drained
2   10-ounce cans cream of mushroom soup
1 cup milk

- Combine dressing mix with water and butter in bowl; mix well. Layer half the dressing mix, green beans, chopped chicken and mushrooms in buttered 9x13-inch baking dish.
- Combine soup and milk in bowl; mix well. Spoon over layers. Top with remaining dressing mix. Chill overnight.
- Bake at 350 degrees for 50 minutes.
- Yield: 10 servings.

Approx Per Serving: Cal 296; Prot 22 g; Carbo 25 g; Fiber 1 g; T Fat 13 g; 38% Calories from Fat; Chol 60 mg; Sod 1058 mg.

*Una Sumner, **Middle Atlantic Region***
GFWC—Oxford Research Club, Oxford PA

HOT CHICKEN SALAD

4 cups chopped cooked chicken
2 cups chopped celery
1 teaspoon finely chopped onion
2 pimentos, finely chopped
4 hard-boiled eggs, sliced
3/4 cup cream of chicken soup

3/4 cup mayonnaise
2 tablespoons lemon juice
1 teaspoon salt
2/3 cup chopped almonds
1 cup shredded Cheddar cheese
1 1/2 cups crushed potato chips

- Combine chicken with next 8 ingredients in bowl; mix well. Spoon into 9x13-inch baking dish.
- Mix almonds, cheese and potato chips in bowl. Spread over casserole.
- Chill, covered, in refrigerator overnight.
- Bake at 400 degrees for 10 to 15 minutes or until bubbly.
- Yield: 8 servings.

Approx Per Serving: Cal 525; Prot 31 g; Carbo 12 g; Fiber 2 g; T Fat 40 g;
68% Calories from Fat; Chol 198 mg; Sod 826 mg.

*Doris L. Holtz, **Middle Atlantic Region***
GFWC—Palatine Literary Society, Palatine Bridge NY

MOM'S HOT CHICKEN SQUARES

3 cups chopped cooked chicken
1/3 cup chopped celery
3/4 cup chopped mushrooms
1 cup cooked rice
3 cups coarse bread crumbs
1/2 cup finely chopped pimento

2 cups chicken broth
Salt and pepper to taste
4 eggs, beaten
1   10-ounce can cream of chicken soup
1/4 cup (about) milk

- Combine chicken with next 5 ingredients in bowl; mix well. Stir in chicken broth, salt and pepper. Fold in eggs. Spoon into 9x13-inch baking dish.
- Bake at 350 degrees for 1 hour or until set.
- Heat soup with enough milk to make of desired consistency in saucepan. Cut casserole into squares. Serve with soup mixture.
- May substitute prepared croutons for bread crumbs.
- Yield: 10 servings.

Approx Per Serving: Cal 294; Prot 21 g; Carbo 31 g; Fiber 2 g; T Fat 9 g;
28% Calories from Fat; Chol 127 mg; Sod 669 mg.

*Mary S. Robinson, **Middle Atlantic Region***
GFWC—Woman's Club of New Kensington, Lower Burrell PA

CHICKEN STRATA

9 slices bread, crusts trimmed
1/4 cup butter, softened
4 cups chopped cooked chicken
1 1/2 cups sliced mushrooms
1 7-ounce can sliced water chestnuts, drained
9 slices sharp Cheddar cheese
1 10-ounce can cream of mushroom soup
1 10-ounce can cream of celery soup
4 eggs
2 cups milk
1 4-ounce can chopped pimento, drained
1 teaspoon salt
1 cup bread crumbs
2 tablespoons melted butter

- Spread both sides of bread with softened butter. Arrange in 9x13-inch baking dish.
- Layer chicken, mushrooms, water chestnuts and cheese in prepared dish.
- Combine mushroom soup and celery soup in saucepan. Heat until bubbly, stirring to mix well. Beat eggs, milk, pimento and salt in mixer bowl. Add soup mixture; mix well. Spread over layers.
- Chill, covered, overnight. Top with mixture of bread crumbs and 2 tablespoons melted butter.
- Bake at 350 degrees for 1 hour or until set. Let stand for 15 minutes before serving.
- Yield: 8 servings.

Approx Per Serving: Cal 604; Prot 38 g; Carbo 33 g; Fiber 2 g; T Fat 35 g; 52% Calories from Fat; Chol 239 mg; Sod 1420 mg.

Ruth Schuldt, **Great Lakes Region**
GFWC—Oak Lawn Woman's Club, Palos Hills IL

FIFTEEN-LAYER HOT DISH

2 cups chopped cooked chicken
1 14-ounce can cut asparagus, drained
1 cup chopped American cheese
5 ounces narrow egg noodles, cooked, drained
1 cup cashews
1 2-ounce can chopped pimento
1 cup chopped celery
1/4 cup chopped onion
1 4-ounce can mushrooms, drained
1/2 cup chopped green bell pepper
1 6-ounce can sliced black olives, drained
1 10-ounce can cream of mushroom soup
1 10-ounce can cream of chicken soup
1/2 cup mayonnaise
2 cups chow mein noodles

- Layer ingredients in order listed in 9x13-inch baking dish sprayed with nonstick cooking spray.
- Bake at 350 degrees for 1 to 1 1/2 hours or until bubbly.
- May substitute ham for chicken or use a combination.
- Yield: 10 servings.

Approx Per Serving: Cal 445; Prot 19 g; Carbo 27 g; Fiber 3 g; T Fat 32 g; 61% Calories from Fat; Chol 71 mg; Sod 1076 mg.

Donna M. Kurth, **Mississippi Valley Region**
GFWC—Knights of Knowledge, Ivanhoe MN

CHILI-CHICKEN CASSEROLE

1/2 cup chopped onion
2 tablespoons margarine
3 10-ounce cans cream of mushroom
  soup
1 4-ounce can chopped pimento,
  drained
2 tablespoons chopped seeded green
  chilies

1 16-ounce package medium noodles,
  cooked, drained
3 cups chopped cooked chicken
2 cups shredded sharp Cheddar cheese
Salt and pepper to taste

- Sauté onion in margarine in large skillet until tender. Stir in soup, pimento and green chilies.
- Layer noodles, chicken, soup mixture and cheese 1/2 at a time in 4-quart baking dish, sprinkling chicken layers with salt and pepper.
- Bake at 350 degrees for 45 minutes.
- May increase chicken to 4 cups and cheese to 3 cups.
- Yield: 8 servings.

Approx Per Serving: Cal 575; Prot 32 g; Carbo 50 g; Fiber 1 g; T Fat 27 g; 43% Calories from Fat; Chol 177 mg; Sod 1124 mg.

Angie Culberson, **South Central Region**
GFWC—Woman's Club of Casa Grande, Casa Grande AZ

CHICKEN CHALUPAS CASSEROLE

1 10-ounce can cream of chicken soup
1 10-ounce can cream of mushroom
  soup
1 4-ounce can chopped green chilies
2/3 cup milk

2/3 cup sour cream
1 cup chopped onion
18 corn tortillas, torn
4 chicken breasts, cooked, chopped
1 pound Cheddar cheese, shredded

- Combine soups, green chilies, milk, sour cream and onion in bowl; mix well.
- Layer tortillas, chicken, soup mixture and cheese in greased 9x13-inch baking dish.
- Bake at 350 degrees for 30 minutes.
- Yield: 8 servings.

Approx Per Serving: Cal 578; Prot 35 g; Carbo 39 g; Fiber 6 g; T Fat 32 g; 49% Calories from Fat; Chol 110 mg; Sod 1071 mg.

Carol Estes Smith, GFWC Treasurer, 1992–94, **South Central Region**
Tempe AZ

1904—*Sixty-three traveling libraries were founded by the North Carolina Federation of Women's Clubs.*

CHICKEN CHALUPAS

2 10-ounce cans tomato soup
3¹/₂ cups milk
2 tablespoons Worcestershire sauce
2 cloves of garlic, pressed
2 teaspoons celery salt
¹/₄ teaspoon black pepper
¹/₈ teaspoon cayenne pepper

2¹/₂ cups chopped cooked chicken
1¹/₂ cups shredded Cheddar cheese
24 flour tortillas
2 cups shredded Cheddar cheese
1 cup finely chopped onion
1 4-ounce can chopped green chilies

- Combine first 7 ingredients in bowl; mix well. Spread half the mixture in buttered 9x13-inch baking dish.
- Toss chicken with 1¹/₂ cups cheese in bowl. Spoon onto tortillas; roll tortillas to enclose filling.
- Layer half the tortillas in prepared dish. Sprinkle with half the remaining 2 cups cheese, onion and green chilies.
- Add remaining soup mixture, tortillas, cheese, onion and green chilies.
- Chill, covered with foil, for 3 to 13 hours.
- Bake, covered, at 350 degrees for 1 hour. Bake, uncovered, for 20 minutes longer or until light brown and bubbly.
- Yield: 12 servings.

Approx Per Serving: Cal 484; Prot 25 g; Carbo 51 g; Fiber 2 g; T Fat 22 g; 39% Calories from Fat; Chol 70 mg; Sod 1197 mg.

*Roberta T. White, **South Central Region***
GFWC—Progress Club, Las Cruces NM

CHICKEN SALSA CASSEROLE

1 cup uncooked rice
2¹/₂ cups (about) chicken broth
3 cups chopped cooked chicken
1 10-ounce can cream of chicken soup
¹/₂ cup milk
1 cup sliced mushrooms
1 small onion, chopped

1 teaspoon chili powder
¹/₂ teaspoon salt
¹/₂ teaspoon pepper
1 16-ounce jar salsa
1 pound Monterey Jack cheese, shredded

- Cook rice in chicken broth in saucepan until tender.
- Combine chicken and next 7 ingredients in bowl; mix well.
- Layer rice, chicken mixture, salsa and cheese ¹/₂ at a time in greased 9x13-inch baking dish.
- Bake at 350 degrees for 20 minutes.
- Yield: 8 servings.

Approx Per Serving: Cal 477; Prot 34 g; Carbo 28 g; Fiber 1 g; T Fat 24 g; 47% Calories from Fat; Chol 104 mg; Sod 1364 mg.

*Trudy James, **Western Region***
GFWC—Pixley Women's Club, Pixley CA

KING RANCH CASSEROLE

2 chickens
15 corn tortillas
1 medium green bell pepper, chopped
1 onion, chopped
1 clove of garlic, chopped
2 tablespoons oil
1½ teaspoons chili powder
1 10-ounce can cream of mushroom soup

1 10-ounce can cream of chicken soup
2 cups shredded Cheddar cheese
½ 10-ounce can Ro-Tel tomatoes with green chilies
½ 16-ounce can tomatoes, drained, crushed
1 8-ounce package corn chips, finely crushed

- Rinse chicken well. Cook in water to cover in saucepan until tender. Drain, reserving broth. Chop chicken into bite-sized pieces, discarding skin and bones.
- Soften tortillas in reserved chicken broth in saucepan. Layer tortillas in 13x23-inch baking dish. Layer chicken over tortillas.
- Sauté green pepper, onion and garlic in oil in skillet. Stir in chili powder. Spread over chicken.
- Layer mushroom soup, chicken soup, half the cheese, Ro-Tel tomatoes, tomatoes and remaining cheese in prepared baking dish. Top with corn chips.
- Bake at 350 degrees for 1 hour.
- Yield: 16 servings.

Approx Per Serving: Cal 415; Prot 32 g; Carbo 25 g; Fiber 3 g; T Fat 21 g; 45% Calories from Fat; Chol 92 mg; Sod 619 mg.

*Shirley Hill, **South Central Region***
GFWC—Corpus Christi Federation of Women's Clubs, Alice TX

MEXICAN CHICKEN CASSEROLE

2 7-ounce cans chicken
2 10-ounce cans cream of chicken soup
1 10-ounce can Ro-Tel tomatoes with green chilies

½ cup chopped onion
1½ cups evaporated milk
1 9-ounce package tortilla chips
1½ cups shredded Cheddar cheese

- Combine all ingredients except cheese in bowl; mix well. Mixture will be soupy. Spoon into 9x13-inch baking dish. Top with cheese.
- Bake at 350 degrees for 30 minutes or until bubbly.
- May substitute one 12-ounce can Milnot for evaporated milk. May prepare in advance adding chips and cheese at baking time.
- Yield: 8 servings.

Approx Per Serving: Cal 438; Prot 25 g; Carbo 32 g; Fiber 2 g; T Fat 25 g; 49% Calories from Fat; Chol 42 mg; Sod 1213 mg.

*Ellen Phelps, **South Central Region***
GFWC—Anadarko Delphian Study Club, Anadarko OK

TAMALE CHICKEN

1 medium onion, chopped
1 green bell pepper, chopped
2 tablespoons oil
1   10-ounce can cream of chicken soup
2 cups sour cream
1 cup sliced black olives
1 cup chopped stewed tomatoes

2 cups shredded sharp Cheddar cheese
8 chicken breast filets, cooked, chopped
1   16-ounce can beef tamales, chopped
1 teaspoon each chili powder, garlic powder and pepper
1/2 cup shredded sharp Cheddar cheese

- Sauté onion and green pepper in oil in skillet.
- Combine soup, sour cream, olives and tomatoes in bowl; mix well. Add sautéed vegetables, 2 cups cheese, chicken, tamales and seasonings; mix gently.
- Spoon into 9x13-inch baking dish; sprinkle with 1/2 cup cheese.
- Bake at 350 degrees for 50 minutes or until bubbly.
- Yield: 8 servings.

Approx Per Serving: Cal 609; Prot 41 g; Carbo 17 g; Fiber 1 g; T Fat 44 g; 63% Calories from Fat; Chol 138 mg; Sod 1157 mg.

Randi Rummage, **South Central Region**
GFWC—Kachina Juniors Club, Phoenix AZ

OKIE TORTILLA CASSEROLE

12 corn tortillas
2 tablespoons oil
1/2 cup chopped onion
2 tablespoons oil
2 large tomatoes, finely chopped
2 cups shredded cooked chicken

1 1/4 cups chicken broth
1 envelope taco seasoning mix
1   4-ounce can chopped green chilies
1 cup sliced black olives
1/2 cup sour cream
1 cup shredded sharp Cheddar cheese

- Cut tortillas into strips. Fry in 2 tablespoons oil in skillet; drain on paper towels.
- Sauté onion in 2 tablespoons oil in saucepan. Add tomatoes. Cook for several minutes. Add chicken, broth, taco seasoning mix and green chilies; mix well.
- Simmer for 15 minutes. Stir in olives.
- Alternate layers of tortillas and chicken mixture in 2-quart baking dish until all ingredients are used. Spread with sour cream; sprinkle with cheese.
- Bake at 375 degrees for 20 minutes. Serve with tomato, onion, cilantro, lime juice and salsa.
- Yield: 6 servings.

Approx Per Serving: Cal 515; Prot 26 g; Carbo 37 g; Fiber 7 g; T Fat 32 g; 53% Calories from Fat; Chol 70 mg; Sod 1264 mg.

Carol J. Duval, **South Central Region**
GFWC—New Century Research Club, Edmond OK

CHICKEN BREASTS SUPREME

4 large chicken breast filets
1 cup flour
1 teaspoon salt
1/2 teaspoon pepper
1 tablespoon butter

1 tablespoon oil
1 cup sweet Marsala
8 ounces Jarlsburg cheese
1 16-ounce can sliced peaches,
   drained

- Rinse chicken and pat dry. Shake with mixture of flour, salt and pepper in bag.
- Brown on both sides in butter and oil in electric skillet heated to 450 degrees. Reduce skillet temperature to 350 degrees. Add wine.
- Simmer, covered, for 20 to 25 minutes or until liquid has evaporated. Remove chicken to baking sheet.
- Cut cheese into strips. Arrange half the strips over chicken. Top with peach slices. Arrange remaining cheese strips in lattice pattern over top.
- Broil for 3 to 5 minutes or until cheese melts. Serve immediately.
- Do not substitute other wine or cheese in this recipe.
- Yield: 4 servings.

Approx Per Serving: Cal 673; Prot 44 g; Carbo 48 g; Fiber 2 g; T Fat 27 g;
36% Calories from Fat; Chol 132 mg; Sod 936 mg.

Mrs. Philip Macdonald, **Middle Atlantic Region**
GFWC—Aronimink Women's Club, Drexel Hill PA

CHICKEN LIVERS WITH APPLES AND ONION RINGS

12 chicken livers
1/4 teaspoon salt
1/4 teaspoon paprika
2 tablespoons flour
2 tablespoons butter

1/2 Spanish onion, sliced into rings
1/2 tablespoon butter
4 1/2-inch apple slices
1/2 tablespoon butter

- Rinse livers and pat dry. Cut large livers into halves. Sprinkle with salt and paprika; coat with flour.
- Brown in 2 tablespoons butter in medium skillet until light brown.
- Sauté onion rings in 1/2 tablespoon butter in small skillet. Add to livers.
- Sauté apple slices in 1/2 tablespoon butter in small skillet. Add to livers. Sprinkle with sugar. Cook until glazed. Serve over rice.
- Yield: 2 servings.

Approx Per Serving: Cal 418; Prot 31 g; Carbo 19 g; Fiber 2 g; T Fat 24 g;
52% Calories from Fat; Chol 803 mg; Sod 473 mg.

Claudia F. Kahn, **Middle Atlantic Region**
GFWC—Glen Rock Woman's Club, Glen Rock NJ

ARIZONA-STYLE TORTILLA PUDDING

1½ pounds ground turkey
1 large onion, chopped
12 flour tortillas
2 tablespoons oil
1 pound Cheddar cheese, shredded
1 cup sour cream

1 16-ounce can enchilada sauce
1 enchilada can water
1 8-ounce can tomato sauce
1 4-ounce can chopped green chilies
2 teaspoons chili powder
Garlic powder to taste

- Brown ground turkey with onion in nonstick skillet, stirring until crumbly.
- Soften tortillas in hot oil in skillet.
- Reserve ⅓ of the cheese for topping. Layer tortillas, turkey mixture, remaining cheese and sour cream ½ at a time in 9x13-inch baking dish. Sprinkle with reserved cheese.
- Bring remaining ingredients to a boil in saucepan. Pour over layers.
- Bake at 350 degrees for 45 to 60 minutes or until bubbly.
- Yield: 8 servings.

Approx Per Serving: Cal 711; Prot 38 g; Carbo 47 g; Fiber 3 g; T Fat 44 g; 54% Calories from Fat; Chol 126 mg; Sod 1623 mg.

*Gertrude Bartlett, **South Central Region***
GFWC—White Mountain Woman's Club, Show Low AZ

SWEET AND SPICY TURKEY LOAF

1 pound ground turkey
½ cup bread crumbs
½ cup finely chopped onion
1 egg
3 tablespoons catsup
1 tablespoon sweet pickle relish

1 tablespoon parsley flakes
1 teaspoon prepared mustard
⅛ teaspoon each ground cloves and
   garlic powder
¼ teaspoon nutmeg and pepper

- Combine all ingredients in bowl; mix well.
- Shape into loaf; place in loaf pan.
- Bake at 350 degrees for 45 minutes or until cooked through.
- Yield: 4 servings.

Approx Per Serving: Cal 286; Prot 26 g; Carbo 15 g; Fiber 1 g; T Fat 13 g; 42% Calories from Fat; Chol 125 mg; Sod 388 mg.

*Shirley Lowder, **Southeastern Region***
GFWC—Fuquay-Varina Woman's Club, Fuquay-Varina NC

1906—*GFWC turned the tide for the passage of the Pure Food and Drug Act.*

RIGATONI WITH TURKEY SAUSAGE AND RED PEPPER

1/2 cup chopped onion
1 pound Italian-seasoned turkey
  sausage
1 teaspoon Italian seasoning
1/2 teaspoon fennel seed, crushed
Crushed red pepper to taste

1 large red bell pepper, julienned
1 35-ounce can salt-free whole
   tomatoes, chopped
1/2 cup dry red wine
1/4 cup chopped fresh parsley
1 16-ounce package rigatoni

- Sauté onion in large skillet sprayed with nonstick cooking spray for 3 minutes. Add sausage, Italian seasoning, fennel seed and red pepper. Cook until sausage is brown and crumbly; remove to bowl.
- Drain and wipe skillet. Spray with nonstick cooking spray. Heat over medium heat. Add bell pepper.
- Sauté bell pepper for 4 minutes. Add sausage mixture, tomatoes and wine; mix well. Bring to a boil; reduce heat.
- Simmer for 15 minutes, stirring occasionally. Stir in parsley. Cook pasta using package directions, omitting butter and salt; drain. Spoon sausage mixture over pasta to serve.
- Yield: 8 servings.

Approx Per Serving: Cal 317; Prot 14 g; Carbo 52 g; Fiber 3 g; T Fat 5 g;
14% Calories from Fat; Chol 22 mg; Sod 206 mg.

*Susan F. Fox, **Middle Atlantic Region***
GFWC—Springfield Township Club, Oreland PA

TURKEY AND CORN CASSEROLE

3 cups cooked corkscrew pasta
1 cup shredded Monterey Jack cheese
1 cup shredded jalapeño pepper cheese
1 1/2 cups chopped cooked turkey
1 10-ounce can cream of chicken soup
1/2 cup sour cream

1 8-ounce can whole kernel corn,
   drained
1/2 cup chopped green onions
1 teaspoon chili powder
1/8 teaspoon garlic powder

- Toss pasta with half the Monterey Jack and half the pepper cheese in bowl. Spoon into 8x12-inch baking dish.
- Combine next 7 ingredients in bowl; mix well. Spoon evenly over pasta.
- Bake at 350 degrees for 35 minutes. Sprinkle with remaining cheeses. Bake for 5 minutes longer. Garnish with chopped tomatoes, chopped black olives and crushed tortilla chips.
- Yield: 8 servings.

Approx Per Serving: Cal 297; Prot 19 g; Carbo 21 g; Fiber 1 g; T Fat 16 g;
47% Calories from Fat; Chol 55 mg; Sod 523 mg.

*Vera D. Ellis, **Southeastern Region***
GFWC—St. Albans Women's Club, St. Albans WV

TURKEY SCALLOP

1 8-ounce package herb-seasoned
   stuffing mix
4 cups chopped cooked turkey
1/2 cup flour
1/4 teaspoon salt
Pepper to taste
1/2 cup butter

4 cups chicken broth
6 eggs, slightly beaten
1 10-ounce can cream of mushroom
   soup
1/4 cup milk
1 cup sour cream
1/4 cup chopped pimento

- Prepare stuffing mix using package directions. Spread in 9x13-inch baking dish. Sprinkle turkey over top.
- Blend flour, salt and pepper into butter in saucepan. Cook until bubbly. Stir in broth.
- Cook until thickened, stirring constantly. Stir a small amount of hot mixture into eggs; stir eggs into hot mixture. Cook until thickened, stirring constantly. Spoon over chicken.
- Bake at 325 degrees for 40 to 45 minutes or until bubbly. Let stand for 5 to 15 minutes.
- Combine remaining ingredients in saucepan. Cook until heated through. Cut casserole into squares. Serve with sauce.
- Yield: 12 servings.

Approx Per Serving: Cal 406; Prot 23 g; Carbo 22 g; Fiber 2 g; T Fat 25 g;
56% Calories from Fat; Chol 187 mg; Sod 1060 mg.

*Eunice Spindler, **Middle Atlantic Region***
GFWC—Delmar Progress Club, Delmar NY

TURKEY STEAKS WITH CRANBERRY SAUCE

1/4 cup oil
3 tablespoons white wine
1/8 teaspoon each thyme, rosemary,
   marjoram and paprika
Salt and pepper to taste
4 6-ounce turkey steaks
2 cups cranberries

1 tablespoon lemon juice
3 tablespoons orange juice
1/2 tablespoon prepared mustard
2 tablespoons cornstarch
5 tablespoons flour
2 tablespoons oil

- Combine first 8 ingredients in shallow dish; mix well. Rinse turkey and pat dry. Place in marinade, coating well. Marinate in refrigerator for 2 hours.
- Cook cranberries in lemon juice and orange juice in saucepan for 5 minutes. Stir in next 2 ingredients. Simmer for 1 minute or until thickened, stirring constantly.
- Drain steaks; coat with flour.
- Brown steaks in 2 tablespoons oil in skillet for 4 to 5 minutes on each side. Remove to serving platter. Serve with cranberry sauce.
- Yield: 4 servings.

Approx Per Serving: Cal 425; Prot 28 g; Carbo 19 g; Fiber 2 g; T Fat 25 g;
55% Calories from Fat; Chol 70 mg; Sod 91 mg.

*Elke Albrecht, **Southeastern Region***
GFWC—Mocksville Woman's Club, Mocksville NC

GEORGIA DOVES

24 doves
2 cups flour
Salt and pepper to taste
Peanut oil for browning
2½ cups chopped onions

1½ cups chopped celery
8 ounces small whole mushrooms
1 teaspoon each thyme and parsley
flakes
2 cups red wine

- Rinse doves inside and out; pat dry. Coat with mixture of flour, salt and pepper.
- Brown in peanut oil in skillet; drain well. Place in Dutch oven.
- Combine remaining ingredients in bowl; mix well. Spoon over doves. Add water to cover; mix well.
- Bake at 300 degrees for 2½ hours or until very tender. Serve pan gravy with rice.
- May substitute 1 tablespoon fresh herbs for dried herbs.
- Yield: 12 servings.

Approx Per Serving: Cal 290; Prot 30 g; Carbo 20 g; Fiber 2 g; T Fat 2 g;
8% Calories from Fat; Chol 109 mg; Sod 17 mg.
Nutritional information does not include peanut oil for browning doves.

Doris P. Blalock, *Southern Region*
GFWC—Metropolitan and Suburban Women's Clubs of Augusta, Evans GA

PHEASANT HOT DISH

2 cups chopped cooked pheasant
1 cup cooked rice
2 cups soft bread crumbs
½ cup chopped celery
4 eggs, beaten
2 cups chicken broth

½ teaspoon crushed basil
Salt and pepper to taste
1   10-ounce can cream of chicken soup
½ cup milk
1 cup crushed potato chips

- Combine first 9 ingredients in bowl; mix well. Spoon into 9x13-inch baking dish.
- Combine soup and milk in bowl; mix well. Spoon over casserole; sprinkle with potato chips.
- Bake at 325 degrees for 1 hour.
- Yield: 10 servings.

Approx Per Serving: Cal 201; Prot 13 g; Carbo 16 g; Fiber 1 g; T Fat 10 g;
43% Calories from Fat; Chol 110 mg; Sod 500 mg.

Opal Fitzgerald, *Mississippi Valley Region*
GFWC—Beresford Study Club, Beresford SD

SEAFOOD

GFWC
Volunteer

Fireplaces with mantelpieces of
"Rouge Royale" Italian marble in
Louis XIV style were imported
from the Paris home of the former
King Alfonso of Spain for the
drawing room. The fireplaces are
enhanced by Louis XVI brass
adornments and fan-shaped
fire screens.

CALIFORNIA BOUILLABAISSE

4 cups water
1 carrot
1 bay leaf
2 teaspoons salt
¼ teaspoon pepper
2 pounds halibut steaks
2 medium onions, sliced
3 tablespoons olive oil

¼ cup flour
1 pound shrimp, deveined
1 cup oysters with liquid
1 16-ounce can tomatoes, chopped
1 tablespoon lemon juice
1²/₃ cups pitted black olives
2 tablespoons chopped parsley

- Bring water, carrot, bay leaf, salt and pepper to a boil in large saucepan.
- Cut halibut into large pieces, discarding skin and bones. Add halibut to saucepan; reduce heat.
- Simmer for 10 minutes. Remove fish and strain stock.
- Sauté onions in olive oil in saucepan until tender but not brown. Stir in flour. Add strained stock gradually. Cook until thickened, stirring constantly.
- Add shrimp. Simmer for 5 minutes. Stir in halibut, undrained oysters, tomatoes, lemon juice and olives. Simmer for 5 minutes. Stir in parsley at serving time.
- Yield: 8 servings.

Approx Per Serving: Cal 303; Prot 37 g; Carbo 11 g; Fiber 2 g; T Fat 13 g;
38% Calories from Fat; Chol 143 mg; Sod 962 mg.

Sara E. Hamilton, **Southeastern Region**
GFWC—Vienna Woman's Club, Vienna VA

CIOPPINO

1 large onion, chopped
1 green bell pepper, chopped
2 cloves of garlic, chopped
¼ cup olive oil
1 16-ounce can stewed tomatoes
2 cups Zinfandel
¼ cup minced parsley

½ teaspoon oregano
¼ teaspoon basil
Salt and pepper to taste
2 pounds halibut, chopped
1 pound shrimp
1 7-ounce can clams

- Sauté onion, green pepper and garlic in olive oil in saucepan. Add next 7 ingredients; mix well.
- Simmer for 1 hour. Add fish, shrimp and clams. Cook until fish flakes easily. Serve with thick slices of French bread or hard rolls.
- May use fresh clams or substitute fresh crabs for shrimp; cook seafood and add to servings.
- Yield: 8 servings.

Approx Per Serving: Cal 305; Prot 36 g; Carbo 8 g; Fiber 1 g; T Fat 12 g;
35% Calories from Fat; Chol 141 mg; Sod 361 mg.

Virginia Kaiser, **Western Region**
GFWC—Kirkland Woman's Club, Kirkland WA

NEW ENGLAND FISH CHOWDER

2 large onions, chopped
1 cup chopped carrots
3 tablespoons margarine
4 cups chopped potatoes

2 pounds haddock, cubed
2 quarts milk, heated
Salt and pepper to taste

- Sauté onions and carrots in margarine in large stockpot. Add potatoes.
- Cook just until potatoes are tender. Add fish, milk, salt and pepper.
- Simmer until fish flakes easily. May thicken with 1 teaspoon cornstarch dissolved in 1 tablespoon water if desired. May substitute codfish for haddock.
- Yield: 10 servings.

Approx Per Serving: Cal 295; Prot 27 g; Carbo 23 g; Fiber 2 g; T Fat 11 g; 32% Calories from Fat; Chol 80 mg; Sod 191 mg.

Frances T. Cronin, **New England Region**
GFWC—Salem Women's Club, Salem NH

ABALONE MEXICANA

2 abalone
8 slices Monterey Jack cheese
1 7-ounce can whole green chilies
1 egg, slightly beaten
1/2 cup flour
2 tablespoons butter

1 6-ounce can tomato paste
1/4 cup sliced olives
1 clove of garlic, pressed
1/4 onion, minced
1/2 cup shredded Monterey Jack cheese

- Clean abalone and slice into eight 1/4-inch steaks. Pound steaks until tender.
- Insert 1 slice cheese into each chili pepper. Place on abalone steaks. Roll abalone to enclose filling. Dip into egg; coat with flour.
- Sauté rolls in butter in skillet until light brown. Place in buttered baking dish.
- Combine next 4 ingredients in bowl; mix well. Spoon over rolls; top with shredded cheese.
- Broil until cheese melts. Serve with lemon wedges.
- Red abalone is preferable in this recipe.
- Yield: 8 servings.

Approx Per Serving: Cal 350; Prot 31 g; Carbo 19 g; Fiber 1 g; T Fat 17 g; 43% Calories from Fat; Chol 163 mg; Sod 793 mg.

Claudia Heller, **Western Region**
GFWC—Duarte Woman's Club, Duarte CA

CATFISH CREOLE

6 catfish filets
2 medium green onions, chopped
2 cloves of garlic, minced
1/4 cup butter
1   15-ounce can stewed tomatoes, crushed

1 tablespoon fresh lemon juice
1 bay leaf
1/2 teaspoon each oregano, basil, salt and freshly ground black pepper
1/4 teaspoon cayenne pepper
12 ounces vermicelli, cooked, drained

- Pat fish dry with paper towel; arrange in 9x13-inch baking dish.
- Sauté green onions and garlic in butter in skillet until tender. Add next 8 ingredients; mix well.
- Simmer until heated through. Spoon over fish.
- Bake at 325 degrees for 20 minutes or until fish flakes easily. Place pasta on 6 serving plates. Place 1 fish filet on each serving; spoon sauce over top, discarding bay leaf.
- Yield: 6 servings.

Approx Per Serving: Cal 326; Prot 25 g; Carbo 49 g; Fiber 3 g; T Fat 12 g; 27% Calories from Fat; Chol 74 mg; Sod 530 mg.

Margaret W. Schaff, **South Central Region**
GFWC—Cum Concilio Club, Nacogdoches TX

CATFISH IN SOUR CREAM

1 pound catfish filets
Salt, pepper and Tabasco sauce to taste
1 cup sour cream
2 tablespoons minced dill pickle
2 tablespoons chopped green bell pepper

2 tablespoons minced onion
1 tablespoon chopped parsley
1 tablespoon lemon juice
1/2 teaspoon sweet basil
1/2 teaspoon dry mustard

- Season fish with salt, pepper and Tabasco sauce; arrange in 8x8-inch baking dish sprayed with nonstick cooking spray.
- Combine remaining ingredients in bowl; mix well. Spoon over fish.
- Bake at 325 degrees for 45 minutes.
- Yield: 4 servings.

Approx Per Serving: Cal 151; Prot 19 g; Carbo 4 g; Fiber <1 g; T Fat 16 g; 62% Calories from Fat; Chol 78 mg; Sod 170 mg.

Marguerite Williams, **Southern Region**
GFWC—Batesville Woman's Club, Batesville MS

CODFISH CAKES

8 ounces salted codfish
3 cups chopped potatoes
1 egg, beaten

2 tablespoons butter
1/4 teaspoon pepper
2 tablespoons oil

- Combine codfish with water to cover in saucepan. Soak in refrigerator overnight. Add potatoes.
- Cook until potatoes are tender; drain. Add egg, butter and pepper; mix until smooth. Shape into cakes.
- Fry in oil in skillet until brown on both sides; drain. May deep-fry by heaping tablespoonfuls if preferred.
- Yield: 4 servings.

Approx Per Serving: Cal 349; Prot 32 g; Carbo 20 g; Fiber 2 g; T Fat 15 g; 39% Calories from Fat; Chol 138 mg; Sod 3258 mg.

Ruth Vernon, **New England Region**
GFWC—Salem Women's Club, Salem NH

FLOUNDER STUFFED WITH CRAB MEAT

1½ tablespoons finely chopped onion
1½ tablespoons chopped celery
1½ tablespoons finely chopped
  parsley
3 tablespoons butter
6 ounces crab meat, flaked

3/4 cup bread crumbs
1 egg, beaten
Salt and pepper to taste
6 flounder filets
2 tablespoons melted butter
Paprika to taste

- Sauté onion, celery and parsley in 3 tablespoons butter in skillet until tender. Add crab meat, bread crumbs, egg, salt and pepper; mix well.
- Spoon stuffing onto fish filets. Roll to enclose filling; secure ends. Arrange fish filet rolls in buttered baking dish. Brush with 1 tablespoon melted butter; sprinkle with paprika.
- Bake at 375 degrees for 30 minutes or until fish flakes easily, brushing with remaining 1 tablespoon melted butter.
- Yield: 6 servings.

Approx Per Serving: Cal 283; Prot 30 g; Carbo 10 g; Fiber 1 g; T Fat 13 g; 42% Calories from Fat; Chol 152 mg; Sod 360 mg.

Betty Asplund, **Middle Atlantic Region**
GFWC—West Essex Woman's Club, West Caldwell NJ

1911—*GFWC supported legislation for the 8-hour work day.*

HADDOCK AU GRATIN

1¹/₂ to 2 pounds haddock filets
Salt and pepper to taste
3 tablespoons butter
3 tablespoons flour

1¹/₂ cups milk
¹/₂ cup toasted bread crumbs
¹/₄ cup shredded Cheddar cheese

- Cut large fish filets into smaller portions. Arrange fish skinned side down in buttered 9x13-inch baking dish, tucking under ends of whole filets. Sprinkle with salt and pepper.
- Melt butter in saucepan; remove from heat. Stir in flour. Add milk.
- Bring to a boil, stirring constantly. Cook for 2 to 3 minutes longer, stirring constantly; sauce will be thick. Season with salt and pepper.
- Spoon sauce over fish, covering completely. Sprinkle with bread crumbs and cheese.
- Bake at 350 degrees for 20 to 25 minutes or until fish flakes easily.
- May layer fish with 1 cup sautéed mushrooms before adding sauce if desired.
- Yield: 4 servings.

Approx Per Serving: Cal 440; Prot 56 g; Carbo 18 g; Fiber 1 g; T Fat 16 g;
33% Calories from Fat; Chol 178 mg; Sod 405 mg.

Donna Minichiello, **New England Region**
GFWC—Bethel Women's Club, Bethel CT

HALIBUT FLORENTINE

1 pound halibut
Salt to taste
2 10-ounce packages frozen chopped
     spinach
6 tablespoons flour
6 tablespoons melted margarine
3 cups milk
1 teaspoon salt

¹/₄ teaspoon pepper
¹/₂ teaspoon nutmeg
¹/₂ teaspoon MSG
¹/₄ cup shredded Cheddar cheese
¹/₄ cup sherry
¹/₄ cup grated Parmesan cheese
2 tablespoons melted margarine

- Poach fish in salted water in saucepan for 5 minutes; drain. Cool fish and break into small pieces. Cook spinach using package directions; drain.
- Blend flour into 6 tablespoons margarine in saucepan. Add milk, 1 teaspoon salt and pepper. Cook until thickened, stirring constantly.
- Combine half the sauce with spinach, nutmeg and MSG in bowl; mix well. Spread in 8x12-inch baking dish. Arrange fish over spinach mixture. Combine remaining sauce with Cheddar cheese and wine in bowl; mix well. Spoon over fish; sprinkle with Parmesan cheese. Drizzle with 2 tablespoons melted margarine.
- Bake at 350 degrees for 20 to 25 minutes or until light brown.
- May omit MSG and salt and use skim milk if preferred.
- Yield: 4 servings.

Approx Per Serving: Cal 587; Prot 40 g; Carbo 26 g; Fiber 4 g; T Fat 36 g;
55% Calories from Fat; Chol 73 mg; Sod 1737 mg.

Alice Breckling, **Western Region**
GFWC—Suburban Woman's Club of Lafayette, Lafayette CA

Alaskan Halibut

2½ pounds halibut
2 quarts water
1 onion, sliced
1 cup celery leaves
3 bay leaves
1 teaspoon thyme
½ teaspoon each onion and celery salt
¼ cup butter
½ cup flour

½ teaspoon salt
⅛ teaspoon pepper
½ teaspoon each onion and celery salt
1 cup plus 2 tablespoons milk
1 chicken bouillon cube
1 4-ounce can mushrooms, drained
1 tablespoon butter
3 tablespoons sherry
1 7-ounce can shrimp

- Tie fish in cheesecloth bag.
- Bring water and next 6 ingredients to a simmer in saucepan. Add fish. Poach for 20 minutes. Strain stock, reserving 1 cup. Cut fish into serving pieces, discarding bones.
- Melt ¼ cup butter in saucepan over low heat. Stir in flour and remaining seasonings; remove from heat. Add milk and bouillon cube dissolved in reserved stock. Cook until thickened, stirring constantly.
- Sauté mushrooms in 1 tablespoon butter and 1 tablespoon wine in skillet. Add to sauce. Spread a thin layer of sauce in buttered baking dish. Arrange fish in prepared dish. Top with remaining sauce. Arrange 3 shrimp on each serving. Sprinkle with remaining 2 tablespoons wine.
- Bake, covered, at 350 degrees for 15 minutes.
- Yield: 6 servings.

Approx Per Serving: Cal 414; Prot 51 g; Carbo 14 g; Fiber 1 g; T Fat 17 g;
37% Calories from Fat; Chol 152 mg; Sod 1226 mg.

Evangeline Landers, **Western Region**
GFWC—Chugiak Ladies Club and Anchorage Woman's Club, Eagle River AK

Italian-Style Orange Roughy

2 cloves of garlic, minced
4 scallions, chopped
1 cup chopped mushrooms
¼ cup butter
¼ cup rosé

3 medium tomatoes, peeled, chopped
Crushed red pepper and salt to taste
1 pound orange roughy filets
1 tablespoon chopped fresh basil

- Sauté garlic, scallions and mushrooms in butter in medium skillet over medium heat for 5 minutes. Stir in wine.
- Cook until most of pan juices have evaporated. Add tomatoes, red pepper and salt; reduce heat. Simmer for 5 minutes.
- Spoon sauce over fish in 9x13-inch baking dish; sprinkle with basil.
- Bake at 375 degrees for 20 to 25 minutes or until fish flakes easily.
- Yield: 4 servings.

Approx Per Serving: Cal 284; Prot 18 g; Carbo 6 g; Fiber 2 g; T Fat 20 g;
64% Calories from Fat; Chol 54 mg; Sod 179 mg.

Mary L. Thorne, **Middle Atlantic Region**
GFWC—Woman's Club of Easton, Easton PA

MACKEREL IN WINE SAUCE

2 large onions, sliced
1 tablespoon oil
2 tablespoons butter
1 cup dry white wine
2 beef bouillon cubes
2 cups water
2 tablespoons melted butter
2 tablespoons flour

1 4-ounce can sliced mushrooms,
   drained
Salt and pepper to taste
2½ pounds mackerel filets
½ cup bread crumbs
1 tablespoon butter
Juice of ½ lemon

- Sauté onions in oil and 2 tablespoons butter in skillet until golden brown. Stir in wine.
- Cook until liquid is reduced to 3 tablespoons. Add bouillon cubes and water. Stir in mixture of 2 tablespoons melted butter and flour.
- Cook over medium heat until thickened, stirring constantly. Add mushrooms, salt and pepper.
- Spread half the sauce in 2-quart baking dish. Arrange fish in prepared dish. Top with remaining sauce. Sprinkle with bread crumbs; dot with 1 tablespoon butter. Drizzle with lemon juice.
- Bake at 375 degrees for 35 to 40 minutes or until fish flakes easily.
- Yield: 6 servings.

Approx Per Serving: Cal 595; Prot 39 g; Carbo 14 g; Fiber 2 g; T Fat 39 g;
63% Calories from Fat; Chol 140 mg; Sod 639 mg.

Victoria R. Morris, **Southeastern Region**
GFWC—Shallotte Junior Woman's Club, Leland NC

GRILLED SALMON STEAKS

4 9-ounce salmon steaks
½ cup melted butter

¼ cup lime juice
1 tablespoon pepper

- Arrange fish in baking dish. Pour mixture of butter, lime juice and pepper over fish. Marinate for several minutes.
- Drain fish, reserving marinade. Place fish on grill.
- Grill until fish flakes easily, brushing with reserved marinade.
- Yield: 4 servings.

Approx Per Serving: Cal 647; Prot 56 g; Carbo 1 g; Fiber <1 g; T Fat 45 g;
64% Calories from Fat; Chol 240 mg; Sod 328 mg.

Jane Cline, **Western Region**
GFWC—Omak Civic League, Okanogan WA

1912—GFWC supported legislation for the rights of married women and uniform marriage and divorce laws.

SALMON IN RED WINE SAUCE

1¼ cups dry red wine
5 tablespoons red wine vinegar
2 shallots, chopped
4 fresh thyme sprigs

6 8-ounce salmon filets
1 tablespoon unsalted butter
1 tablespoon olive oil
12 tablespoons butter

- Bring wine, vinegar, shallots and thyme to a boil in small saucepan. Cook until liquid is reduced to ½ cup; set aside.
- Brown fish in unsalted butter and olive oil in skillet for 4 minutes on each side. Remove to warm dish.
- Bring sauce to a simmer; remove from heat. Whisk in 2 tablespoons cold butter. Place over low heat.
- Whisk in remaining 10 tablespoons butter 1 tablespoon at a time, removing from heat if necessary to prevent sauce from separating.
- Serve with salmon.
- May reduce sauce base and hold for up to 6 hours before whisking in butter.
- Yield: 6 servings.

Approx Per Serving: Cal 686; Prot 51 g; Carbo 6 g; Fiber <1 g; T Fat 47 g;
65% Calories from Fat; Chol 225 mg; Sod 319 mg.

Charlotte Pritz, **Western Region**
GFWC—Orange Cove Women's Club, Orange Cove CA

STUFFED FILETS OF SOLE

2 tablespoons chopped red or green
   bell pepper
2 tablespoons chopped onion
¼ cup butter
½ cup crushed butter crackers
1 6-ounce can crab meat
2 pounds sole filets

3 tablespoons flour
3 tablespoons melted butter
1½ cups milk, heated
⅓ cup dry white wine
1 cup shredded Swiss cheese
Paprika to taste

- Sauté bell pepper and onion in ¼ cup butter in skillet until golden brown. Stir in cracker crumbs and crab meat.
- Spoon onto fish filets. Roll up fish to enclose filling. Arrange seam side down in buttered baking dish.
- Blend flour into 3 tablespoons melted butter in saucepan. Cook until bubbly. Stir in milk. Cook until thickened, stirring constantly. Add wine and cheese. Cook until cheese melts.
- Spoon sauce over fish; sprinkle with paprika.
- Bake at 400 degrees for 30 minutes or until fish flakes easily.
- Yield: 6 servings.

Approx Per Serving: Cal 456; Prot 44 g; Carbo 12 g; Fiber <1 g; T Fat 25 g;
51% Calories from Fat; Chol 170 mg; Sod 480 mg.

Midge Klein, **New England Region**
GFWC—Harvard Woman's Club, Harvard MA

MARINATED AND GRILLED SWORDFISH

2 pounds swordfish, 1¹/₂ inches thick **1 tablespoon lemon juice**
1 teaspoon olive oil **¹/₂ cup country-style Dijon mustard**

- Rub both sides of fish with olive oil; sprinkle with lemon juice. Coat generously with mustard; place in shallow dish. Marinate in refrigerator for 1 hour or longer.
- Place fish on grill sprayed with nonstick cooking spray. Grill for 7 minutes on each side for thick portions.
- Garnish with fresh peaches.
- Yield: 4 servings.

Approx Per Serving: Cal 342; Prot 48 g; Carbo 2 g; Fiber <1 g; T Fat 15 g; 39% Calories from Fat; Chol 91 mg; Sod 1009 mg.

*Bette Pease, **New England Region***
GFWC—Southington Woman's Club, Southington CT

SWORDFISH KABOBS IN ORANGE SAUCE

4 small white onions **2 tablespoons oil**
10 to 12 ounces swordfish **1 tablespoon soy sauce**
1 green bell pepper **¹/₂ teaspoon each oregano and paprika**
8 kumquats **Freshly ground pepper to taste**
¹/₂ cup orange juice

- Cook onions in water in saucepan for 5 minutes; drain. Cut swordfish and green pepper into 8 pieces.
- Thread fish, green pepper, onions and kumquats alternately onto 4 skewers. Place in 8x10-inch broiler pan.
- Combine remaining ingredients in bowl; mix well. Pour over kabobs. Marinate, covered with plastic wrap, for several hours to overnight; drain.
- Broil kabobs for 10 to 12 minutes or until fish flakes easily. Garnish with orange wedges and chopped parsley or watercress. Serve with rice pilaf and salad.
- May substitute pineapple chunks for kumquats.
- This recipe won first place in the Essex County Senior Citizens Recipe Contest held at the COOKINGS Supermarket Studio in Short Hills, New Jersey.
- Yield: 2 servings.

Approx Per Serving: Cal 502; Prot 39 g; Carbo 39 g; Fiber 7 g; T Fat 22 g; 38% Calories from Fat; Chol 68 mg; Sod 681 mg.

*Effie Vlahakes, **Middle Atlantic Region***
GFWC—Women's Club of Livingston Township, Livingston NJ

1915—*The Georgia Federation of Women's Clubs opened and operated the Tallulah Falls Industrial School for grades 7–12. The school, still in existence, fills a need for educational opportunities, particularly in rural areas.*

SEAFOOD ALFREDO WITH LINGUINE

1 large onion, chopped
1 stalk celery, chopped
8 ounces small scallops
2 tablespoons oil
1 envelope Alfredo sauce mix

8 ounces cooked peeled shrimp
8 ounces cooked lobster meat
1   4-ounce can mushrooms, drained
8 ounces linguine, cooked

- Sauté onion, celery and scallops in oil in skillet until vegetables are tender.
- Prepare Alfredo sauce mix in saucepan using package directions.
- Cook sauce for several minutes, adding sautéed mixture, shrimp, lobster and mushrooms. Cook until thickened, stirring constantly.
- Serve over pasta.
- Yield: 6 servings.

Approx Per Serving: Cal 461; Prot 34 g; Carbo 35 g; Fiber 3 g; T Fat 20 g; 40% Calories from Fat; Chol 114 mg; Sod 764 mg.

*Eileen McDevitt, **Middle Atlantic Region***
GFWC—Pocono Mountain Women's Club, Pocono Lake PA

SEAFOOD LASAGNA

1 onion, chopped
2 tablespoons butter
8 ounces cream cheese
15 ounces ricotta cheese
1 egg
1½ teaspoons basil
⅛ teaspoon pepper
10 ounces scallops

8 ounces shrimp, cooked
8 ounces crab meat
2   10-ounce cans cream of mushroom soup
⅔ cup white wine
½ cup grated Parmesan cheese
9 lasagna noodles, cooked, drained
⅔ cup shredded mozzarella cheese

- Sauté chopped onion in butter in skillet. Stir in cream cheese, ricotta cheese, egg, basil and pepper.
- Chop large scallops. Reserve 4 shrimp. Combine remaining shrimp with scallops, crab meat, soup, wine and Parmesan cheese in bowl; mix well.
- Arrange 3 noodles in shallow baking pan. Layer seafood mixture, 3 noodles, cheese mixture, remaining 3 noodles, mozzarella cheese and reserved shrimp in prepared pan.
- Bake, covered with foil, at 325 degrees for 1¼ hours. Let stand for 15 minutes before serving.
- Yield: 8 servings.

Approx Per Serving: Cal 572; Prot 36 g; Carbo 34 g; Fiber <1 g; T Fat 31 g; 50% Calories from Fat; Chol 189 mg; Sod 1053 mg.

*Alice Glaser, **New England Region***
GFWC—Simsbury Woman's Club, Simsbury CT

MARYLAND SEAFOOD CASSEROLE

8 ounces mushrooms
1 tablespoon butter
1/4 cup flour
1/4 cup melted butter
1 1/2 cups milk
1/8 teaspoon each dry mustard, thyme
  and pepper
1/2 teaspoon salt

1 1/2 cups shredded Cheddar cheese
2 egg yolks, slightly beaten
1 pound shrimp, cooked
1 pound crab meat, cooked
1 quart oysters, poached
2 tablespoons lemon juice
2 ounces dry sherry
1/2 cup shredded Cheddar cheese

- Sauté mushrooms in 1 tablespoon butter in saucepan; drain and set aside.
- Cook mixture of flour and 1/4 cup melted butter in saucepan for several minutes. Stir in milk. Cook until thickened, stirring constantly. Add dry mustard, thyme, pepper and salt. Stir in 1 1/2 cups cheese until melted.
- Stir a small amount of hot mixture into egg yolks; stir egg yolks into hot mixture.
- Cook for 5 minutes, stirring constantly. Add mushrooms, seafood, lemon juice and wine. Spoon into shallow 3-quart baking dish. Top with 1/2 cup cheese.
- Bake at 450 degrees for 10 minutes or until golden brown. Serve with rice and salad.
- Yield: 8 servings.

Approx Per Serving: Cal 449; Prot 37 g; Carbo 9 g; Fiber 9 g; T Fat 130 g;
  86% Calories from Fat; Chol 703 mg; Sod 781 mg.

Juanita A. Eagles, **Southeastern Region**
GFWC—Rossmoor Woman's Club, Silver Spring MD

SEAFOOD QUICHE WITH SOUFFLÉ SAUCE

1 recipe 1-crust pie pastry
1 1/2 cups sealegs
1/2 cup chopped onion
1 cup chopped tomato
Salt and pepper to taste
3/4 cup shredded mozzarella cheese

3 eggs, beaten
1/2 cup flour
1 1/2 cups milk
3/4 cup mayonnaise
2 egg whites, stiffly beaten
2 tablespoons sweet pickle relish

- Spray large quiche pan with nonstick cooking spray. Line with pastry.
- Sprinkle sealegs, onion, tomato, salt, pepper and cheese in prepared pan.
- Combine eggs, flour and milk in bowl; beat until smooth. Pour over seafood mixture.
- Bake at 300 degrees for 30 minutes or until top is golden brown and center is set.
- Fold mayonnaise into egg whites. Add relish; mix gently. Spread over quiche. Increase oven temperature to 350 degrees.
- Bake at 350 degrees just until golden brown; watch carefully. Garnish with lemon pinwheels and parsley.
- This recipe won First Place at the Pittsfield Egg Festival.
- Yield: 8 servings.

Approx Per Serving: Cal 419; Prot 13 g; Carbo 25 g; Fiber 1 g; T Fat 30 g;
  65% Calories from Fat; Chol 112 mg; Sod 598 mg.

Phyllis A. Oliveira, **New England Region**
GFWC—Pittsfield Arts Club, Pittsfield ME

CALIFORNIA SEAFOOD BRUNCH BAKE

8 ounces fresh mushrooms, sliced
2 tablespoons butter
12 ounces crab meat, flaked
2/3 cup sliced green onions
2 cups shredded Gruyère cheese
5 to 6 cups 1-inch French bread cubes
4 eggs

2½ cups milk
1 teaspoon dry mustard
½ teaspoon hot pepper sauce
½ teaspoon nutmeg
¾ teaspoon salt
¼ teaspoon pepper

- Sauté mushrooms in butter in skillet over low heat for 8 minutes; remove from heat. Stir in crab meat, green onions and cheese.
- Layer bread cubes and seafood mixture ½ at a time in 9x13-inch baking dish, pressing down layers.
- Whisk eggs and remaining ingredients in bowl. Pour over layers.
- Chill, covered, for 4 hours to overnight.
- Bake at 350 degrees for 40 to 50 minutes or until set.
- May substitute 6 ounces flaked salmon for 4 ounces crab meat or sourdough bread for French bread.
- Yield: 12 servings.

Approx Per Serving: Cal 232; Prot 17 g; Carbo 12 g; Fiber 1 g; T Fat 13 g;
50% Calories from Fat; Chol 132 mg; Sod 424 mg.

Genevieve Doty, **Western Region**
GFWC—San Dieguito Woman's Club, Encinitas CA

WISCONSIN INDOOR FISH BOIL

½ ounce whole allspice
1½ ounces shrimp and crab boil
　seasoning
8 ounces salt
3 pounds small onions

2 pounds small carrots
3 pounds egg-sized red potatoes,
　unpeeled
5 pounds codfish, cut into 3 or
　4-ounce portions

- Bring enough water to cover ingredients to a boil in large stockpot. Tie allspice and shrimp and crab boil seasoning in cheesecloth bag. Add to water with salt. Add vegetables.
- Bring to a boil. Cook until vegetables are tender-crisp. Add codfish.
- Cook for 10 minutes or until fish flakes easily and vegetables are tender; drain. Serve with melted butter.
- May cook outside in large pot over open fire if preferred.
- Yield: 12 servings.

Approx Per Serving: Cal 349; Prot 38 g; Carbo 45 g; Fiber 7 g; T Fat 2 g;
5% Calories from Fat; Chol 83 mg; Sod 326 mg.
Nutritional information does not include 8 ounces salt for fish boil.

Diane M. Mayer, **Great Lakes Region**
GFWC—Port Washington Women's Club, Port Washington WI

NEW ENGLAND LOBSTER BOIL

6 chicken thighs
6 live 1¼-pound lobsters
6 Italian sausage links
5 medium red potatoes
6 small yams
6 onions

6 dozen steamer clams
1 cup water
1 cup dry white wine
4 bay leaves
2 tablespoons salt
1 medium red potato

- Rinse chicken well. Layer lobsters, sausage, chicken, 5 red potatoes, yams, onions and clams in order listed in 20-quart stockpot.
- Combine water, wine, bay leaves and salt in bowl; mix well. Pour over layers. Top with 1 potato.
- Cook, tightly covered, for 45 minutes. Discard bay leaves.
- Yield: 12 servings.

Approx Per Serving: Cal 449; Prot 46 g; Carbo 32 g; Fiber 3 g; T Fat 13 g; 29% Calories from Fat; Chol 80 mg; Sod 1868 mg.

Sandra L. Cruz, **New England Region**
GFWC—Woman's Club of Woodbury, Bethlehem CT

LINGUINE WITH CLAM SAUCE

3 6-ounce cans minced clams
1 medium onion, chopped
¼ cup olive oil
2 large cloves of garlic, minced
¼ cup dry white wine
2 tablespoons flour

½ cup black olive halves
1 tablespoon chopped parsley
¼ teaspoon each basil and oregano
⅛ teaspoon pepper
12 ounces linguine, cooked

- Drain clams, reserving liquid.
- Sauté onion in olive oil in large skillet for 1 to 2 minutes. Add garlic. Sauté for 1 minute or until tender but not brown.
- Add reserved clam juice and wine. Stir in flour.
- Cook until mixture thickens, stirring constantly. Simmer, covered, for 10 minutes. Stir in clams and next 5 ingredients. Heat to serving temperature.
- Combine with pasta in serving bowl; toss to coat well. Serve with grated Parmesan cheese.
- Yield: 4 servings.

Approx Per Serving: Cal 557; Prot 22 g; Carbo 74 g; Fiber 5 g; T Fat 26 g; 38% Calories from Fat; Chol 80 mg; Sod 138 mg.

Lillian Torres, **New England Region**
GFWC—Dover Woman's Club, Dover NH

PACIFIC RED CLAM SAUCE

1 cup chopped onion
1 tablespoon olive oil
1 clove of garlic, minced
1 15-ounce can tomatoes, drained, chopped

2 cups sliced fresh mushrooms
1 6-ounce can tomato paste
1/4 cup parsley flakes
2 6-ounce cans minced clams

- Sauté onion in olive oil in 10-inch skillet until tender. Stir in next 5 ingredients in order listed. Drain clams, reserving liquid. Stir liquid into skillet.
- Simmer for 15 minutes. Add clams. Cook, covered, over medium heat for 10 minutes longer.
- Serve over linguine.
- Yield: 6 servings.

Approx Per Serving: Cal 103; Prot 7 g; Carbo 13 g; Fiber 3 g; T Fat 7 g; 43% Calories from Fat; Chol 36 mg; Sod 160 mg.

Lydia Ruscillo, **Western Region**
GFWC—Kitsap Peninsula Club, Bremerton WA

WHITE CLAM SAUCE

4 10-ounce cans whole clams
1 medium onion, coarsely chopped
1/4 cup olive oil
4 cloves of garlic, minced
1 4-ounce bottle of clam juice
1/2 cup vermouth
1 bunch parsley, finely chopped

5 tablespoons butter
1 1/2 tablespoons anchovy paste
2 teaspoons oregano
1/4 teaspoon tarragon
1/2 teaspoon thyme
1 16-ounce package linguine, cooked

- Drain clams, reserving liquid from 3 cans.
- Sauté onion in olive oil in large sauté pan until tender. Add minced garlic. Sauté for 30 seconds.
- Add clams, reserved liquid, clam juice and next 7 ingredients.
- Simmer for 15 to 20 minutes. Combine with pasta in serving bowl; mix gently.
- Serve with salad and crusty bread for dipping.
- Yield: 6 servings.

Approx Per Serving: Cal 637; Prot 35 g; Carbo 68 g; Fiber 4 g; T Fat 31 g; 40% Calories from Fat; Chol 147 mg; Sod 243 mg.

Elaine Sulat, **Middle Atlantic Region**
GFWC—Allaire Woman's Club, Wall NJ

1918—*Rutgers College established the New Jersey College for Women after much effort by the New Jersey Federation of Women's Clubs.*

CRAWFISH ÉTOUFFÉ QUICHES

1 large onion, chopped
1/3 cup chopped celery
1/3 cup chopped green bell pepper
1 cup melted margarine
1 cube chicken bouillon
1/2 6-ounce can tomato paste
1 tablespoon sugar
Chopped garlic, salt and pepper to taste
1/2 teaspoon liquid crab boil seasoning
1/4 cup flour

4 to 6 cups water
1 pound crawfish tails
1/4 cup chopped parsley
1/4 cup chopped shallots
2 unbaked 9-inch pie shells
1/2 cup each shredded Cheddar and
    mozzarella cheeses
6 eggs
3/4 cup each milk and cream
Parsley flakes to taste

- Combine onion, celery and green pepper in blender; process until smooth.
- Sauté purée in margarine in saucepan for 20 minutes or until tender. Stir in next 7 ingredients; mix well. Cook for 15 minutes. Stir in flour and water. Add crawfish.
- Cook for 10 minutes or until thickened, stirring constantly. Add 1/4 cup parsley and shallots.
- Spoon into pie shells. Sprinkle with cheeses.
- Beat eggs with milk and cream in bowl. Pour over seafood filling. Sprinkle with parsley flakes to taste.
- Bake at 375 degrees for 35 to 45 minutes or until set.
- Yield: 12 servings.

Approx Per Serving: Cal 481; Prot 16 g; Carbo 21 g; Fiber 1 g; T Fat 37 g; 69% Calories from Fat; Chol 190 mg; Sod 580 mg.

Donna Waguespack, **South Central Region**
GFWC—Bayou Junior Woman's Club, Baton Rouge LA

CRAWFISH FETTUCINI

1 onion, chopped
1 stalk celery, chopped
1/2 green bell pepper, chopped
1/2 cup butter
1 tablespoon flour
1 1/3 tablespoons chopped parsley
1 pound crawfish tails

1 1/3 cups half and half
8 ounces Velveeta cheese, cubed
1 tablespoon chopped jalapeño pepper
1 clove of garlic, minced
Salt and pepper to taste
6 ounces fettucini, cooked
1/4 cup grated Parmesan cheese

- Sauté onion, celery and green pepper in butter in skillet until tender. Stir in flour.
- Cook for 15 minutes, stirring frequently. Stir in parsley and crawfish.
- Cook for 20 minutes. Add next 6 ingredients. Cook for 20 minutes. Add pasta; mix gently. Spoon into 9x13-inch baking dish. Sprinkle with Parmesan cheese.
- Bake at 350 degrees for 20 to 30 minutes or until bubbly.
- Yield: 8 servings.

Approx Per Serving: Cal 414; Prot 22 g; Carbo 21 g; Fiber 1 g; T Fat 27 g; 58% Calories from Fat; Chol 154 mg; Sod 617 mg.

Becky Johnson, **South Central Region**
GFWC—Vinton Literary Club, Vinton LA

MUSSELS MARINARA

1 pound mussels
3 cloves of garlic, chopped
1 to 2 tablespoons chopped parsley
4 tomatoes, chopped

2 onions, chopped
5 or 6 basil leaves
6 tablespoons olive oil
1 cup white wine

- Steam mussels, covered, in 2 inches water in large saucepan for 20 minutes.
- Sauté garlic, parsley, tomatoes, onions and basil in olive oil in saucepan for 1 to 2 minutes. Stir in wine. Cook until onions are tender.
- Drain mussels and place on serving plate. Spoon sauce over top.
- Yield: 2 servings.

Approx Per Serving: Cal 861; Prot 48 g; Carbo 38 g; Fiber 6 g; T Fat 50 g; 52% Calories from Fat; Chol 102 mg; Sod 699 mg.

*Liz Martin, **Southern Region***
GFWC—Charlotte County Junior Women's Club, Inc., Punta Gorda FL

MOTHER'S OYSTER POTPIE

3 cups 1/2-inch potato cubes
16 ounces oysters
1 1/4 cups (about) milk
1 tablespoon margarine
1/4 cup flour

2 tablespoons melted butter
Salt and pepper to taste
2 1/3 cups baking mix
2/3 cup skim milk

- Cook potatoes in water in saucepan just until tender; drain.
- Drain oysters, reserving liquid. Add enough milk to reserved liquid to measure 1 3/4 cups.
- Sauté oysters in 1 tablespoon margarine in skillet until edges curl. Layer oysters and potatoes in 9x10-inch baking dish.
- Blend flour into 2 tablespoons melted margarine in saucepan. Stir in milk mixture.
- Cook until thickened, stirring constantly. Season with salt and pepper. Spoon over layers in baking dish.
- Combine baking mix and skim milk in bowl; stir for 30 seconds to form dough. Knead 10 times on surface sprinkled with additional baking mix.
- Roll 1/2 inch thick; cut into 2-inch circles. Prick tops with fork. Place on casserole.
- Bake at 450 degrees for 20 to 25 minutes or until golden brown.
- Yield: 4 servings.

Approx Per Serving: Cal 700; Prot 24 g; Carbo 84 g; Fiber 9 g; T Fat 121 g; 72% Calories from Fat; Chol 507 mg; Sod 1268 mg.

*Hettie A. Collins, **Southeastern Region***
GFWC—Women's Club of Glen Hill, Baltimore MD

SCALLOPED OYSTERS

1 cup soft bread crumbs
1 cup cracker crumbs
1/2 cup melted margarine
1 quart oysters
2 tablespoons chopped parsley

Mace to taste
1 teaspoon salt
1 tablespoon lemon juice
1/4 cup milk

- Mix bread crumbs, cracker crumbs and margarine in bowl. Spread half the mixture in shallow baking pan.
- Drain oysters, reserving 1/2 cup liquid. Arrange oysters in 2 layers in prepared pan. Top with parsley, mace and salt; drizzle with lemon juice. Pour reserved oyster liquid and milk over layers. Top with remaining crumb mixture.
- Bake at 400 degrees for 30 minutes.
- Yield: 6 servings.

Approx Per Serving: Cal 405; Prot 21 g; Carbo 17 g; Fiber 11 g; T Fat 163 g; 91% Calories from Fat; Chol 758 mg; Sod 1009 mg.

*Marie S. Lewis, **New England Region***
GFWC—Woman's Club of Plainville, Farmington CT

OYSTER STEW

1 pint oysters
1/8 teaspoon paprika
1/2 teaspoon celery salt
1/2 teaspoon onion salt

2 tablespoons melted butter
1 teaspoon Worcestershire sauce
Hot pepper sauce to taste
2 cups milk, scalded

- Drain oysters, reserving liquid. Stir oysters, paprika, celery salt and onion salt into melted butter in 2-quart saucepan; mix well.
- Cook until edges of oysters begin to curl. Stir in reserved oyster liquid, Worcestershire sauce and hot pepper sauce. Add scalded milk.
- Serve over oyster crackers in soup bowls.
- May make seasoned oyster crackers by baking mixture of 12 ounces oyster crackers, 1 envelope salad dressing mix and 1/2 cup oil at 200 degrees for 15 minutes. Store in airtight container.
- Yield: 2 servings.

Approx Per Serving: Cal 531; Prot 37 g; Carbo 16 g; Fiber 16 g; T Fat 239 g; 91% Calories from Fat; Chol 1129 mg; Sod 1446 mg.
Nutritional information does not include oyster crackers.

*Frances Smith, **Southeastern Region***
GFWC—Westmoreland Woman's Club, Montross VA

PANNED OYSTERS OVER HAM

1/2 cup butter
1 quart select oysters, drained

Salt and pepper to taste
6 thin slices Virginia ham

- Heat butter in medium skillet just until butter begins to brown. Add oysters.
- Cook oysters for 2 to 5 minutes or until edges begin to curl. Sprinkle with salt and pepper.
- Spoon over ham on serving platter. Serve with spoon bread, batter bread or corn cakes.
- Yield: 6 servings.

Approx Per Serving: Cal 363; Prot 26 g; Carbo 3 g; Fiber 11 g; T Fat 163 g; 93% Calories from Fat; Chol 767 mg; Sod 805 mg.

Doris R. Young, **Southeastern Region**
GFWC—Ravenscroft Federated Woman's Club, Petersburg VA

SCALLOPS WITH SPINACH

1 pound fresh sea scallops
Juice of 1 lemon
1/4 cup white wine
1   10-ounce can cream of shrimp soup
1   10-ounce package frozen chopped spinach, cooked, drained
1 medium onion, finely chopped

2 eggs, beaten
Paprika, basil, thyme and white pepper to taste
1/2 cup shredded Cheddar cheese
1 cup bread crumbs
2 tablespoon melted butter

- Cut large scallops into smaller pieces.
- Simmer scallops with lemon juice and wine in water to cover in saucepan for 5 minutes. Drain, reserving cooking liquid.
- Combine soup with enough reserved liquid to make a medium-thick mixture in saucepan. Add spinach and onion.
- Cook just until mixture comes to a simmer; do not boil. Stir 2 tablespoons hot mixture into eggs; stir eggs into hot mixture.
- Stir in scallops and seasonings. Spoon into baking dish. Top with cheese and mixture of bread crumbs and melted butter.
- Bake at 400 degrees for 20 minutes or until golden brown and bubbly.
- Yield: 4 servings.

Approx Per Serving: Cal 444; Prot 35 g; Carbo 34 g; Fiber 4 g; T Fat 19 g; 38% Calories from Fat; Chol 187 mg; Sod 1147 mg.

Nancy L. Blomquist, **New England Region**
GFWC—Castine Woman's Club, Castine ME

CRAB MEAT AU GRATIN

2 tablespoons flour
1/4 cup melted butter
2 cups milk
1 tablespoon Dijon mustard
1 tablespoon Worcestershire sauce
Pepper to taste

1 pound fresh crab meat
8 ounces sharp Cheddar cheese, shredded
Nutmeg to taste
3/4 cup soft bread crumbs
2 tablespoons butter, softened

- Stir flour into 1/4 cup melted butter in saucepan.
- Cook for several minutes, stirring constantly. Stir in milk gradually. Cook until thickened, stirring constantly. Cool slightly.
- Add mustard, Worcestershire sauce and pepper; mix gently. Fold in crab meat and cheese. Spoon into greased baking dish.
- Sprinkle casserole with nutmeg. Top with mixture of bread crumbs and 2 tablespoons butter.
- Bake at 350 degrees for 30 to 40 minutes or just until bubbly.
- Yield: 6 servings.

Approx Per Serving: Cal 396; Prot 25 g; Carbo 10 g; Fiber <1 g; T Fat 28 g; 65% Calories from Fat; Chol 142 mg; Sod 654 mg.

*Mary Anne McGovern, **Middle Atlantic Region***
GFWC—Village Improvement Association, Rehoboth Beach DE

JW CRAB CAKES

1 1/4 cups fine Italian bread crumbs
1 cup mayonnaise
1 egg white
1/4 teaspoon lemon juice
1/8 teaspoon each dry mustard and ground celery seed

Cayenne pepper to taste
1 pound lump crab meat
1 1/2 tablespoons (or more) dry bread crumbs
6 tablespoons clarified butter

- Combine first 7 ingredients in bowl; mix well. Fold in crab meat. Shape into 8 cakes. Coat with 1 1/2 tablespoons bread crumbs.
- Brown on both sides in butter in skillet.
- Yield: 8 servings.

Approx Per Serving: Cal 349; Prot 15 g; Carbo 13 g; Fiber 1 g; T Fat 33 g; 74% Calories from Fat; Chol 97 mg; Sod 517 mg.

*Carole Carter, **Southeastern Region***
GFWC—Harpers Ferry Women's Club, Harpers Ferry WV

MARYLAND CRAB CAKES

1 pound crab meat
2 eggs, beaten
1/4 cup chopped onion
1 tablespoon chopped green bell
    pepper

1/2 cup cracker crumbs
3 tablespoons mayonnaise
1 tablespoon prepared mustard
Worcestershire sauce to taste
3 tablespoons margarine

- Combine crab meat with next 7 ingredients in large bowl; mix well. Shape into 6 large cakes.
- Brown on both sides in margarine in skillet.
- Yield: 6 servings.

Approx Per Serving: Cal 237; Prot 18 g; Carbo 6 g; Fiber <1 g; T Fat 15 g;
58% Calories from Fat; Chol 153 mg; Sod 463 mg.

Edna Jean McCaslin, **Southeastern Region**
GFWC—Woman's Club of Glenhill, Baltimore MD

CRAB IMPERIAL

1/4 green bell pepper
1/4 cup butter
1 cup mayonnaise
1 egg
1/4 cup chopped onion
1 tablespoon lemon juice
2 teaspoons Worcestershire sauce

1 teaspoon dry mustard
1 teaspoon salt
3/4 teaspoon pepper
2 tablespoons minced pimento
1 pound fresh crab meat
2 tablespoons sherry
1/4 cup cracker crumbs

- Cook green pepper in water in small saucepan until tender. Chop green pepper to measure 2 tablespoons.
- Melt butter in double boiler over boiling water. Stir in next 8 ingredients.
- Cook for several minutes, stirring constantly. Add pimento, green pepper, crab meat and wine; remove from heat.
- Spoon mixture into greased seafood shells; place on baking sheet. Sprinkle with cracker crumbs.
- Bake at 400 degrees for 25 to 30 minutes or until bubbly.
- Yield: 4 servings.

Approx Per Serving: Cal 669; Prot 26 g; Carbo 7 g; Fiber <1 g; T Fat 59 g;
80% Calories from Fat; Chol 232 mg; Sod 1369 mg.

Virginia H. Clarke, **Southeastern Region**
GFWC—Federated Woman's Club of Petersburg, Church Road VA

CRAB MEAT WITH SHERRY

1 pound fresh crab meat, flaked
1/2 cup sherry
3 slices white bread
1/2 cup half and half
Juice of 1/2 lemon
1/4 cup melted butter
1/2 cup mayonnaise

1/2 cup shredded mild Cheddar cheese
1 teaspoon Worcestershire sauce
Salt and pepper to taste
2 cups cooked shrimp
1 cup bread crumbs
2 tablespoons melted butter

- Mix crab meat and wine in bowl. Marinate in refrigerator for several minutes.
- Combine bread with half and half, lemon juice and 1/4 cup melted butter in bowl. Let stand for several minutes.
- Add next 5 ingredients; mix well. Fold in crab meat and shrimp. Spoon into greased 3-quart baking dish. Top with mixture of bread crumbs and 2 tablespoons melted butter.
- Bake at 350 degrees for 20 to 30 minutes or until bubbly.
- Yield: 8 servings.

Approx Per Serving: Cal 405; Prot 23 g; Carbo 16 g; Fiber 1 g; T Fat 26 g; 60% Calories from Fat; Chol 169 mg; Sod 571 mg.

*Frances Kunzler, **Southeastern Region***
GFWC—Oriental Woman's Club, Oriental NC

SPAGHETTI WITH CRAB SAUCE

1 tablespoon chopped celery
1 medium onion, chopped
1 teaspoon chopped garlic
1 tablespoon chopped parsley
1/4 cup olive oil
1 cup solid-pack tomatoes

1 cup tomato sauce
1 1/2 cups water
Salt and pepper to taste
1 pound fresh dungeness crab meat
1/4 cup sherry
1 16-ounce package spaghetti

- Sauté celery, onion, garlic and parsley in olive oil in large skillet. Add tomatoes, tomato sauce, water, salt and pepper; mix well.
- Simmer for 1 hour. Fold in crab meat and wine. Simmer until bubbly.
- Cook spaghetti in salted water in large saucepan; drain. Add to sauce; mix well.
- Spoon onto heated platter. Garnish with grated Parmesan cheese.
- Yield: 6 servings.

Approx Per Serving: Cal 463; Prot 23 g; Carbo 64 g; Fiber 5 g; T Fat 11 g; 23% Calories from Fat; Chol 61 mg; Sod 485 mg.

*Donna Shehan, **Western Region***
GFWC—Benicia Women's Club, Benicia CA

TILLAMOOK CRAB DELIGHT

2 tablespoons chopped green bell pepper
2 tablespoons butter
2 tablespoons flour
1 cup tomato sauce
1 cup shredded Tillamook cheese
1 egg, beaten

1/2 teaspoon Worcestershire sauce
1/2 teaspoon mustard
1/4 teaspoon salt
Cayenne pepper to taste
3/4 cup milk, scalded
1 cup crab meat

- Sauté green pepper in butter in saucepan for 5 minutes. Add next 8 ingredients; mix well.
- Cook for several minutes. Add scalded milk. Fold in crab meat. Serve on toast or in pastry shells.
- Yield: 4 servings.

Approx Per Serving: Cal 281; Prot 18 g; Carbo 10 g; Fiber 1 g; T Fat 19 g; 60% Calories from Fat; Chol 138 mg; Sod 872 mg.

Mrs. L. W. Vearrier, **Western Region**
GFWC—Albany Woman's Club, Albany OR

CRAB MEAT SUPREME

1/4 cup butter
3 tablespoons flour
2 cups milk
2 tablespoons minced onion
1 tablespoon chopped parsley
1 tablespoon minced green bell pepper
1 pimento, minced
2 tablespoons sherry

1/8 teaspoon grated orange rind
1/2 teaspoon celery salt
1 egg, beaten
3 cups fresh or frozen King crab meat
1/2 teaspoon salt
Pepper to taste
1/2 cup bread crumbs
1 tablespoon melted butter

- Melt 1/4 cup butter in double boiler over boiling water. Stir in flour and milk.
- Cook until thickened, stirring constantly. Stir in onion, parsley, green pepper, pimento, wine, orange rind and celery salt; remove from heat.
- Stir a small amount of hot mixture into egg; stir egg into hot mixture. Stir in crab meat, salt and pepper.
- Spoon into greased 1 1/2-quart baking dish. Top with mixture of bread crumbs and 1 tablespoon butter.
- Bake at 350 degrees for 15 to 20 minutes or until bubbly. Serve with rice, green salad and rolls.
- Yield: 6 servings.

Approx Per Serving: Cal 255; Prot 16 g; Carbo 13 g; Fiber 1 g; T Fat 15 g; 53% Calories from Fat; Chol 127 mg; Sod 641 mg.

Shirley M. Mitchell, **New England Region**
GFWC—New Canaan Woman's Club, New Canaan CT

CRAB MEAT CASSEROLE

2 tablespoons flour
1/4 cup melted butter
1 cup milk
1 teaspoon prepared horseradish
1 teaspoon mustard
1 to 4 teaspoons parsley flakes

2 teaspoons lemon juice
1 teaspoon salt
Pepper to taste
1 pound crab meat
1/2 cup bread crumbs
2 teaspoons melted butter

- Blend flour into 1/4 cup melted butter in saucepan.
- Cook for several minutes. Add milk. Cook for several minutes or until thickened, stirring constantly. Add next 6 ingredients.
- Bring to a boil. Stir in crab meat. Spoon into buttered 2-quart baking dish. Top with mixture of bread crumbs and 2 teaspoons butter.
- Bake at 400 degrees for 20 to 25 minutes or until bubbly.
- Yield: 6 servings.

Approx Per Serving: Cal 225; Prot 18 g; Carbo 10 g; Fiber <1 g; T Fat 12 g;
49% Calories from Fat; Chol 106 mg; Sod 731 mg.

*Elsie Lewis, **Southeastern Region***
GFWC—Woman's Club of Newport News, Newport News VA

BARBECUED SHRIMP

1 cup melted margarine
1/4 cup olive oil
2 tablespoons Worcestershire sauce
Tabasco sauce to taste
1/2 cup white wine
2 large onions, chopped
Juice of 1 lemon
Sugar to taste
1 tablespoon each paprika and rosemary

1 teaspoon each oregano, MSG and
thyme
1/8 teaspoon red pepper
2 bay leaves
Salt to taste
2 pounds uncooked jumbo shrimp
with heads
Black pepper to taste

- Combine margarine, olive oil, Worcestershire sauce, Tabasco sauce, wine, onions, lemon juice, sugar, paprika, rosemary, oregano, MSG, thyme, red pepper, bay leaves and salt in bowl; mix well. Pour into large shallow baking pan.
- Add shrimp, mixing gently. Sprinkle generously with black pepper.
- Marinate in refrigerator for 8 hours to overnight.
- Bake at 350 degrees for 45 minutes. Discard bay leaves.
- Yield: 4 servings.

Approx Per Serving: Cal 763; Prot 36 g; Carbo 9 g; Fiber 1 g; T Fat 61 g;
75% Calories from Fat; Chol 316 mg; Sod 2047 mg.
Nutritional information includes entire amount of marinade.

*Roberta S. Atkinson, **Southern Region***
GFWC—Shades Mountain Junior Women's Club, Hoover AL

SHRIMP AND ARTICHOKE CASSEROLE

1 14-ounce can artichokes, drained
1¹/₂ to 2 pounds shrimp, cooked, peeled
8 ounces fresh mushrooms
2 tablespoons butter
¹/₄ teaspoon flour
4¹/₂ tablespoons melted butter
4¹/₂ tablespoons flour

1 cup whipping cream
¹/₂ cup half and half
Salt and pepper to taste
¹/₄ cup sherry
1 tablespoon Worcestershire sauce
¹/₄ cup shredded Cheddar cheese
Paprika to taste

- Cut artichokes into halves. Layer artichokes and shrimp in 8x10-inch baking dish.
- Sauté mushrooms in 2 tablespoons butter in skillet. Sprinkle with ¹/₄ teaspoon flour; mix well. Layer over shrimp.
- Blend 4¹/₂ tablespoons melted butter and 4¹/₂ tablespoons flour in saucepan.
- Cook for several minutes. Stir in cream and half and half. Cook until thickened, stirring constantly. Add salt and pepper. Stir in wine and Worcestershire sauce.
- Spoon sauce over casserole; top with cheese and paprika.
- Bake at 375 degrees for 20 minutes.
- Yield: 6 servings.

Approx Per Serving: Cal 468; Prot 28 g; Carbo 13 g; Fiber 1 g; T Fat 33 g;
65% Calories from Fat; Chol 311 mg; Sod 591 mg.

*Betty Alfonsi, **New England Region***
GFWC—Southington Woman's Club, Southington CT

CANTONESE SHRIMP AND BEANS

1¹/₂ teaspoons chicken stock base
1 cup boiling water
¹/₄ cup thinly sliced green onions
1 clove of garlic, pressed
1¹/₂ pounds peeled deveined shrimp
1 teaspoon oil
1 9-ounce package frozen cut green
   beans

¹/₂ teaspoon ginger
1 teaspoon salt
Pepper to taste
1 teaspoon cornstarch
1 tablespoon cold water

- Dissolve chicken stock base in boiling water in small bowl.
- Sauté green onions, garlic and shrimp in oil in skillet for 3 minutes, adding a small amount of chicken stock mixture if necessary to prevent sticking. Add remaining chicken stock and next 4 ingredients.
- Simmer, covered, for 5 to 7 minutes or until beans are tender-crisp. Stir in mixture of cornstarch and cold water.
- Cook until thickened, stirring constantly.
- Yield: 6 servings.

Approx Per Serving: Cal 124; Prot 21 g; Carbo 4 g; Fiber 1 g; T Fat 2 g;
17% Calories from Fat; Chol 177 mg; Sod 822 mg.

*Phyllis W. Miller, **Middle Atlantic Region***
GFWC—Woman's Club of Pennsville, Pennsville NJ

SAVANNAH SHRIMP CREOLE

1 pound unpeeled shrimp	1 16-ounce can tomatoes
2 medium onions, chopped	1 4-ounce can tomato sauce
1 green bell pepper, chopped	1 teaspoon oregano
1/4 cup oil	1/2 teaspoon salt
2 tablespoons flour	1/4 teaspoon pepper

- Cook shrimp in boiling water in saucepan for 3 to 5 minutes or until pink; drain. Peel and devein shrimp.
- Sauté onions and green pepper in oil in skillet until tender. Stir in flour. Cook for several minutes.
- Add remaining ingredients; mix well. Stir in shrimp.
- Simmer for 20 minutes. Serve over rice or vermicelli.
- Yield: 4 servings.

Approx Per Serving: Cal 277; Prot 20 g; Carbo 17 g; Fiber 3 g; T Fat 15 g; 48% Calories from Fat; Chol 158 mg; Sod 806 mg.

Angela Dearing, **Southern Region**
GFWC—Huntingdon Woman's Guild, Savannah GA

CURRIED SHRIMP

3/4 cup finely chopped onion	1/2 teaspoon salt
1 cup chopped apple	1/8 teaspoon pepper
1/2 cup chopped celery	1/2 cup milk
1/4 cup butter	11/2 cups chicken bouillon
2 tablespoons flour	1 teaspoon Worcestershire sauce
1/4 teaspoon ginger	12 ounces shrimp, cooked
2 teaspoons curry powder	

- Sauté onion, apple and celery in butter in skillet for 5 to 10 minutes or until tender. Sprinkle with mixture of flour, ginger, curry powder, salt and pepper; mix well.
- Combine milk, chicken bouillon and Worcestershire sauce in bowl; mix well. Stir into skillet.
- Cook until thickened, stirring constantly. Add shrimp. Cook until heated through. Serve over rice.
- Yield: 4 servings.

Approx Per Serving: Cal 180; Prot 18 g; Carbo 14 g; Fiber 2 g; T Fat 6 g; 30% Calories from Fat; Chol 149 mg; Sod 798 mg.

Frances Riebe, **New England Region**
GFWC—R.I. Ex Club, Foster RI

1922—*GFWC purchased historic Headquarters building at 1734 N Street, NW in Washington, DC.*

CRESCENT SHRIMP SQUARES

3 ounces cream cheese, softened
3 tablespoons melted butter
2 tablespoons milk
2 cups chopped cooked shrimp
2 tablespoons chopped onion
2 tablespoons chopped celery
1/4 teaspoon salt
1/8 teaspoon pepper
1   8-count can crescent rolls
2 tablespoons melted butter
3/4 cup seasoned croutons, crushed

- Blend cream cheese and butter in bowl. Add next 6 ingredients; mix well.
- Separate roll dough into 4 rectangles. Spoon shrimp into middle of rectangles. Pull up corners of dough to enclose filling; twist to seal.
- Brush with melted butter; sprinkle with crushed croutons. Place on ungreased baking sheet.
- Bake at 350 degrees for 20 minutes.
- Yield: 4 servings.

Approx Per Serving: Cal 473; Prot 22 g; Carbo 24 g; Fiber <1 g; T Fat 32 g; 61% Calories from Fat; Chol 221 mg; Sod 958 mg.

*Bertie Broaddus, **Southern Region***
GFWC—Miracle Strip Junior Women's Club, Panama City Beach FL

EGGPLANT AND SHRIMP CASSEROLE

1 large onion, chopped
3 stalks celery, chopped
2 tablespoons butter
1 large eggplant, cut into 1-inch cubes
1 1/2 pounds shrimp, peeled, deveined
2 tablespoons chopped parsley
Salt and pepper to taste
1 cup bread crumbs
1 tablespoon butter

- Sauté onion and celery in 2 tablespoons butter in skillet until light brown. Add eggplant. Cook until eggplant is tender. Add shrimp.
- Cook for several minutes. Add parsley, salt, pepper and 3/4 cup bread crumbs; mix well.
- Spoon into baking dish; sprinkle with remaining 1/4 cup bread crumbs. Dot with 1 tablespoon butter.
- Bake at 350 degrees for 30 to 35 minutes or until light brown.
- Yield: 6 servings.

Approx Per Serving: Cal 232; Prot 22 g; Carbo 18 g; Fiber 3 g; T Fat 8 g; 30% Calories from Fat; Chol 193 mg; Sod 395 mg.

*Shirley C. Tolpin, **Southern Region***
GFWC—Wistaria Study Club, Mobile AL

SHRIMP FLORENTINE

4 10-ounce packages frozen chopped
   spinach, thawed, drained
3 pounds shrimp, cooked, peeled,
   deveined
1/2 cup butter
1/2 cup flour

3 cups milk
1 cup dry white wine
1/2 cup chopped scallions
Paprika, salt and pepper to taste
2 cups shredded Cheddar cheese

- Layer spinach and shrimp in 1¹/2 to 2-quart baking dish.
- Melt butter in saucepan. Stir in flour. Add milk, wine and scallions.
- Cook until thickened, stirring constantly. Add paprika, salt and pepper. Spoon over layers in baking dish. Sprinkle with cheese.
- Bake at 350 degrees for 35 minutes or until bubbly.
- Yield: 8 servings.

> *Approx Per Serving:* Cal 481; Prot 41 g; Carbo 19 g; Fiber 4 g; T Fat 26 g;
> 49% Calories from Fat; Chol 310 mg; Sod 706 mg.

*Margaret M. Kelly, **Middle Atlantic Region***
GFWC—Women's Club of Huntington, Huntington NY

SAN DIEGO SPICY SHRIMP

1/2 cup finely chopped onion
1 cup sliced mushrooms
2 pounds shrimp, peeled
1/4 cup margarine
2 10-ounce cans cream of mushroom
   soup
1/4 cup lemon juice

2 tablespoons Worcestershire sauce
2 teaspoons curry powder
2 teaspoons dry mustard
1/2 teaspoon cumin
1/4 teaspoon pepper
2 tablespoons cornstarch
1/3 cup water

- Sauté onion, mushrooms and shrimp in margarine in 4-quart saucepan over medium heat for 3 minutes or just until shrimp turn pink; do not overcook. Add next 7 ingredients; mix well.
- Cook until bubbly. Stir in mixture of cornstarch and water. Cook until thickened, stirring constantly.
- Serve in pastry shells or over toast points or brown rice.
- May substitute imitation crab meat for shrimp.
- Yield: 6 servings.

> *Approx Per Serving:* Cal 300; Prot 25 g; Carbo 13 g; Fiber 1 g; T Fat 16 g;
> 49% Calories from Fat; Chol 212 mg; Sod 1146 mg.

*Lillian Burroughs, **Western Region***
GFWC—Allied Gardens Woman's Club, San Diego CA

SPAGHETTI WITH SHRIMP

1 pound medium shrimp in shells
Coarse salt to taste
1 medium red onion, chopped
1 large clove of garlic, chopped
1/2 cup olive oil

1 1/2 pounds fresh tomatoes or drained canned Italian tomatoes
Salt and freshly ground pepper to taste
1   16-ounce package spaghetti, cooked

- Combine shrimp with cold water to cover and coarse salt to taste in bowl. Let stand in refrigerator for 30 minutes.
- Sauté onion and garlic in olive oil in large skillet over medium heat for 5 minutes.
- Process tomatoes in food processor until smooth. Add to skillet with salt and pepper to taste.
- Simmer for 15 minutes.
- Drain and rinse shrimp in cold water. Peel and devein. Add to skillet.
- Simmer, covered for 2 minutes or until shrimp are pink. Adjust seasonings. Add pasta; mix with wooden spoon. Cook until heated through. Garnish servings with leaves of Italian parsley.
- Yield: 6 servings.

Approx Per Serving: Cal 523; Prot 22 g; Carbo 64 g; Fiber 5 g; T Fat 20 g;
34% Calories from Fat; Chol 105 mg; Sod 132 mg.

*Ingeborg Schwab, **Middle Atlantic Region***
GFWC—Pompton Lakes Woman's Club, Pompton Lakes NJ

SHRIMP STROGANOFF

1/2 cup chopped onion
1 clove of garlic, minced
2 tablespoons butter
1/4 cup flour
2 teaspoons dillweed

Salt to taste
1   10-ounce can beef broth
1   2-ounce can sliced mushrooms
2 cups cooked shrimp
1 cup sour cream, at room temperature

- Sauté onion and garlic in butter in large skillet until onion is tender. Stir in flour, dillweed and salt; remove from heat. Stir in beef broth and undrained sliced mushrooms gradually.
- Cook over medium heat until thickened, stirring constantly. Add shrimp. Cook over low heat for 5 to 10 minutes or until bubbly. Stir in sour cream.
- Heat just to serving temperature; do not boil. Serve over buttered noodles or rice. Garnish with parsley sprigs.
- May substitute 1 cup plain yogurt for sour cream.
- Yield: 4 servings.

Approx Per Serving: Cal 259; Prot 13 g; Carbo 11 g; Fiber 1 g; T Fat 19 g;
64% Calories from Fat; Chol 120 mg; Sod 462 mg.

*Johanna A. Pangborn, **Southeastern Region***
GFWC—Southport Woman's Club, Southport NC

SHRIMP-STUFFED PEPPERS

6 medium green bell peppers
Salt to taste
2 cups chopped cooked shrimp
2 cups cooked rice
1 cup mayonnaise-type salad dressing

2 tablespoons chopped onion
Tabasco sauce to taste
Pepper to taste
1 8-ounce can seasoned tomato sauce

- Cut off tops of green peppers and discard seed and membranes. Parboil in a small amount of salted boiling water in saucepan for 5 minutes; drain. Sprinkle inside of peppers with salt.
- Combine shrimp, rice, salad dressing and onion in bowl; mix well. Add Tabasco sauce, salt and pepper.
- Spoon shrimp mixture into peppers. Arrange in 6x10-inch baking dish. Top with tomato sauce.
- Bake at 350 degrees for 30 minutes. Spoon tomato sauce over peppers to serve.
- May omit parboiling step for firmer green peppers.
- Yield: 6 servings.

Approx Per Serving: Cal 311; Prot 14 g; Carbo 33 g; Fiber 2 g; T Fat 14 g;
40% Calories from Fat; Chol 115 mg; Sod 630 mg.

Naomi Murray, **Southeastern Region**
GFWC—Winston-Salem Woman's Club, Winston-Salem NC

VODKA AND SOY SHRIMP

1 pound shrimp
1 tablespoon garlic powder
Parsley flakes, ginger, red pepper and
cayenne pepper to taste
1 tablespoon onion salt
2 teaspoons black pepper

2 tablespoons peanut oil
1 tablespoon chopped garlic
2 tablespoons vodka
2 tablespoons sherry
5 tablespoons soy sauce

- Peel and devein shrimp; cut into bite-sized pieces. Combine with next 7 seasonings in bowl; mix well.
- Heat peanut oil in wok over high heat. Add garlic.
- Stir-fry until garlic is golden brown. Add shrimp mixture. Stir-fry for 2 minutes or until shrimp turn pink. Add vodka, sherry and soy sauce.
- Cook just until heated through; do not overcook.
- Yield: 4 servings.

Approx Per Serving: Cal 111; Prot 3 g; Carbo 4 g; Fiber <1 g; T Fat 7 g;
55% Calories from Fat; Chol 11 mg; Sod 2493 mg.

Medora M. Kaltenbach, **Southeastern Region**
GFWC—Outer Banks Woman's Club, Kill Devil Hills NC

CAPE COD SHRIMP AND SCALLOPS

1¹/₂ pounds peeled uncooked shrimp
1¹/₂ pounds bay scallops
6 tablespoons butter
2 tablespoons oil
2 cups thinly sliced mushrooms
1 clove of garlic, chopped
3 green onions, minced

1 cup fish stock
¹/₂ cup dry white wine
1 cup cream
1¹/₂ cups unsalted butter, softened
Lemon juice to taste
¹/₄ cup fresh dill
Salt and pepper to taste

- Sauté shrimp and scallops in 6 tablespoons butter in large skillet until shrimp turn pink and scallops are firm. Remove with slotted spoon.
- Add oil and mushrooms to skillet.
- Sauté for 2 minutes. Add garlic and green onions. Sauté for 1 minute. Stir in fish stock and wine.
- Cook mixture for 5 minutes or until reduced by ¹/₂. Add cream. Cook until slightly thickened.
- Whisk in butter gradually over low heat. Add shrimp and scallops, lemon juice, dill, salt and pepper; mix well.
- Cook just until heated through. Serve over sautéed spinach or rice.
- Yield: 6 servings.

Approx Per Serving: Cal 907; Prot 43 g; Carbo 6 g; Fiber 1 g; T Fat 79 g;
78% Calories from Fat; Chol 427 mg; Sod 633 mg.

*Jane Drew, **New England Region***
GFWC—Chatham Women's Club, Chatham MA

CHESAPEAKE BAY SEAFOOD BAKE

1 pound crab meat
1 pound deveined cooked shrimp
1 cup mayonnaise
¹/₂ cup chopped green bell pepper
¹/₄ cup minced onion
1¹/₂ cups finely chopped celery

3 tablespoons margarine
1 tablespoon Worcestershire sauce
¹/₂ teaspoon salt
1 cup dry bread crumbs
1 tablespoon melted margarine
Paprika to taste

- Combine crab meat and shrimp with mayonnaise in large bowl; mix well.
- Sauté green pepper, onion and celery in 3 tablespoons margarine in medium skillet until tender.
- Add sautéed mixture to seafood with Worcestershire sauce and salt; mix well.
- Spoon into 2-quart baking dish sprayed with nonstick cooking spray. Top with bread crumbs. Drizzle with 1 tablespoon margarine; sprinkle with paprika.
- Bake at 400 degrees for 20 to 25 minutes or until bubbly.
- Yield: 8 servings.

Approx Per Serving: Cal 419; Prot 26 g; Carbo 12 g; Fiber 1 g; T Fat 30 g;
64% Calories from Fat; Chol 184 mg; Sod 772 mg.

*Rosanne Ferris, **Southeastern Region***
GFWC—Junior Woman's Club of Rockville, Olney MD

ENCHILADAS DEL MAR

2 medium white onions, chopped
1   7-ounce can chopped green chilies, drained
1¹/₂ tablespoons butter
1 pound imitation crab meat
1 pound medium shrimp, cooked
1   12-ounce can medium black olives, drained
1 pound Monterey Jack cheese, shredded

1 pound Cheddar cheese, shredded
16   6-inch flour tortillas
1   12-ounce can evaporated skim milk
1 cup low-fat sour cream
1¹/₂ teaspoons oregano
1 teaspoon garlic salt
1 avocado, sliced
1 bunch green onions, chopped
1   4-ounce can sliced black olives

- Sauté onions and green chilies in butter in skillet until onions are tender; remove from heat. Add crab meat, shrimp and 1 can black olives.
- Mix cheeses in bowl. Reserve 1¹/₂ cups for topping. Stir remaining cheese mixture into seafood mixture.
- Microwave tortillas, wrapped in plastic wrap, on High for 30 seconds or until warm.
- Spoon filling onto tortillas. Wrap tortillas to enclose filling. Place seam side down in 2 greased 10x15-inch baking pans. Heat next 4 ingredients in medium saucepan until lukewarm. Pour over enchiladas. Sprinkle with reserved cheese mixture.
- Bake at 350 degrees for 30 minutes. Top with avocado slices, green onions and 1 can black olives.
- Yield: 8 servings.

Approx Per Serving: Cal 975; Prot 54 g; Carbo 50 g; Fiber 7 g; T Fat 67 g;
59% Calories from Fat; Chol 242 mg; Sod 2375 mg.

*Lee Jordan, **Western Region***
GFWC—Clayton Woman's Club, Concord CA

SEAFOOD LINGUINE

¹/₂ medium onion, chopped
2 cloves of garlic, chopped
1 tablespoon oil
8 ounces small bay scallops
8 ounces peeled medium shrimp
1 teaspoon Dijon mustard
1 teaspoon chopped parsley

1 cup white wine
¹/₂ teaspoon dillweed
¹/₂ teaspoon lemon pepper
¹/₄ teaspoon seafood seasoning
12 ounces linguine, cooked
¹/₂ cup grated Parmesan cheese

- Sauté onion and garlic in oil in skillet until tender. Add scallops.
- Sauté for 5 minutes, stirring occasionally. Stir in next 7 ingredients.
- Cook for 5 minutes; remove from heat. Stir in pasta; mix well. Let stand for 5 minutes.
- Toss with cheese. Serve with tossed green salad and French bread.
- May add Szechuan seasoning or MSG to taste.
- Yield: 4 servings.

Approx Per Serving: Cal 537; Prot 35 g; Carbo 68 g; Fiber 4 g; T Fat 9 g;
14% Calories from Fat; Chol 116 mg; Sod 506 mg.

*Sue Bishop, **Western Region***
GFWC—Amalak Women's Club, Kalama WA

SHRIMP AND WILD RICE CASSEROLE

1   7-ounce can crab meat, flaked
1 pound peeled shrimp, partially
    cooked
1   7-ounce package long grain and
    wild rice mix, cooked
1 green bell pepper, chopped
1/2 cup chopped onion
1 cup chopped celery
1   4-ounce can chopped mushrooms
1 cup mayonnaise
1 tablespoon Worcestershire sauce
3/4 cup evaporated milk
1/2 teaspoon salt

■ Combine all ingredients in bowl; mix well. Spoon into 9x13-inch baking dish.
■ Bake at 375 degrees for 30 minutes.
■ Yield: 10 servings.

Approx Per Serving: Cal 319; Prot 16 g; Carbo 20 g; Fiber 1 g; T Fat 20 g;
56% Calories from Fat; Chol 107 mg; Sod 788 mg.

Rowena Caraway, **South Central Region**
GFWC—Silsbee Woman's Club, Silsbee TX

CAROLINA CASSEROLE FROM THE SEA

1 pound bay scallops
2 tablespoons margarine
1 pound backfin crab meat
1 pound cooked peeled shrimp
3   9-ounce jars marinated artichoke
    hearts, drained, sliced
2   7-ounce cans sliced water
    chestnuts, drained
1/2 small onion, grated
1/2 cup margarine
1/2 cup flour
1 teaspoon salt
1 teaspoon pepper
2 cups buttermilk
1/2 cup dry sherry
3/4 cup shredded Cheddar cheese
1 cup Italian bread crumbs
2 tablespoons melted butter
1/4 cup grated Parmesan cheese

■ Sauté scallops in 2 tablespoons margarine in skillet for 3 to 5 minutes. Sprinkle crab meat, shrimp, scallops, artichokes and water chestnuts in 2 lightly buttered 8x12-inch baking dishes.
■ Sauté onion in 1/2 cup margarine in saucepan. Stir in flour, salt and pepper. Cook for several minutes. Add buttermilk and wine.
■ Cook until thickened, stirring constantly. Stir in Cheddar cheese until melted. Pour over seafood. Top with mixture of bread crumbs and butter; sprinkle with Parmesan cheese.
■ Bake at 350 degrees for 35 to 40 minutes or until bubbly.
■ Yield: 16 servings.

Approx Per Serving: Cal 305; Prot 22 g; Carbo 17 g; Fiber 4 g; T Fat 16 g;
48% Calories from Fat; Chol 105 mg; Sod 803 mg.

Janet R. Smalley, **Southern Region**
GFWC—Walhalla Woman's Club, Walhalla SC

These 18th-century coffee and tea
urns on display in the dining
room were a gift of the
Nebraska Federation of Women's
Clubs in 1927.

ARIZONA BEANS

2 pounds dried pinto beans
2 large onions, chopped
4 cloves of garlic, minced
2 teaspoons salt
Pepper to taste

1/2 teaspoon cumin
1 4-ounce can taco sauce
1 4-ounce can chopped green chilies
1 28-ounce can tomatoes

- Soak beans in water to cover in saucepan overnight. Drain and rinse.
- Add water to 2 inches over beans.
- Cook over medium heat for 1 hour, stirring occasionally. Add onions, garlic, seasonings, taco sauce, green chilies and tomatoes.
- Simmer for 4 to 6 hours longer or until beans are tender, stirring occasionally.
- May add browned ground beef if desired. May also be cooked in slow cooker on Low for 6 to 8 hours.
- Yield: 24 servings.

Approx Per Serving: Cal 142; Prot 10 g; Carbo 26 g; Fiber 9 g; T Fat 1 g;
4% Calories from Fat; Chol 0 mg; Sod 312 mg.

Helen M. Gibbs, **South Central Region**
GFWC—Las Noches Woman's Club, Tempe AZ

BOSTON BAKED BEANS

2 pounds dried California pea beans
1 teaspoon baking soda
1 pound salt pork, chopped
1 medium onion,
1/2 cup sugar

2/3 cup molasses
2 teaspoons dry mustard
4 teaspoons salt
1/2 teaspoon pepper

- Soak beans in water to cover in saucepan overnight.
- Add baking soda to beans. Parboil for 10 minutes. Drain and rinse.
- Layer half the chopped salt pork, whole onion, beans and remaining salt pork in bean pot.
- Mix sugar and remaining ingredients with enough water to cover beans. Pour over beans.
- Bake at 300 degrees for 6 hours.
- Yield: 10 servings.

Approx Per Serving: Cal 476; Prot 24 g; Carbo 80 g; Fiber 3 g; T Fat 8 g;
15% Calories from Fat; Chol 12 mg; Sod 1167 mg.

Eda M. Wells, **New England Region**
GFWC—Northborough Woman's Club, Northborough MA

SOUTHERN BAKED BEANS

1 pound ground beef
2 30-ounce cans pork and beans
1 small onion, finely chopped
1 small green bell pepper, finely
   chopped
2 tablespoons mustard

3 tablespoons brown sugar
2 teaspoons honey
2 cups barbecue sauce
1 teaspoon garlic powder
1 teaspoon celery salt
6 slices bacon

- Brown ground beef in skillet, stirring until crumbly; drain.
- Combine ground beef, pork and beans, onion, green pepper, mustard, brown sugar, honey, barbecue sauce, garlic powder and celery salt in bowl; mix well.
- Spray 9x13-inch baking dish with nonstick cooking spray. Pour in bean mixture. Arrange bacon slices on top.
- Bake at 350 degrees for 45 minutes.
- Yield: 25 servings.

Approx Per Serving: Cal 145; Prot 8 g; Carbo 19 g; Fiber 4 g; T Fat 5 g;
29% Calories from Fat; Chol 18 mg; Sod 502 mg.

Sue McMichael, **Southern Region**
GFWC—Saraland Woman's Club, Saraland AL

VERMONT BAKED BEANS

2 pounds dried beans
1 cup maple syrup
³/4 cup sugar
1 tablespoon salt

1 teaspoon dry mustard
1 teaspoon ginger
8 ounces salt pork or bacon, chopped

- Soak beans in water to cover in saucepan overnight.
- Parboil beans until skins crack, stirring occasionally.
- Stir in maple syrup and remaining ingredients.
- Pour into 3-quart casserole.
- Bake at 350 degrees for 6 to 8 hours, adding additional water as needed.
- May also be cooked in slow cooker. May be frozen.
- Yield: 8 servings.

Approx Per Serving: Cal 601; Prot 30 g; Carbo 112 g; Fiber 25 g; T Fat 5 g;
8% Calories from Fat; Chol 7 mg; Sod 969 mg.

Shirley L. Kenyon, **New England Region**
GFWC—Better Homes of South Royalton, South Royalton VT

World War II—*GFWC raised over one million dollars in the Buy a Bomber campaign.*

BEST-EVER GREEN BEANS

16 ounces mushrooms, sliced
1 medium onion, sliced
1/2 cup melted butter
1/4 cup flour
1 cup cream
1 teaspoon MSG
1/8 teaspoon Tabasco sauce
12 ounces Cheddar cheese, shredded
2 teaspoons soy sauce

Salt to taste
1/2 teaspoon pepper
3 to 5   16-ounce cans green beans,
    drained
2   8-ounce cans sliced water
    chestnuts, drained
1   3-ounce jar chopped pimento,
    drained

- Sauté mushrooms and onion in butter in skillet. Add flour, blending well.
- Add cream, blending well. Cook until slightly thickened, stirring constantly.
- Add MSG, Tabasco sauce, cheese, soy sauce, salt and pepper, mixing well.
- Layer green beans, water chestnuts and pimento in 3-quart casserole. Pour cheese sauce over layers.
- Bake at 350 degrees for 15 minutes.
- Yield: 12 servings.

Approx Per Serving: Cal 332; Prot 11 g; Carbo 19 g; Fiber 5 g; T Fat 25 g;
65% Calories from Fat; Chol 78 mg; Sod 1142 mg.

Frances L. Plooster, **Mississippi Valley Region**
GFWC—White River Women's Club, White River SD

HOPPIN JOHN

16 ounces dried black-eyed peas
6 cups water
3 pounds smoked ham hocks
1 cup finely chopped onion

1 cup finely chopped green pepper
2 bay leaves
1 teaspoon salt
1 1/2 cups uncooked rice

- Sort and rinse peas. Soak peas in water to cover by 2 inches in saucepan overnight; drain.
- Add 6 cups water and next 5 ingredients; mix well.
- Cook, covered, over medium heat until mixture comes to a boil.
- Reduce heat. Simmer for 1 hour or until peas are tender, stirring occasionally and adding water if needed to keep peas covered.
- Discard bay leaves. Remove ham hocks. Cut ham from ham hocks; chop and return ham to peas.
- Cook rice using package directions.
- May add rice to peas or serve peas over rice.
- Yield: 10 servings.

Approx Per Serving: Cal 312; Prot 17 g; Carbo 51 g; Fiber 13 g; T Fat 4 g;
12% Calories from Fat; Chol 13 mg; Sod 472 mg.

Louise Carter, **Southern Region**
GFWC—East Point Woman's Club, East Point GA

HARVARD BEETS

2 pounds small beets
3 tablespoons cornstarch
1/2 cup sugar

Salt and pepper to taste
1 cup white wine vinegar
2 tablespoons butter

- Cut off tops of beets. Place beets in water to cover in saucepan.
- Cook, covered, over medium heat until beets come to a boil.
- Reduce heat. Simmer for 30 to 40 minutes or until beets are tender, adding water if needed to keep beets covered.
- Drain beets, reserving 3/4 cup cooking liquid. Let beets cool slightly.
- Peel beets and cut into 1/4-inch slices or chop.
- Combine cornstarch, sugar, salt, pepper, white wine vinegar and reserved beet liquid in saucepan.
- Cook over medium heat until thickened, stirring constantly.
- Add beets. Cook for 5 minutes or until heated through.
- Stir in butter. Serve immediately.
- Yield: 4 servings.

Approx Per Serving: Cal 245; Prot 2 g; Carbo 49 g; Fiber 5 g; T Fat 6 g;
21% Calories from Fat; Chol 16 mg; Sod 162 mg.

*Gertrude H. McDermott, **New England Region***
GFWC—Salem Women's Club, Salem NH

BROCCOLI CASSEROLE

2 10-ounce packages frozen chopped broccoli
2 eggs, beaten
1 10-ounce can mushroom soup

1 cup shredded sharp Cheddar cheese
1/2 cup mayonnaise
1/2 cup crushed butter crackers
1 tablespoon butter

- Cook broccoli for 5 minutes using package directions; drain.
- Combine eggs, mushroom soup, cheese and mayonnaise in bowl. Fold in broccoli.
- Pour into 1 1/2-quart casserole.
- Top with cracker crumbs; dot with butter.
- Bake at 350 degrees for 30 minutes.
- Yield: 6 servings.

Approx Per Serving: Cal 360; Prot 11 g; Carbo 15 g; Fiber 3 g; T Fat 31 g;
73% Calories from Fat; Chol 107 mg; Sod 735 mg.

*Irene P. Axelson, **Middle Atlantic Region***
GFWC—Wildwood Civic Club, North Wildwood NJ

1944—*GFWC first endorsed a resolution supporting equal rights and responsibilities for women.*

NEW YORK'S BEST BROCCOLI CASSEROLE

1 20-ounce package frozen cut
   broccoli
2 eggs, beaten
1 cup mayonnaise
1 teaspoon Worcestershire sauce
1 10-ounce can cream of mushroom
   soup

3 tablespoons dried minced onion
1/8 teaspoon pepper
1 cup shredded sharp Cheddar cheese
3/4 roll butter crackers, crushed
1/4 cup butter

- Cook broccoli in boiling salted water for 8 minutes or until tender-crisp; drain.
- Combine eggs, mayonnaise, Worcestershire sauce, soup, onion, pepper and cheese in bowl; mix well. Stir in broccoli.
- Pour into greased 2-quart casserole.
- Top with cracker crumbs; dot with butter.
- Bake at 350 degrees for 45 minutes or until hot and bubbly.
- Yield: 4 servings.

Approx Per Serving: Cal 861; Prot 18 g; Carbo 30 g; Fiber 5 g; T Fat 79 g;
79% Calories from Fat; Chol 201 mg; Sod 1420 mg.

*Bobbie Zachensky, **Middle Atlantic Region***
GFWC—Pocantico Hills Women's Club, Elmsford NY

SMOTHERED CABBAGE WEDGES

1 medium head cabbage
1/2 cup chopped green bell pepper
1/4 cup chopped red bell pepper
1/4 cup chopped onion
1/4 cup butter
1/4 cup flour
1/2 teaspoon salt

1/8 teaspoon pepper
2 cups milk
1/2 cup mayonnaise
3/4 cup shredded Cheddar cheese
3 tablespoons chili sauce
2 tablespoons chopped green and red
   bell pepper

- Cut cabbage into 8 wedges.
- Cook cabbage in 1/2 to 3/4 cup boiling water in saucepan for 12 minutes or until tender-crisp; drain. Place in greased 9x13-inch baking dish.
- Sauté 1/2 cup green pepper, 1/4 cup red pepper and onion in butter in skillet until tender. Blend in flour, salt and pepper. Add milk all at once, stirring to blend. Cook until thickened, stirring constantly. Pour over cabbage.
- Bake, uncovered, at 375 degrees for 20 minutes.
- Combine mayonnaise, cheese and chili sauce in bowl; mix well. Spoon over top. Sprinkle with remaining green and red bell pepper. Bake for 5 minutes longer.
- Yield: 8 servings.

Approx Per Serving: Cal 263; Prot 6 g; Carbo 11 g; Fiber 1 g; T Fat 22 g;
75% Calories from Fat; Chol 43 mg; Sod 443 mg.

*Esther P. Gelatt, **Mid Atlantic Region***
GFWC—The Woman's Club of Honesdale, Honesdale PA

CABBAGE AND DUMPLINGS

1 medium onion, chopped
1/2 cup butter
1 small head cabbage, thinly shredded
2 eggs, beaten
1 teaspoon salt

1 tablespoon melted butter, cooled
1/2 cup milk
2 cups flour
Salt and pepper to taste

- Sauté onion in 1/2 cup butter in large skillet until tender. Add cabbage. Cook, covered, over medium heat until tender-crisp.
- Combine eggs, 1 teaspoon salt, melted butter and milk in bowl; mix well. Add enough flour to make a sticky heavy dough.
- Drop dough by 1/2 teaspoonfuls several at a time into boiling salted water in saucepan. Cook for 10 minutes after dumplings return to surface of water. Remove with slotted spoon; place in colander. Rinse in cold water to remove starch.
- Combine dumplings and cabbage in slow cooker. Season with salt and pepper. Heat on Low until serving time. May add additional butter if desired. Serve with smoked sausage or hot dogs.
- Yield: 6 servings.

Approx Per Serving: Cal 360; Prot 8 g; Carbo 37 g; Fiber 2 g; T Fat 20 g;
51% Calories from Fat; Chol 120 mg; Sod 539 mg.

*Jean Borland, **Great Lakes Region***
GFWC—Canton Junior Guild, Louisville OH

CABBAGE TACOS

4 green onions
8 zucchini slices
1 cup refried beans
4 teaspoons hot taco sauce

8 slices Colby or Cheddar cheese
4 tomato slices
2 taco shells, split
4 cabbage leaves

- Cut green onions into halves lengthwise and crosswise.
- Layer green onions, 2 zucchini slices, 1/4 cup refried beans, 1 teaspoon taco sauce, 2 cheese slices and 1 tomato slice on each taco half. Top each with cabbage leaf.
- Yield: 1 serving.

Approx Per Serving: Cal 1332; Prot 75 g; Carbo 82 g; Fiber 28 g; T Fat 82 g;
54% Calories from Fat; Chol 216 mg; Sod 2660 mg.

*Charlotte Cox Haynes, **South Central Region***
GFWC—The Woman's Club of Boulder, Boulder CO

1945—*The Utah Federation of Women's Clubs provided magazine subscriptions to the libraries of Veteran's Homes and held birthday parties for veterans.*

CELERY CASSEROLE

3 cups chopped celery, cooked
    tender-crisp
1/4 cup blanched almonds
1/2 cup sliced water chestnuts
1 tablespoon flour
1 cup chicken broth

3/4 cup half and half
5 tablespoons melted butter
1/2 cup sliced mushrooms
1/2 cup grated Parmesan cheese
1/2 cup bread crumbs

- Layer drained celery, almonds and water chestnuts in buttered 2-quart casserole.
- Pour mixture of next 5 ingredients over layers. Bake at 350 degrees for 20 to 25 minutes or until hot and bubbly. Top with cheese and bread crumbs.
- Yield: 6 servings.

Approx Per Serving: Cal 251; Prot 8 g; Carbo 14 g; Fiber 2 g; T Fat 19 g;
66% Calories from Fat; Chol 43 mg; Sod 464 mg.

*Jane Ball, **Southeastern Region***
GFWC—The Woman's Club of Fairmont, Fairmont WV

BAKED CORN SUPREME

1 20-ounce can cream-style corn
1 20-ounce can whole kernel corn,
    drained
1 large onion, chopped

1 green bell pepper, chopped
3 eggs
1 cup sour cream
1 7-ounce package Jiffy corn muffin mix

- Combine all ingredients in bowl in order given, mixing well; do not beat.
- Pour into greased casserole. Bake at 325 degrees for 1 1/2 to 1 3/4 hours or until brown.
- Yield: 10 servings.

Approx Per Serving: Cal 206; Prot 6 g; Carbo 31 g; Fiber 3 g; T Fat 8 g;
34% Calories from Fat; Chol 74 mg; Sod 415 mg.

*Mrs. Neil A. Webster, **Mississippi Valley Region***
GFWC—Ingleside Study Club, Guttenberg IA

LANCASTER COUNTY CORN PIE

3 large cooked potatoes, sliced
Kernels of 6 ears of corn
4 hard-boiled eggs, sliced

2 tablespoons butter
1 recipe 2-crust pie pastry
1/2 cup (or more) milk

- Layer first 4 ingredients in pastry-lined pie plate. Add salt and pepper to taste and milk. Top with remaining pastry, sealing edge and cutting vents.
- Bake at 350 degrees for 20 minutes or until brown.
- Yield: 6 servings.

Approx Per Serving: Cal 510; Prot 12 g; Carbo 58 g; Fiber 5 g; T Fat 27 g;
47% Calories from Fat; Chol 155 mg; Sod 468 mg.

*Janet E. Grosh, **Middle Atlantic Region***
GFWC—Lititz Woman's Club, Lititz PA

FRIED CORN

4 slices bacon
Kernels of 4 large ears of corn
1¹/₂ cups water
1 tablespoon sugar

1 teaspoon salt
1 tablespoon cornstarch
1 tablespoon cold water

- Cook bacon in skillet until crisp; drain, reserving 2 tablespoons bacon drippings.
- Add corn, 1¹/₂ cups water, sugar and salt to bacon drippings in skillet. Bring to a boil. Simmer, covered, for 20 to 25 minutes, stirring occasionally.
- Combine cornstarch and 1 tablespoon water in bowl; mix well. Stir into corn mixture. Cook for 1 minute, stirring constantly. Pour into serving bowl. Crumble bacon over top.
- Yield: 4 servings.

Approx Per Serving: Cal 202; Prot 5 g; Carbo 24 g; Fiber 3 g; T Fat 11 g;
46% Calories from Fat; Chol 47 mg; Sod 717 mg.

*Mary Garrison, **Southern Region***
GFWC—Woman's Club of Auburndale, Auburndale FL

COLONIAL CORN SOUFFLÉ

¹/₂ cup butter
¹/₂ cup sugar
1 tablespoon flour
¹/₂ cup evaporated milk
2 eggs, beaten

1¹/₂ teaspoons baking powder
2   12-ounce cans whole kernel corn
1 tablespoon melted butter
¹/₄ cup sugar
¹/₂ teaspoon cinnamon

- Heat ¹/₂ cup butter and ¹/₂ cup sugar in saucepan until butter is melted, stirring constantly. Blend in flour. Remove from heat.
- Stir in evaporated milk, eggs and baking powder, mixing well. Fold in corn.
- Pour into buttered 1-quart casserole. Bake at 350 degrees for 50 to 60 minutes or until knife inserted near center comes out clean.
- Brush with melted butter; sprinkle with ¹/₄ cup sugar and cinnamon.
- Yield: 6 servings.

Approx Per Serving: Cal 379; Prot 6 g; Carbo 45 g; Fiber 1 g; T Fat 21 g;
48% Calories from Fat; Chol 124 mg; Sod 560 mg.

*Jean W. Drayer, **Southeastern Region***
GFWC—The Woman's Club of Williamsburg, Williamsburg VA

1949—*The Build a Better Community Program was initiated. This program later became GFWC's successful and long-running Community Improvement Program.*

SOUTHERN EGGPLANT CASSEROLE

1 medium eggplant, peeled, cubed
1 teaspoon salt
3 tablespoons melted margarine
2 tablespoons chopped green bell
  pepper
1¹/₂ cups canned tomatoes

1 egg, beaten
1 cup dry bread crumbs
1 medium onion, finely chopped
¹/₂ cup shredded mild Cheddar cheese
Salt and pepper to taste

- Cook eggplant with 1 teaspoon salt in water to cover in saucepan until tender-crisp, stirring occasionally; drain.
- Add remaining ingredients; mix well. Pour into greased 2-quart casserole.
- Bake at 350 degrees for 30 minutes.
- Yield: 6 servings.

Approx Per Serving: Cal 202; Prot 7 g; Carbo 21 g; Fiber 4 g; T Fat 11 g;
47% Calories from Fat; Chol 46 mg; Sod 715 mg.

Julene B. McPhaul, **Southeastern Region**
GFWC—Woman's Club of Raleigh, Raleigh NC

MUSHROOM SOUFFLÉ

¹/₄ cup butter, softened
8 slices bread, crusts trimmed
1 pound mushrooms, chopped
¹/₄ cup butter
¹/₂ cup chopped celery
¹/₂ cup chopped green bell pepper
¹/₂ cup chopped onion

¹/₂ cup mayonnaise
³/₄ teaspoon salt
¹/₂ teaspoon pepper
2 eggs, beaten
1¹/₂ cups milk
1   10-ounce can mushroom soup
¹/₂ cup shredded Cheddar cheese

- Spread ¹/₄ cup butter on bread slices; cut 3 slices bread into cubes. Spread bread cubes in buttered 3-quart casserole.
- Sauté mushrooms in ¹/₄ cup butter in skillet. Remove from heat. Stir in celery, green pepper, onion, mayonnaise, salt and pepper. Cut 3 slices bread into cubes. Layer vegetable mixture and bread cubes in casserole.
- Combine eggs and milk in bowl; beat well. Pour over layers.
- Chill, covered, in refrigerator for 1 hour or longer.
- Spoon undiluted soup over layers. Cut remaining 2 slices bread into cubes. Sprinkle over top.
- Bake at 325 degrees for 50 minutes. Sprinkle with cheese. Bake for 10 minutes longer.
- Yield: 6 servings.

Approx Per Serving: Cal 514; Prot 12 g; Carbo 25 g; Fiber 3 g; T Fat 42 g;
72% Calories from Fat; Chol 142 mg; Sod 1136 mg.

Ida M. Findley, **Middle Atlantic Region**
GFWC—Woman's Club of Southern Butler County, Butler PA

CAJUN OKRA OVER RICE

4 cups sliced okra
1/2 cup chopped onion
1/4 teaspoon each salt and pepper

1/4 cup vegetable oil
3 medium tomatoes, chopped
3 cups cooked rice

- Cook okra and onion with salt and pepper in hot oil in skillet over low heat for 20 to 25 minutes, stirring frequently. Stir in tomatoes.
- Cook, covered, for 10 to 15 minutes, stirring occasionally. Serve over hot rice.
- Yield: 4 servings.

Approx Per Serving: Cal 380; Prot 8 g; Carbo 58 g; Fiber 7 g; T Fat 15 g; 33% Calories from Fat; Chol 0 mg; Sod 147 mg.

*Sue Carter, **South Central Region***
GFWC—Elsie McCain Club, Hazen AR

GOLDEN PARMESAN POTATOES

6 large potatoes
1/4 cup sifted flour
1/4 cup grated Parmesan cheese

3/4 teaspoon salt
1/8 teaspoon pepper
1/3 cup butter

- Peel potatoes; cut into quarters. Mix flour, cheese, salt and pepper in plastic bag.
- Moisten potatoes with water. Place potatoes several at a time in mixture in plastic bag, shaking to coat.
- Melt butter in 9x13-inch baking dish in 375-degree oven. Layer potatoes in butter.
- Bake for 1 hour or until brown, turning 1 time. Garnish with chopped parsley.
- Yield: 6 servings.

Approx Per Serving: Cal 268; Prot 5 g; Carbo 37 g; Fiber 3 g; T Fat 11 g; 38% Calories from Fat; Chol 30 mg; Sod 423 mg.

*Ellen Sparks, **Western Region***
GFWC—Peninsula Hills Women's Club, San Carlos CA

POTATOES ROMANOFF

6 large boiled potatoes, peeled, shredded
2 cups sour cream
1 bunch green onions, chopped

1 cup shredded sharp Cheddar cheese
1 1/2 teaspoons salt
1/4 teaspoon pepper

- Combine all ingredients in bowl; mix well.
- Pour into 2-quart casserole. Chill, covered, in refrigerator for several hours.
- Bake, uncovered, at 350 degrees for 30 to 40 minutes or until brown.
- Yield: 10 servings.

Approx Per Serving: Cal 218; Prot 6 g; Carbo 19 g; Fiber 1 g; T Fat 14 g; 55% Calories from Fat; Chol 32 mg; Sod 418 mg.

*Norine Wise, **Western Region***
GFWC—St. John, St. John WA

CREAMY POTATO CASSEROLE

7 medium cooked potatoes
1 10-ounce can cream of chicken soup
1/4 cup butter
2 cups sour cream

1/3 cup chopped green onions
1 1/2 cups shredded Cheddar cheese
3/4 cup crushed potato chips

- Peel and coarsely grate potatoes.
- Heat soup with butter in saucepan until butter melts, stirring frequently.
- Add sour cream, green onions and cheese to soup; blend well. Stir in potatoes. Spoon into buttered casserole; top with crushed potato chips.
- Bake at 350 degrees for 45 minutes.
- Yield: 8 servings.

Approx Per Serving: Cal 425; Prot 11 g; Carbo 32 g; Fiber 2 g; T Fat 29 g; 60% Calories from Fat; Chol 66 mg; Sod 519 mg.

*Martha Rohrer, **Western Region***
GFWC—Woman's Club of Bellflower, Fullerton CA

FLUFFY POTATO CASSEROLE

2 cups mashed potatoes
8 ounces cream cheese, softened
1 small green onion, finely chopped
2 eggs, beaten

2 tablespoons flour
Salt and pepper to taste
1 2-ounce can French-fried onion
  rings

- Combine mashed potatoes, cream cheese, green onion, eggs, flour, salt and pepper in bowl; mix well.
- Spoon into greased 9x11-inch baking dish; top with onion rings.
- Bake at 300 degrees for 35 minutes.
- May be prepared and refrigerated for 2 to 3 hours before needed. Add onion rings just before baking.
- Yield: 4 servings.

Approx Per Serving: Cal 420; Prot 11 g; Carbo 29 g; Fiber 2 g; T Fat 30 g; 63% Calories from Fat; Chol 170 mg; Sod 613 mg.

*Kathryn Reardon, **Western Region***
GFWC—Fortnightly Woman's Club, Gig Harbor WA

1956—*In order to prevent juvenile delinquency, the Woman's Club of Idaho Falls, Idaho, sponsored the development of a girls' summer camp which served a ten-county area.*

POTATIS BULLAR

1/4 cup butter, softened
2 egg yolks, beaten
1/2 cup fine dry bread crumbs
1/2 cup packed mashed potatoes

1/4 teaspoon salt
1 cup 1/2-inch ham cubes
3 cups beef broth

- Cream butter until light and fluffy. Add egg yolks; beat well. Stir in bread crumbs, mashed potatoes and salt, mixing well.
- Knead mixture; shape into long roll. Cut into walnut-sized pieces, flattening each piece. Place ham cube in center of each piece. Shape dough around ham to enclose completely.
- Bring broth to a simmer in saucepan. Drop dumplings into simmering broth. Cook, uncovered, for 10 minutes. Cook, covered, for 5 minutes longer.
- May use broth or soup of your choice for cooking.
- Yield: 6 servings.

Approx Per Serving: Cal 183; Prot 10 g; Carbo 10 g; Fiber 1 g; T Fat 12 g;
57% Calories from Fat; Chol 106 mg; Sod 984 mg.

Avis R. Olson, **Great Lakes Region**
GFWC—Ashland Monday Club, Ashland WI

MASHED POTATOES IN ADVANCE

5 pounds potatoes, peeled
2/3 cup butter, softened
1 1/2 cups hot milk

1 teaspoon salt
1/2 teaspoon pepper

- Cook potatoes in water to cover in large saucepan for 20 to 30 minutes or until tender; drain.
- Add butter, milk, salt and pepper; mash with potato masher until smooth. Spoon into 3-quart casserole.
- Bake at 350 degrees for 30 minutes or until heated through.
- Garnish with paprika and several pats of butter.
- Potatoes may be refrigerated for up to 2 days before baking. Remove and let stand at room temperature for 1 1/2 hours before baking. Bake as above.
- Yield: 12 servings.

Approx Per Serving: Cal 272; Prot 4 g; Carbo 39 g; Fiber 3 g; T Fat 11 g;
37% Calories from Fat; Chol 32 mg; Sod 286 mg.

Helen L. Long, **Mississippi Valley Region**
GFWC—Beta GFWC of Beemer, Beemer NE

POTATO PANCAKES

¼ cup milk
2 eggs
3 cups chopped uncooked potatoes
1 small onion, cut into quarters

¼ cup flour
1 teaspoon salt
¼ teaspoon baking powder
Oil for frying

- Combine all ingredients in blender container in order listed. Process, covered, at high speed just until potatoes are finely chopped. Do not overprocess.
- Drop by tablespoonfuls onto hot oiled griddle or skillet. Fry until brown on both sides, turning once. Garnish with applesauce or raspberry sauce. Serve hot.
- Yield: 18 (3-inch) servings.

Approx Per Serving: Cal 44; Prot 2 g; Carbo 8 g; Fiber 1 g; T Fat 1 g;
16% Calories from Fat; Chol 24 mg; Sod 134 mg.
Nutritional analysis does not include oil for frying.

*Gladys Willeke, **Mississippi Valley Region***
GFWC—Aplington Woman's Club, Aplington IA

TOP-HAT POTATOES

4 cups seasoned mashed potatoes
2 eggs, beaten
2 tablespoons minced onion
1 cup shredded sharp Cheddar cheese

8 thick tomato slices
6 tablespoons fine dry bread crumbs
2 teaspoons melted butter
Salt, seasoned salt and MSG to taste

- Combine potatoes, eggs and onion in bowl; mix well. Shape into 4 balls; place on greased baking sheet.
- Make deep hole in each potato ball. Fill with cheese.
- Top with tomato slices. Sprinkle mixture of bread crumbs, butter and seasonings over top.
- Bake at 350 degrees for 30 minutes.
- Yield: 4 servings.

Approx Per Serving: Cal 455; Prot 19 g; Carbo 48 g; Fiber 0 g; T Fat 26 g;
51% Calories from Fat; Chol 180 mg; Sod 964 mg.

*Kate Skupny, **Western Region***
GFWC—Federated Women's Club, St. Helena CA

1956—*The GFWC President appeared regularly on the NBC-TV "Home" show starring Arlene Francis.*

Spinach and Artichokes en Casserole

2 10-ounce packages frozen chopped spinach
1/2 cup melted unsalted butter
8 ounces cream cheese, softened

1 teaspoon lemon juice
1 16-ounce can artichokes, drained
1/2 cup cracker crumbs
2 tablespoons butter

- Cook spinach using package directions; drain. Add melted butter, cream cheese and lemon juice; mix well.
- Arrange artichokes in greased 1 1/2-quart casserole. Top with spinach mixture. Sprinkle with cracker crumbs; dot with butter.
- Bake at 350 degrees for 25 to 30 minutes or until hot and bubbly.
- Yield: 6 servings.

Approx Per Serving: Cal 384; Prot 8 g; Carbo 15 g; Fiber 3 g; T Fat 34 g; 77% Calories from Fat; Chol 95 mg; Sod 507 mg.

*Barbara A. Kiefer, **Southeastern Region***
GFWC—Woman's Club of Asheville, Asheville NC

Spinach Gnocchi with Gorgonzola Sauce

1 pound spinach
Salt, pepper and nutmeg to taste
3 tablespoons butter, softened
8 ounces ricotta cheese
3/4 to 1 cup flour
1 egg, beaten

1 egg yolk, beaten
2 tablespoons butter
3 ounces Gorgonzola cheese, crumbled
1 cup cream
6 ounces pignoli nuts, toasted

- Rinse spinach, discarding stalks. Cook in a small amount of water with salt, pepper and nutmeg in saucepan until tender; drain, squeezing out moisture. Chop very fine. Add 3 tablespoons butter; mix well.
- Press ricotta cheese through sieve into bowl. Beat with spoon until smooth. Add spinach, flour, egg and egg yolk, beating well after addition.
- Shape with floured hands into walnut-sized dumplings. Drop into boiling salted water several at a time. Remove with a slotted spoon as they rise to surface, placing in colander to drain.
- Place dumplings in buttered casserole. Keep warm in 200-degree oven.
- Melt 2 tablespoons butter in small saucepan. Add crumbled cheese and cream. Cook over low heat for 4 to 5 minutes or until thickened, stirring constantly.
- Sprinkle dumplings with pignoli nuts. Serve accompanied by sauce in sauceboat.
- Yield: 4 servings.

Approx Per Serving: Cal 907; Prot 32 g; Carbo 37 g; Fiber 5 g; T Fat 76 g; 71% Calories from Fat; Chol 274 mg; Sod 685 mg.

*Mary Lou DeNardis, **New England Region***
GFWC—New Haven Woman's Club, Hamden CT

SOUTHERN SPINACH MADELEINE

2   10-ounce packages frozen chopped
   spinach
¼ cup butter
2 tablespoons flour
2 tablespoons chopped onion
½ cup evaporated milk
½ teaspoon black pepper

¾ teaspoon celery salt
¾ teaspoon garlic salt
Salt to taste
1 teaspoon Worcestershire sauce
Red pepper to taste
1   6-ounce roll jalapeño cheese, cubed

- Cook spinach using package directions; drain, reserving ½ cup cooking liquid.
- Melt butter in saucepan over medium heat. Blend in flour. Add onion. Cook until onion is soft, stirring constantly. Stir in reserved spinach cooking liquid and evaporated milk. Cook until thickened, stirring constantly. Add seasonings and cheese. Cook until cheese is melted, stirring constantly.
- Combine sauce and spinach in serving dish.
- May place in 9x9-inch casserole and top with buttered crumbs. Chill in refrigerator overnight or freeze. Bake at 350 degrees for 30 minutes or until hot and bubbly.
- Yield: 8 servings.

Approx Per Serving: Cal 180; Prot 9 g; Carbo 7 g; Fiber 2 g; T Fat 14 g;
65% Calories from Fat; Chol 40 mg; Sod 579 mg.

Polly Williams, **South Central Region**
GFWC—Lagniappe Woman's Club, Baton Rouge LA

TOMATOES AU GRATIN

4 large ripe tomatoes
1 onion, chopped
3 tablespoons butter
1 cup shredded Swiss cheese

1 cup soft bread crumbs
1 cup sour cream
2 eggs, beaten
Salt and pepper to taste

- Peel tomatoes; cut into slices.
- Sauté onion in butter in skillet until soft.
- Combine cheese and bread crumbs in bowl; mix well.
- Layer tomato slices, onion and cheese mixture ½ at a time in greased 8x8-inch baking dish.
- Combine sour cream, eggs, salt and pepper in bowl; mix well. Pour over layers.
- Bake at 350 degrees for 10 to 15 minutes or until hot and bubbly.
- Garnish with parsley.
- Yield: 6 servings.

Approx Per Serving: Cal 276; Prot 10 g; Carbo 12 g; Fiber 2 g; T Fat 21 g;
69% Calories from Fat; Chol 121 mg; Sod 187 mg.

Jan Hanson, **Middle Atlantic Region**
GFWC—Jr. Woman's Club of the Merchantville Area, Inc., Pennsauken NJ

JERSEY TOMATO BAKE

4 tomatoes
1 medium onion, cut into rings
1/8 teaspoon basil
1/2 teaspoon salt
1/4 teaspoon pepper

2 tablespoons butter, softened
4 slices white bread
1/4 cup shredded Cheddar cheese
1/4 cup water

- Core 4 tomatoes; slice into halves crosswise. Place bottom halves of tomatoes cut side up in 2-quart casserole sprayed with nonstick cooking spray.
- Arrange half the onion rings on tomatoes in prepared dish. Sprinkle with half the seasonings.
- Spread butter lightly on 1 side of bread. Place bread buttered side up over onions. Layer remaining onion rings, seasonings and tomatoes cut side down over bread. Dot butter in core cavities of tomatoes; sprinkle with Cheddar cheese. Pour water around tomatoes.
- Bake, uncovered, at 350 degrees for 30 minutes. Bake, covered, for 30 minutes longer.
- Yield: 4 servings.

Approx Per Serving: Cal 192; Prot 6 g; Carbo 22 g; Fiber 3 g; T Fat 10 g;
44% Calories from Fat; Chol 23 mg; Sod 513 mg.

Grace Mathis Williams, **Middle Atlantic Region**
GFWC—Woman's Club of Westville, Westville NJ

SOUTH JERSEY FRIED TOMATOES

3 firm ripe tomatoes
1/4 cup (or more) flour
Butter for frying

3/4 cup sugar
Salt and pepper to taste
1 cup (or more) milk

- Cut tomatoes into 1/2-inch slices. Reserve 2 tomato slices; chop coarsely. Coat remaining tomatoes with flour.
- Sauté coated tomatoes several at a time in hot butter in skillet until light brown. Turn tomatoes; sprinkle cooked side with sugar, salt and pepper. Cook until brown; remove to warm platter.
- Add milk to drippings in skillet, stirring to deglaze. Mix a small amount of flour with water. Add to skillet. Add chopped tomatoes. Cook until thickened, stirring constantly. Pour over fried tomatoes. Serve with crusty bread or rolls.
- Yield: 4 servings.

Approx Per Serving: Cal 228; Prot 4 g; Carbo 50 g; Fiber 2 g; T Fat 2 g;
9% Calories from Fat; Chol 8 mg; Sod 34 mg.
Nutritional analysis does not include butter for frying.

Roe Kitchen, **Middle Atlantic Region**
Haddon Heights NJ

FRIED GREEN TOMATO

1 medium green tomato
1/2 cup flour

2 tablespoons margarine
Salt and pepper to taste

- Cut tomato into 1/2-inch slices. Coat tomato slices with flour, shaking off excess flour.
- Fry in hot margarine in skillet over medium heat until brown, turning frequently.
- Remove to paper towels to drain. Season with salt and pepper. Serve immediately.
- Yield: 2 servings.

Approx Per Serving: Cal 231; Prot 4 g; Carbo 27 g; Fiber 1 g; T Fat 12 g; 46% Calories from Fat; Chol 0 mg; Sod 142 mg.

*Hilda Reynolds, **Southern Region***
GFWC—Wistaria Study Club, Mobile AL

ESCALLOPED TURNIPS

6 large turnips, peeled, chopped
1/4 teaspoon baking soda
1/2 teaspoon salt
1/2 cup (about) milk

1/4 cup sugar
1 1/2 tablespoons flour
1 tablespoon (about) cream

- Combine turnips and baking soda with water to cover in saucepan. Bring to a boil; drain. Add fresh water to cover and salt. Cook until tender-crisp, stirring occasionally; drain. Place in greased 2-quart casserole. Add milk to just cover.
- Mix sugar, flour and enough cream to form paste in bowl. Stir gently into turnips.
- Bake at 275 degrees for 45 to 60 minutes or until thickened.
- Yield: 6 servings.

Approx Per Serving: Cal 95; Prot 2 g; Carbo 19 g; Fiber 3 g; T Fat 2 g; 16% Calories from Fat; Chol 6 mg; Sod 310 mg.

*Ruth N. Duffy, **Mississippi Valley Region***
GFWC—Bellevue Woman's Club, Bellevue NE

TURNIP GREENS CASSEROLE

2 cups drained cooked turnip greens
1   10-ounce can cream of celery soup
1/2 cup mayonnaise
1 tablespoon horseradish

2 tablespoons pepper sauce
2 eggs, beaten
2 corn bread muffins, crumbled
1/2 cup margarine

- Mix turnip greens, soup, mayonnaise, horseradish, pepper sauce and eggs in bowl. Pour into 8x8-inch casserole. Sprinkle with crumbled corn bread; dot with margarine.
- Bake at 350 degrees for 30 minutes.
- Yield: 6 servings.

Approx Per Serving: Cal 386; Prot 5 g; Carbo 14 g; Fiber 2 g; T Fat 36 g; 81% Calories from Fat; Chol 94 mg; Sod 759 mg.

*Edwina Crisler, **Southern Region***
GFWC—Heritage Club of Clinton, Clinton MS

SUMMER SQUASH CASSEROLE

2 pounds yellow squash, sliced
¼ cup chopped onion
1   10-ounce can cream of chicken soup
1 cup sour cream

1 cup shredded carrot
½ cup melted butter
1   8-ounce package herb-seasoned
    stuffing mix

- Cook squash with onion in a small amount of water in saucepan for 5 minutes; drain.
- Combine soup, sour cream and shredded carrot in bowl; mix well. Fold in squash and onion mixture.
- Combine melted butter and stuffing mix in bowl; mix well.
- Layer half the stuffing mix, all the squash mixture and remaining stuffing mix in greased 7x12-inch casserole.
- Bake at 350 degrees for 25 to 30 minutes or until heated through.
- Yield: 6 servings.

Approx Per Serving: Cal 442; Prot 10 g; Carbo 41 g; Fiber 3 g; T Fat 28 g;
55% Calories from Fat; Chol 62 mg; Sod 1034 mg.

Marion E. Boyce, **Middle Atlantic Region**
GFWC—Northampton Township Woman's Club, Churchville PA

BUTTERNUT SQUASH CASSEROLE

3 cups mashed cooked squash
3 eggs, beaten
½ cup milk
1 cup sugar

½ cup coconut
½ to 1 teaspoon ginger
1 teaspoon vanilla extract
½ cup margarine

- Combine squash, eggs, milk, sugar, coconut, ginger and vanilla in bowl; mix well.
- Melt margarine in baking dish in 350-degree oven. Spoon squash mixture into melted margarine.
- Bake at 350 degrees for 1 hour.
- Yield: 6 servings.

Approx Per Serving: Cal 396; Prot 5 g; Carbo 50 g; Fiber 4 g; T Fat 21 g;
46% Calories from Fat; Chol 109 mg; Sod 228 mg.

Jane Lassiter, **Southeastern Region**
GFWC—Tarrara Woman's Club, Boykins VA

1961—GFWC crusade for automobile seat belts and cancer awareness campaign is launched.

FRIED SQUASH FRITTERS

4 cups mashed cooked yellow squash
2 eggs, beaten
1/2 cup cornmeal
1/2 cup flour

1 small onion, chopped
Salt and pepper to taste
1/2 cup vegetable oil

- Combine squash, eggs, cornmeal, flour, onion, salt and pepper in bowl; mix well. Shape into patties. Fry patties in hot oil in skillet until brown on both sides.
- Serve hot with butter.
- May substitute 3 cups squash and 1 cup cooked corn for 4 cups squash.
- Yield: 12 servings.

Approx Per Serving: Cal 161; Prot 3 g; Carbo 15 g; Fiber 3 g; T Fat 11 g; 57% Calories from Fat; Chol 36 mg; Sod 13 mg.

*Marian H. Carrington, **Southeastern Region***
GFWC—Burkeville Woman's Club, Burkeville VA

FRIED SWEET POTATOES

3 large sweet potatoes, peeled, sliced
1 cup vegetable oil

4 teaspoons brown sugar
3/4 cup milk

- Fry sweet potatoes in hot oil in skillet until brown on both sides. Sprinkle with brown sugar. Add milk. Simmer on low heat until tender. Serve hot.
- Yield: 6 servings.

Approx Per Serving: Cal 431; Prot 2 g; Carbo 23 g; Fiber 2 g; T Fat 38 g; 77% Calories from Fat; Chol 4 mg; Sod 24 mg.

*Carolyn Dischar, **Southeastern Region***
GFWC—Town and Country Club, Brooksville KY

SWEET POTATO SOUFFLÉ

1 29-ounce can sweet potatoes, drained
1 17-ounce can sweet potatoes, drained
1/2 cup packed dark brown sugar

1/2 cup applesauce
2 teaspoons vanilla extract
1/4 cup melted butter
3/4 cup flaked coconut
20 large marshmallows

- Mash sweet potatoes in bowl until smooth. Add brown sugar, applesauce, vanilla and butter; mix well. Spoon into greased 8x12-inch baking dish.
- Bake at 325 degrees for 25 minutes. Sprinkle with coconut; arrange marshmallows on top. Bake for 10 to 15 minutes longer or until marshmallows are golden brown.
- Yield: 8 servings.

Approx Per Serving: Cal 383; Prot 4 g; Carbo 75 g; Fiber 5 g; T Fat 8 g; 19% Calories from Fat; Chol 16 mg; Sod 194 mg.

*Barbara A. Porach, **Southeastern Region***
GFWC—Ravenscroft Federated Woman's Club, Chester VA

CHEESE STRATA WITH ZUCCHINI

1 small onion, thinly sliced
3 tablespoons butter
1 zucchini, thinly sliced
1/4 teaspoon marjoram
1/4 teaspoon oregano
8 slices firm white bread
4 eggs, beaten

2 cups milk
1 teaspoon salt
1/8 teaspoon pepper
Nutmeg to taste
8 ounces Swiss cheese, shredded
2 tablespoons butter

- Sauté onion in 3 tablespoons butter in skillet for 2 minutes or until tender. Add zucchini, marjoram and oregano. Cook for 6 to 8 minutes or until zucchini is tender and brown.
- Cut bread into 1/2-inch cubes. Combine next 5 ingredients in bowl; beat well.
- Layer bread cubes, zucchini mixture and cheese in greased 9x13-inch baking dish. Pour eggs mixture over all; dot with 2 tablespoons butter.
- Bake at 375 degrees for 30 minutes or until brown.
- Yield: 6 servings.

Approx Per Serving: Cal 443; Prot 21 g; Carbo 27 g; Fiber 1 g; T Fat 28 g; 57% Calories from Fat; Chol 213 mg; Sod 808 mg.

*Marie R. Scott, **Mid Atlantic Region***
GFWC—Wallsholm Club, Vineland NJ

ZUCCHINI LASAGNA

1 medium onion, chopped
1 clove of garlic, minced
1 teaspoon vegetable oil
1 15-ounce can tomato sauce
1 teaspoon oregano
Pepper to taste

2 cups cottage cheese
1/2 cup grated Parmesan cheese
1 egg
3 medium zucchini, unpeeled
2 teaspoons flour
1 cup shredded mozzarella cheese

- Sauté onion and garlic in oil in skillet for 2 minutes. Stir in tomato sauce, oregano and pepper. Bring to a boil. Simmer, uncovered, until thickened, stirring frequently.
- Process cottage cheese, Parmesan cheese and egg in blender until smooth.
- Spray 9x13-inch baking dish with nonstick cooking spray.
- Cut zucchini into 1/4-inch slices. Layer half the zucchini in baking dish. Coat remaining zucchini lightly with flour.
- Layer half the cottage cheese mixture, half the sauce, half the mozzarella cheese and remaining zucchini in prepared baking dish. Repeat layers with remaining ingredients ending with mozzarella cheese.
- Bake at 350 degrees for 40 minutes. Let stand at room temperature for 15 minutes before serving. May top with bread crumbs before baking.
- Yield: 10 servings.

Approx Per Serving: Cal 137; Prot 12 g; Carbo 9 g; Fiber 2 g; T Fat 7 g; 42% Calories from Fat; Chol 39 mg; Sod 554 mg.

*Bettie Bintrim, **Mid Atlantic Region***
GFWC—Ellwood City Municipal Women's Club, Ellwood City PA

ZUCCHINI BAKE

4 cups thinly sliced zucchini
1 cup chopped onion
1/2 cup butter
1/2 cup chopped fresh parsley
1/2 teaspoon salt
1/2 teaspoon garlic powder
1/2 teaspoon pepper

1/4 teaspoon basil
1/4 teaspoon oregano
2 eggs, beaten
2 cups shredded mozzarella cheese
1 8-count can crescent rolls
2 teaspoons Dijon mustard

- Sauté zucchini and onion in butter in large skillet until tender; drain. Stir in parsley and seasonings.
- Combine eggs and cheese in bowl; mix well. Stir in zucchini mixture.
- Unroll crescent roll dough. Separate into rectangles. Press onto bottom and up sides of 8x12-inch baking dish, sealing perforations.
- Spread mustard over dough. Spoon in zucchini mixture.
- Bake at 375 degrees for 18 to 20 minutes or until brown. Let stand at room temperature for 10 minutes before cutting into squares.
- Yield: 16 servings.

Approx Per Serving: Cal 160; Prot 5 g; Carbo 8 g; Fiber 1 g; T Fat 12 g;
69% Calories from Fat; Chol 53 mg; Sod 310 mg.

Donita Sanders, Mid Atlantic Region
GFWC—Community Women's Club of Level Green, Level Green PA

ZUCCHINI CASSEROLE

1 8-ounce package chicken-flavored
   stove-top stuffing mix
1/2 cup finely chopped onion
1/2 cup grated carrot
4 cups chopped zucchini

1/2 cup butter
1 cup sour cream
1 10-ounce can cream of chicken soup
Salt and pepper to taste
3/4 cup shredded Cheddar cheese

- Prepare and cook stuffing mix using package directions.
- Sauté onion, carrot and zucchini in butter in skillet until carrot is tender.
- Combine vegetables, sour cream, soup, salt and pepper in bowl; mix lightly.
- Spoon into greased 9x13-inch baking dish. Spoon stuffing onto top; sprinkle with Cheddar cheese.
- Bake at 350 degrees for 45 minutes.
- Yield: 10 servings.

Approx Per Serving: Cal 345; Prot 8 g; Carbo 22 g; Fiber 3 g; T Fat 26 g;
66% Calories from Fat; Chol 63 mg; Sod 874 mg.

Louise Oras, Mid Atlantic Region
GFWC—Clara Barton Woman's Club, Edison NJ

VEGGIES SUPREME

1 10-ounce package frozen chopped
   broccoli
1 10-ounce package frozen lima beans
1 10-ounce can cream of mushroom
   soup

1 cup sour cream
1/2 envelope dried vegetable soup mix
1 8-ounce can sliced water chestnuts
1/2 cup crushed crisp rice cereal
2 tablespoons melted butter

- Cook broccoli and lima beans using package directions until just tender-crisp.
- Combine mushroom soup, sour cream, soup mix and water chestnuts in bowl; mix well.
- Combine crushed cereal and butter in bowl; mix well.
- Layer vegetables, soup mixture and cereal in greased 9x13-inch casserole.
- Bake at 350 degrees for 30 minutes or until hot and bubbly.
- Yield: 10 servings.

Approx Per Serving: Cal 171; Prot 5 g; Carbo 18 g; Fiber 4 g; T Fat 10 g;
49% Calories from Fat; Chol 17 mg; Sod 458 mg.

Maxine S. Scarbro, **Southeastern Region**
GFWC Second Vice President, 1992–94, Charleston WV

CHEESE PUDDING

1 cup saltine cracker crumbs
2 cups medium white sauce
8 ounces American cheese, shredded
4 hard-boiled eggs, grated

1 7-ounce can pimentos, grated
1/2 cup cracker crumbs
1 tablespoon butter

- Combine cracker crumbs and white sauce in bowl; mix well to moisten cracker crumbs, adding milk if necessary to moisten.
- Layer cracker crumbs mixture, cheese, eggs and pimentos 1/2 at a time in greased casserole. Top with mixture of cracker crumbs and butter.
- Bake at 350 degrees for 30 minutes.
- This was a favorite of President Eisenhower.
- Yield: 4 servings.

Approx Per Serving: Cal 582; Prot 25 g; Carbo 38 g; Fiber 2 g; T Fat 36 g;
56% Calories from Fat; Chol 294 mg; Sod 1681 mg.

Martha L. Hamilton, **Southeastern Region**
GFWC—Hodgenville Woman's Club, Hodgenville KY

1962—*GFWC Juniors raised $25,913 for Project Hope, to support
the hospital teaching and training ship S.S. HOPE.*

CHILIES RELLENOS

12 large chilies with stems, roasted
16 ounces Cheddar cheese, cubed
1 small onion, chopped
³/₄ teaspoon baking powder
¹/₄ cup flour

¹/₄ teaspoon salt
4 egg yolks, beaten
4 egg whites, stiffly beaten
Oil for deep frying

- Peel chilies; open small slits below stems and remove seed.
- Combine cheese and onion in bowl; mix well. Fill chilies carefully to avoid breaking; fasten with wooden picks.
- Sift baking powder, flour and salt together in bowl. Add egg yolks; mix well. Fold in stiffly beaten egg whites.
- Dip stuffed chilies into batter to coat.
- Fry in 360 to 365-degree oil until golden brown; drain. Serve hot.
- May also place chilies stuffed with cheese or ground cooked meat in greased casserole. Pour batter over chilies. Bake at 325 degrees until light brown.
- Yield: 6 servings.

Approx Per Serving: Cal 419; Prot 26 g; Carbo 15 g; Fiber 2 g; T Fat 29 g;
62% Calories from Fat; Chol 222 mg; Sod 644 mg.
Nutritional analysis does not include oil for deep frying.

*Diane Turner, **South Central Region***
GFWC—White Sands Jr. Woman's Club, Alamogordo NM

SPECIAL CHILIES RELLENOS CASSEROLE

1 27-ounce can Ortega green chilies
16 ounces sharp Cheddar cheese,
    shredded
4 eggs, beaten
2 tablespoons flour
1 12-ounce can evaporated milk

16 ounces Monterey Jack cheese,
    shredded
1 bunch cilantro, chopped
2 8-ounce cans tomato sauce or
   1 16-ounce jar salsa

- Split chilies; remove seed. Rinse and drain on paper towels.
- Layer chilies and Cheddar cheese ¹/₂ at a time in greased 9x13-inch casserole.
- Combine eggs, flour and evaporated milk in bowl; mix well. Pour over layers.
- Bake at 400 degrees for 30 minutes.
- Sprinkle with Monterey Jack cheese and chopped cilantro. Pour tomato sauce over top. Bake for 15 minutes longer. Cool at room temperature for 10 minutes before cutting.
- Yield: 12 servings.

Approx Per Serving: Cal 392; Prot 24 g; Carbo 12 g; Fiber 1 g; T Fat 28 g;
64% Calories from Fat; Chol 154 mg; Sod 1173 mg.

*Emma V. Howe, **Western Region***
GFWC—Los Molinos Woman's Club, Los Molinos CA

EGGS SAN FRANCISCO

¹/2 cup chopped onion
¹/2 cup chopped green bell pepper
2 tablespoons butter
8 eggs, beaten
¹/4 cup milk
¹/2 teaspoon salt

¹/2 teaspoon basil
Pepper to taste
3 ounces cream cheese, cubed
1 medium tomato, peeled and chopped
8 ounces crab meat, drained

- Sauté onion and green pepper in butter in skillet until tender.
- Combine eggs, milk, salt, basil and pepper in bowl; mix well. Add to onion and green pepper mixture in skillet. Add cream cheese, tomato and crab meat.
- Cook gently over medium heat until eggs are scrambled, lifting with spatula as eggs set on bottom. Remove from skillet when soft cooked.
- Serve with sourdough or Italian bread or English muffins.
- Yield: 4 servings.

Approx Per Serving: Cal 366; Prot 26 g; Carbo 6 g; Fiber 1 g; T Fat 26 g;
64% Calories from Fat; Chol 524 mg; Sod 683 mg.

Ruth Williams, **Western Region**
GFWC—Peninsula Hills Women's Club, Redwood City CA

HUEVOS RANCHEROS NUEVOS

1 onion, chopped
2 tablespoons oil
1   30-ounce can tomatoes, chopped
1   4-ounce can green chilies, cut into
    strips
¹/2 teaspoon oregano
1 teaspoon salt

1 teaspoon chili powder
6 eggs
8 ounces Monterey Jack cheese, cut
    into strips
1   16-ounce can refried beans
6 corn tortillas

- Sauté onion in oil in skillet until tender. Add tomatoes, green chilies, oregano, salt and chili powder; mix well. Simmer for 15 to 20 minutes or until mixture is thickened, stirring frequently.
- Break eggs 1 at a time into small dish. Slide carefully into sauce. Poach, covered, on low heat for 10 minutes or until firm.
- Add cheese strips. Cook, covered, for several minutes or until cheese is melted.
- Heat refried beans and tortillas while eggs are cooking.
- Spoon egg and sauce onto tortilla on serving plate. Spoon beans onto top of egg.
- Yield: 6 servings.

Approx Per Serving: Cal 447; Prot 24 g; Carbo 37 g; Fiber 11 g; T Fat 24 g;
47% Calories from Fat; Chol 248 mg; Sod 1313 mg.

Jean Burhop, **Western Region**
GFWC—Fallbrook Woman's Club, Fallbrook CA

CALIFORNIA DRIED APRICOT STUFFING

1 cup dried apricots
1 1/2 cups Grand Marnier liqueur
1 turkey heart
1 turkey liver
2 cups water
1 pound pork sausage
1 large onion, chopped

2 cups coarsely chopped celery
1/2 cup butter
1 pound prepared herb-seasoned
   stuffing mix
1 cup slivered almonds
1/2 teaspoon thyme
Salt and pepper to taste

- Combine apricots and 1 cup liqueur in small saucepan. Bring to a boil. Remove from heat.
- Combine turkey heart and liver with water in saucepan. Simmer until heart and liver are tender, stirring occasionally; drain, reserving stock. Chop heart and liver.
- Brown sausage in skillet, stirring until crumbly; drain.
- Sauté onion and celery in butter in skillet until tender.
- Combine apricot mixture, remaining liqueur, chopped heart and liver, reserved stock, sausage, onion and celery, stuffing mix, almonds, thyme, salt and pepper in bowl; mix well.
- Use to stuff 20 to 24-pound turkey and roast.
- Yield: 40 servings.

Approx Per Serving: Cal 152; Prot 3 g; Carbo 12 g; Fiber 1 g; T Fat 8 g;
50% Calories from Fat; Chol 23 mg; Sod 198 mg.

Alice T. Allen, **Western Region**
GFWC—Norwalk Woman's Club, Whittier CA

TEXAS CORN BREAD DRESSING

1   10-inch round corn bread
5 slices white bread, toasted
1 medium onion, chopped
1 1/2 cups celery, chopped
1 quart chicken broth

1 tablespoon sugar
Salt to taste
1 teaspoon pepper
6 eggs, beaten

- Crumble corn bread and toasted white bread into bowl. Add onion, celery, chicken broth, sugar, salt and pepper; mix well. Add eggs; mix well.
- Spoon into greased 9x13-inch baking dish.
- Bake at 350 degrees for 1 hour or until crusty around edges.
- Yield: 12 servings.

Approx Per Serving: Cal 188; Prot 8 g; Carbo 24 g; Fiber 1 g; T Fat 7 g;
34% Calories from Fat; Chol 120 mg; Sod 527 mg.

Frances Rudisill, **South Central Region**
GFWC—Cum Concilio Club, Nacogdoches TX

BAKED CHEESE GRITS

2 cups water
1 teaspoon salt
1 cup quick-cooking grits
3 cups shredded Cheddar cheese
1 or 2 cloves of garlic, minced

2 tablespoons Worcestershire sauce
Tabasco sauce to taste
Freshly ground pepper to taste
2 egg whites

- Bring water and salt to a boil in large saucepan. Stir in grits; return to a boil. Cook for 2½ minutes, stirring occasionally.
- Add cheese, garlic, Worcestershire sauce and seasonings; stir until well mixed. Let stand until cool.
- Beat egg whites until stiff peaks form. Fold into grits mixture.
- Pour into buttered 1½-quart casserole.
- Bake at 400 degrees for 20 minutes or until lightly browned.
- Yield: 8 servings.

Approx Per Serving: Cal 251; Prot 13 g; Carbo 17 g; Fiber 2 g; T Fat 14 g;
52% Calories from Fat; Chol 45 mg; Sod 579 mg.

Jeannine C. Faubion, GFWC President-Elect, 1992–94, **Southern Region**
Fort Myers FL

GREEN CHILIES AND HOMINY CASSEROLE

2 15-ounce cans golden hominy, drained
1 4-ounce can chopped green chilies, drained
¼ cup finely chopped onion

½ cup sour cream
¼ to ½ teaspoon chili powder
¼ cup chopped parsley
¾ cup shredded Cheddar cheese

- Combine hominy, green chilies, onion, sour cream, chili powder, parsley and half the cheese in bowl; mix well.
- Pour into lightly greased 2½-quart casserole. Sprinkle with remaining cheese.
- Bake, covered, at 350 degrees for 30 minutes.
- Yield: 6 servings.

Approx Per Serving: Cal 181; Prot 6 g; Carbo 19 g; Fiber <1 g; T Fat 9 g;
45% Calories from Fat; Chol 23 mg; Sod 644 mg.

Mildred Litt, **South Central Region**
GFWC—The Woman's Club of Albuquerque, Albuquerque NM

1965—*GFWC celebrated its Diamond Jubilee with a commemorative U.S. postage stamp.*

NOODLE SURPRISE CASSEROLE

8 ounces uncooked noodles, cooked
1 small head cabbage, finely shredded
4 green, yellow or red bell peppers, chopped
4 stalks celery, finely chopped
4 carrots, finely chopped

1 small zucchini
2 10-ounce cans broccoli-cheese soup
1 10-ounce can chicken broth
8 ounces Cheddar cheese, shredded
1 cup croutons

- Rinse cabbage in cold water; drain.
- Combine cabbage, bell peppers, celery and carrots in a small amount of water in saucepan. Cook until just tender; drain, reserving liquid.
- Cook zucchini in a small amount of water in saucepan until just tender; drain. Pat dry with paper towel. Cut into thin slices.
- Combine broccoli-cheese soup and mixture of reserved vegetable liquid and chicken broth in bowl to make sauce; mix well.
- Layer soup mixture, noodles and vegetable mixture 1/3 at a time in greased 8x14-inch casserole, adding 1/4 of the cheese on each vegetable mixture layer. Top with zucchini and remaining cheese. Sprinkle with croutons.
- Bake at 350 degrees for 30 minutes or until hot and bubbly.
- Yield: 8 servings.

Approx Per Serving: Cal 280; Prot 14 g; Carbo 32 g; Fiber 3 g; T Fat 12 g;
36% Calories from Fat; Chol 80 mg; Sod 379 mg.
Nutritional information does not include broccoli-cheese soup.

*Elizabeth K. McKinney, **Mid Atlantic Region***
GFWC—Glenside Woman's Club, Philadelphia PA

PASTA WITH BROCCOLI IN SWEET TOMATO SAUCE

4 cups broccoli flowerets
2 cloves of garlic, minced
1 tablespoon olive oil
1 28-ounce can tomatoes, chopped
2 tablespoons golden raisins, chopped

1/8 teaspoon cayenne pepper
1 1/2 tablespoons whole pine nuts or chopped almonds
6 ounces uncooked spaghetti
2 tablespoons minced parsley

- Cook broccoli in water to cover in saucepan for 2 to 3 minutes or until tender-crisp. Rinse under cold running water; drain.
- Sauté garlic in olive oil for 3 minutes or until golden brown. Add undrained tomatoes, raisins and cayenne pepper. Simmer for 15 minutes. Add pine nuts. Simmer for 5 minutes longer.
- Cook spaghetti using package directions; drain. Pour into warm serving bowl.
- Add broccoli to tomato sauce, tossing to mix well. Pour over spaghetti; sprinkle with parsley.
- Yield: 4 servings.

Approx Per Serving: Cal 286; Prot 10 g; Carbo 50 g; Fiber 8 g; T Fat 7 g;
20% Calories from Fat; Chol 0 mg; Sod 350 mg.

*Rita D'Arconte, **Mid Atlantic Region***
GFWC—The Woman's Club of Clinton, Inc., Lebanon NJ

ARROZ BLANCO CON ALCACHOFAS

2 cups uncooked rice
1/4 cup olive oil
1 medium onion, finely chopped
2 cloves of garlic, minced
5 cups chicken broth
1 cup fresh or frozen peas
12 fresh or frozen artichoke hearts, cooked

1 4-ounce can pimentos, cut into strips
Salt and pepper to taste
1/8 to 1/4 teaspoon saffron
1 tablespoon water

- Fry rice in oil in skillet until light brown. Add onion and garlic. Cook for 2 to 3 minutes longer or until onion is tender.
- Bring chicken broth to a boil in saucepan.
- Combine rice mixture, boiling broth, peas, artichoke hearts, pimentos, salt and pepper in bowl; mix well.
- Dissolve saffron in 1 tablespoon water. Add to mixture; mix well.
- Pour into greased 2-quart casserole.
- Bake at 350 degrees for 40 to 45 minutes or until all liquid has been absorbed.
- Yield: 6 servings.

Approx Per Serving: Cal 445; Prot 14 g; Carbo 75 g; Fiber 16 g; T Fat 11 g; 22% Calories from Fat; Chol 1 mg; Sod 762 mg.

Lori Hagge, **Western Region**
GFWC—Clayton Women's Club, Concord CA

WILD RICE AND BARLEY CASSEROLE

1 4-ounce can mushroom pieces
1 medium onion, chopped
1/2 cup butter

3 cups chicken stock
1/2 cup uncooked wild rice
1/2 cup uncooked barley

- Drain mushrooms, reserving liquid.
- Sauté mushrooms and onion in butter in skillet until onion is tender.
- Combine reserved mushroom liquid, mushrooms and onion, chicken stock, rice and barley in bowl; mix well.
- Pour into greased 2-quart casserole.
- Bake, covered, at 325 degrees for 1 1/2 hours. Garnish with minced parsley and celery leaves.
- Yield: 6 servings.

Approx Per Serving: Cal 274; Prot 7 g; Carbo 27 g; Fiber 3 g; T Fat 16 g; 53% Calories from Fat; Chol 42 mg; Sod 599 mg.

Esther B. Mork, **Mississippi Valley Region**
GFWC—Bonaventure Club, Marine on St. Croix MN

WILD RICE CASSEROLE

1 cup uncooked wild rice
4 cups seasoned chicken broth
2 cups sliced celery
1/2 cup thinly sliced onion
1/2 cup butter
1 4-ounce can sliced mushrooms
1 8-ounce can sliced water chestnuts
1/3 cup julienned pimento

1/3 cup chopped parsley
1 10-ounce can cream of mushroom soup
1/2 cup dry sherry or Sauterne
Marjoram and garlic salt to taste
3/4 cup sliced blanched almonds, toasted

- Combine wild rice and chicken broth in saucepan. Simmer on low heat for 1 1/2 to 2 hours or until rice is tender and fluffy. Remove from heat.
- Sauté celery and onion in butter in skillet until onion is tender. Drain mushrooms and water chestnuts, reserving liquid. Add mushrooms to onion mixture. Sauté for 5 minutes longer.
- Combine rice, sautéed vegetables, water chestnuts, pimento, parsley, mushroom soup, reserved liquid, sherry, marjoram and garlic salt in bowl; mix well. Pour into buttered casserole. Top with almonds.
- Bake at 350 degrees for 45 to 60 minutes or until hot and bubbly.
- Yield: 8 servings.

Approx Per Serving: Cal 326; Prot 9 g; Carbo 27 g; Fiber 3 g; T Fat 20 g; 56% Calories from Fat; Chol 32 mg; Sod 866 mg.

Virginia Weber Davis, **Great Lakes Region**
GFWC—Shawano Woman's Club, Shawano WI

SOUTHERN FRUIT RELISH

4 16-ounce cans chunky mixed fruit in light syrup
1/4 cup butter
1 cup minced dried apricots

1/2 cup golden raisins
3/4 cup molasses
3 tablespoons dry mustard

- Drain mixed fruit in colander for 1 hour.
- Melt butter in 3-quart saucepan over medium heat. Add drained fruit, apricots and raisins. Cook for 2 to 3 minutes or until fruit is hot and coated with butter, stirring gently. Stir in molasses and mustard. Bring to a boil. Reduce heat. Simmer for 15 minutes or until most of liquid is evaporated and fruit is glazed.
- Serve warm.
- Yield: 6 servings.

Approx Per Serving: Cal 456; Prot 3 g; Carbo 97 g; Fiber 5 g; T Fat 9 g; 18% Calories from Fat; Chol 21 mg; Sod 89 mg.

Pat Lewis, **Southern Region**
GFWC—Coterie Club, Athens AL

APRICOT AND RHUBARB JAM

6 cups chopped rhubarb
4 cups sugar
1 21-ounce can apricot pie filling

Grated rind of 1 orange
1 3-ounce package apricot or orange
   gelatin

- Combine chopped rhubarb and sugar in bowl; mix well. Let stand, covered, in refrigerator overnight.
- Pour into saucepan. Bring to a boil over medium heat. Add apricot filling and orange rind. Bring to a boil, stirring frequently. Add gelatin, stirring until dissolved.
- Pour into 6 hot sterilized 8-ounce jars, leaving ½ inch headspace; seal with 2-piece lids. Process in boiling water bath for 10 minutes.
- May store in refrigerator instead of sealing in jars. May vary by substituting cherry or strawberry pie filling mix and gelatin.
- Yield: 48 servings.

Approx Per Serving: Cal 86; Prot <1 g; Carbo 22 g; Fiber 1 g; T Fat <1 g;
0% Calories from Fat; Chol 0 mg; Sod 10 mg.

*Clarice Yttreness, **Mississippi Valley Region***
GFWC—Pleasant Study Club, Sioux Falls SD

STRAWBERRY WINE JELLY

4 cups sliced strawberries
4½ cups sugar
¼ cup Sangria

1 box powdered fruit pectin
½ cup water

- Layer strawberries and sugar in 6-quart saucepan. Add wine; let stand at room temperature for 4 to 5 hours. Bring to a full rolling boil over medium heat. Boil for 2 minutes, stirring constantly. Remove from heat.
- Mix fruit pectin and water in saucepan. Bring to a full rolling boil over medium heat. Boil for 1 minute, stirring constantly. Add to hot fruit mixture; mix well. Skim with metal spoon.
- Pour into 6 to 8 hot sterilized jelly jars, leaving ½ inch headspace; seal with 2-piece lids. Process in boiling water bath for 10 minutes.
- Yield: 50 servings.

Approx Per Serving: Cal 82; Prot <1 g; Carbo 21 g; Fiber 1 g; T Fat <1 g;
1% Calories from Fat; Chol 0 mg; Sod 9 mg.

*Marty Walker, **Southeastern Region***
GFWC—North Carolina Junior Sorosis, Wilmington NC

CRANBERRY CHUTNEY

3 cups fresh or frozen cranberries
1/2 cup chopped dates
1 cup chopped dried apricots
1/2 cup chopped onion
1/2 cup cider vinegar
1/2 cup light corn syrup

3/4 cup packed brown sugar
1 tablespoon grated orange rind
3/4 cup orange juice
1/2 teaspoon dry mustard
1/2 teaspoon salt
1/2 teaspoon ginger

- Combine all ingredients in large saucepan; mix well.
- Bring to a boil over medium heat. Reduce heat. Simmer, uncovered, for 15 to 20 minutes or until thickened and cranberries have popped.
- Chill in refrigerator. Serve with turkey or pork.
- Yield: 10 servings.

Approx Per Serving: Cal 236; Prot 1 g; Carbo 62 g; Fiber 4 g; T Fat <1 g; 1% Calories from Fat; Chol 0 mg; Sod 126 mg.

*Margaret Long Arnold, Honorary Past President, **New England Region**
GFWC—The Woman's Club, Concord NH*

CORN RELISH

Kernels of 6 ears of sweet corn
1 large stalk celery, finely chopped
1 1/3 large white onions, finely chopped
1 small green bell pepper, finely chopped

1/3 large red bell pepper, finely chopped
1/2 pound sugar
1 tablespoon plus 1 teaspoon salt
1 heaping teaspoon dry mustard
2 1/4 cups vinegar

- Combine all ingredients in saucepan; mix well. Bring to a boil over medium heat. Boil for 15 to 20 minutes, stirring frequently.
- Pour into 3 hot sterilized 1-pint jars leaving 1/2 inch headspace; seal with 2-piece lids. Process in boiling water bath for 10 minutes.
- Yield: 12 servings.

Approx Per Serving: Cal 128; Prot 2 g; Carbo 33 g; Fiber 2 g; T Fat 1 g; 4% Calories from Fat; Chol 0 mg; Sod 721 mg.

*Thelma M. Kennedy, **Mississippi Valley Region**
GFWC—Ogden Women's Club, Ogden IA*

1966—GFWC helped establish and fund the Congressional Medal of Honor Grove at Freedoms Foundation, Valley Forge, Pennsylvania. Funded building of archives to house records of Congressional Medal of Honor recipients.

OKRA PICKLES

3 pounds okra, rinsed, stems cut off
3 teaspoons dillseed
2 tablespoons salt

4 cups vinegar
4 cups water

- Place cleaned okra in 6 clean 1-pint jars. Add dillseed and salt to okra.
- Heat vinegar and water together in saucepan. Pour over okra, leaving ½ inch headspace; seal with 2-piece lids. Shake. Process in boiling water bath for 15 minutes. Cool. Store in cool place.
- Yield: 24 servings.

Approx Per Serving: Cal 23; Prot 1 g; Carbo 6 g; Fiber 1 g; T Fat <1 g;
3% Calories from Fat; Chol 0 mg; Sod 536 mg.

*Treva Kintner, **Southern Region***
GFWC—Kissimmee Woman's Club, Inc., Kissimmee FL

ZUCCHINI RELISH

12 cups finely ground zucchini
4 cups finely ground onions
4 red bell peppers, finely ground
4 green bell peppers, finely ground
½ cup salt

4 cups sugar
2¾ cups vinegar
1 tablespoon celery seed
2 teaspoons turmeric
1 teaspoon nutmeg

- Combine ground zucchini, onions, bell peppers and salt in bowl; mix well. Let stand, covered, in refrigerator for 12 hours; drain.
- Add sugar, vinegar, celery seed, turmeric and nutmeg; mix well. Pour into saucepan. Bring to a boil over medium heat, stirring occasionally. Reduce heat. Simmer for 30 minutes, stirring occasionally.
- Pour into 10 hot sterilized 1-pint jars, leaving ½ inch headspace; seal with 2-piece lids. Process in boiling water bath for 10 minutes.
- Serve on hot dogs and hamburgers. Mix with mayonnaise or salad dressing for tartar sauce.
- Yield: 160 (2-tablespoon) servings.

Approx Per Serving: Cal 25; Prot <1 g; Carbo 6 g; Fiber <1 g; T Fat <1 g;
2% Calories from Fat; Chol 0 mg; Sod 321 mg.

*Eleanor A. Shaner, **Middle Atlantic Region***
GFWC—Woman's Club of Oley Valley, Fleetwood PA

BREADS

The solarium on the second floor
is the setting for this Louis XIV
style fruitwood finish wingback
chair and a specially inscribed
Wesleyan Wedgwood Blue
Calico teapot, given by
Mrs. Anna Onstott of Indiana.

FLATBROD

4 cups flour	1 teaspoon baking soda
1 tablespoon sugar	5 tablespoons shortening
1/2 teaspoon salt	1³/4 cups buttermilk

- Combine flour, sugar, salt and baking soda in bowl; mix well.
- Cut in shortening until crumbly. Add enough buttermilk to make a stiff dough, stirring to mix well. Pinch off walnut-sized pieces of dough. Roll very thin on floured surface. Place on baking sheet.
- Bake at 325 degrees for 10 minutes or until crisp but not brown.
- Remove to wire rack to cool completely. Store in covered container.
- Yield: 20 servings.

Approx Per Serving: Cal 130; Prot 3 g; Carbo 21 g; Fiber 1 g; T Fat 4 g; 25% Calories from Fat; Chol 1 mg; Sod 117 mg.

Gladys Solyst, **Mississippi Valley Region**
GFWC—KIP Study Club, Kerkhoven MN

LEFSE

8 cups hot riced potatoes	1 tablespoon salt
1 cup margarine, softened	4 cups (scant) flour

- Combine hot potatoes, margarine and salt in bowl; mix well. Let stand, uncovered to avoid steaming, until cold. Add flour; mix well.
- Shape into 1/3-cup-sized balls. Place on large plate. Chill, covered, in refrigerator.
- Remove potato balls from refrigerator 1 at a time. Roll paper-thin on lightly floured surface.
- Bake on 450 to 475-degree griddle until brown on both sides. Remove to large plate. Cover with towel and large pan cover. Let steam until cool. Fold; store in plastic bags. May be frozen.
- Yield: 30 (plate-size) servings.

Approx Per Serving: Cal 177; Prot 3 g; Carbo 27 g; Fiber 2 g; T Fat 6 g; 32% Calories from Fat; Chol 0 mg; Sod 289 mg.

Elaine J. Gehler, **Great Lakes Region**
GFWC—Ladysmith Women's Study Club, Ladysmith WI

1966—*The Heeko Club of Pawhuska, Oklahoma, established a museum to show their area's cultural heritage and Indian artifacts. The project was part of a program the club initiated to revive the economic and cultural aspects of their town.*

APPLE AND NUT COFFEE CAKE

1/2 cup butter, softened
1 cup sugar
2 eggs
1 teaspoon vanilla extract
2 cups flour
1 teaspoon baking powder
1 teaspoon baking soda

1/4 teaspoon salt
1 cup sour cream
2 cups finely chopped apples
1/2 cup packed brown sugar
2 tablespoons butter
1 teaspoon cinnamon
1/2 cup chopped pecans

- Cream 1/2 cup butter and sugar in mixer bowl until light and fluffy. Beat in eggs 1 at a time. Add vanilla; mix well.
- Mix flour, baking powder, baking soda and salt together. Add to creamed mixture alternately with sour cream. Stir in apples. Pour into greased and floured 9x13-inch baking dish.
- Combine brown sugar, 2 tablespoons butter and cinnamon in bowl; mix well. Stir in pecans. Sprinkle over coffee cake.
- Bake at 350 degrees for 35 to 40 minutes or until brown.
- Yield: 15 servings.

Approx Per Serving: Cal 295; Prot 3 g; Carbo 39 g; Fiber 1 g; T Fat 15 g;
44% Calories from Fat; Chol 56 mg; Sod 199 mg.

Patricia G. Pinkston, **Great Lakes Region**
GFWC—Sesser Woman's Club, Sesser IL

BLUEBERRY BUCKLE COFFEE CAKE

3/4 cup sugar
1/4 cup shortening
1 egg
1/2 cup milk
2 cups sifted flour
2 teaspoons baking powder

1/2 teaspoon salt
2 cups well drained blueberries
1/2 cup sugar
1/3 cup sifted flour
1/2 teaspoon cinnamon
1/4 cup butter, softened

- Beat 3/4 cup sugar, shortening and egg in bowl until well blended. Add milk and mixture of 2 cups flour, baking powder and salt alternately, mixing well after each addition.
- Fold in blueberries. Pour into greased 9-inch round or square baking dish.
- Mix 1/2 cup sugar, 1/3 cup flour and cinnamon in small bowl. Add butter; mix until crumbly. Sprinkle over batter.
- Bake at 375 degrees for 45 minutes.
- May substitute other favorite fruit for blueberries.
- Yield: 8 servings.

Approx Per Serving: Cal 391; Prot 5 g; Carbo 63 g; Fiber 2 g; T Fat 14 g;
31% Calories from Fat; Chol 44 mg; Sod 283 mg.

Joan Anello, **Middle Atlantic Region**
GFWC—Latham Woman's Club, Latham NY

WILD BLUEBERRY COFFEE CAKE

1/4 cup corn oil
1/2 cup milk
1 egg, beaten
3/4 cup sugar
1 1/2 cups flour
2 teaspoons baking powder

1/2 teaspoon salt
1 cup blueberries
1/2 cup sugar
1 tablespoon flour
1/2 teaspoon cinnamon
1 1/2 tablespoons melted butter

- Combine corn oil, milk and egg in mixer bowl; beat well.
- Mix 3/4 cup sugar, flour, baking powder and salt together. Add to liquid ingredients; mix well.
- Fold in blueberries. Pour into greased 9x9-inch baking dish.
- Combine 1/2 cup sugar, 1 tablespoon flour, cinnamon and butter in bowl; mix well. Sprinkle over top of coffee cake.
- Bake at 375 degrees for 25 minutes.
- Yield: 9 servings.

Approx Per Serving: Cal 284; Prot 4 g; Carbo 47 g; Fiber 1 g; T Fat 9 g;
29% Calories from Fat; Chol 31 mg; Sod 223 mg.

Polly C. Spratt, ***New England Region***
GFWC—Norumbega-Bangori Woman's Club, Bucksport ME

SOUR CREAM-CRANBERRY COFFEE CAKE

1/2 cup margarine, softened
1 cup sugar
2 eggs
1 teaspoon baking soda
1 teaspoon baking powder
1/2 teaspoon salt
2 cups flour

2 cups sour cream
1 teaspoon almond extract
1 8-ounce can whole cranberry sauce
1/2 cup chopped pecans
3/4 cup confectioners' sugar
2 tablespoons warm water
1/2 teaspoon almond extract

- Cream margarine and sugar in mixer bowl until light and fluffy. Beat in eggs 1 at a time.
- Mix baking soda, baking powder, salt and flour together. Add to creamed mixture alternately with sour cream and 1 teaspoon almond extract, beating well after each addition.
- Layer batter and cranberry sauce 1/2 at a time in greased and floured 8-inch tube pan. Sprinkle with pecans.
- Bake at 350 degrees for 55 minutes. Cool in pan for 10 minutes. Remove to serving plate to cool completely.
- Combine confectioners' sugar, warm water and 1/2 teaspoon almond extract in mixer bowl; beat well. Spread over coffee cake.
- Yield: 16 servings.

Approx Per Serving: Cal 297; Prot 4 g; Carbo 38 g; Fiber 1 g; T Fat 15 g;
45% Calories from Fat; Chol 39 mg; Sod 234 mg.

Hazel A. Muise, ***New England Region***
GFWC—Cosmo Club, Wakefield MA

MESILLA VALLEY NUT RING

1/2 cup butter
3/4 cup packed brown sugar
1/3 cup maple-flavored syrup
1 cup broken pecans

2 10-count cans butter-flavored
  biscuits
1/2 cup sugar
Cinnamon to taste

■ Melt butter in saucepan over medium heat. Add brown sugar and syrup, stirring until smooth. Stir in pecans. Pour syrup into greased bundt pan.
■ Separate biscuits; dip in sugar to coat both sides. Sprinkle with cinnamon on both sides; stand biscuits on edge around bundt pan.
■ Bake at 350 degrees for 35 minutes. Cool in pan for 5 minutes.
■ Remove to buttered serving plate.
■ Yield: 16 servings.

Approx Per Serving: Cal 274; Prot 2 g; Carbo 38 g; Fiber 1 g; T Fat 13 g; 43% Calories from Fat; Chol 17 mg; Sod 369 mg.

Brenda Gail Hatcher, **South Central Region**
GFWC—Mesilla Valley Woman's Club, Las Cruces NM

SOUR CREAM-PUMPKIN COFFEE CAKE

1/2 cup margarine, softened
3/4 cup sugar
1 teaspoon vanilla extract
3 eggs
2 cups flour
1 teaspoon baking powder
1 teaspoon baking soda
1 cup sour cream

1 16-ounce can pumpkin
1 egg, beaten
1/3 cup sugar
1 teaspoon pumpkin pie spice
1 cup packed brown sugar
1/3 cup margarine, softened
2 teaspoons cinnamon
1 cup chopped walnuts

■ Cream 1/2 cup margarine, 3/4 cup sugar and vanilla in mixer bowl until light and fluffy. Beat in 3 eggs 1 at a time.
■ Mix flour, baking powder and baking soda together. Add to creamed mixture alternately with sour cream.
■ Combine pumpkin, 1 egg, 1/3 cup sugar and pie spice in bowl; mix well.
■ Combine brown sugar, 1/3 cup margarine and cinnamon in small bowl; mix well. Stir in walnuts.
■ Layer half the batter, half the brown sugar mixture, all the pumpkin mixture, remaining batter and brown sugar mixture in greased 9x13-inch baking dish, spreading each layer to corners of dish.
■ Bake at 325 degrees for 45 to 50 minutes or until brown.
■ Yield: 15 servings.

Approx Per Serving: Cal 392; Prot 5 g; Carbo 50 g; Fiber 1 g; T Fat 20 g; 45% Calories from Fat; Chol 64 mg; Sod 233 mg.

Barbara A. Chivalette, **Middle Atlantic Region**
GFWC—Aston Woman's Club, Aston PA

RASPBERRY-CREAM CHEESE COFFEE CAKE

2¹/₄ cups flour	1 egg
³/₄ cup sugar	1 teaspoon almond extract
³/₄ cup margarine	8 ounces cream cheese, softened
¹/₂ teaspoon baking powder	¹/₄ cup sugar
¹/₂ teaspoon baking soda	1 egg
¹/₄ teaspoon salt	¹/₂ cup raspberry preserves
³/₄ cup sour cream	¹/₂ cup sliced almonds

- Grease and flour bottom and sides of springform pan.
- Combine flour and ³/₄ cup sugar in bowl; mix well. Cut in margarine until crumbly. Reserve 1 cup crumb mixture. Add baking powder, baking soda, salt, sour cream, 1 egg and almond extract to remaining mixture; mix well. Spread batter over bottom and 2 inches up sides of prepared pan. Batter should be ¹/₄ inch thick on sides.
- Combine cream cheese, ¹/₄ cup sugar and 1 egg in mixer bowl; mix well. Pour over batter layer.
- Spoon raspberry preserves over cream cheese layer; top with reserved crumb mixture. Sprinkle with almonds.
- Bake at 350 degrees for 45 to 55 minutes or until coffee cake tests done. Cool in pan for 15 minutes. Remove sides of pan. Serve warm or cold.
- Yield: 16 servings.

Approx Per Serving: Cal 316; Prot 5 g; Carbo 35 g; Fiber 1 g; T Fat 18 g;
51% Calories from Fat; Chol 47 mg; Sod 228 mg.

*Linda S. Love, **Southeastern Region***
GFWC—Rutherford Women's Club, Smyrna TN

BLUEBERRY JOHNNYCAKES

1 pint blueberries	1 teaspoon salt
1 cup sugar	³/₄ cup plus 2 tablespoons milk
1 cup white cornmeal	2 eggs, beaten
1 cup flour	¹/₄ cup melted butter
1 teaspoon baking powder	

- Rinse blueberries; drain. Combine blueberries and sugar in bowl, tossing gently to coat blueberries.
- Sift cornmeal, flour, baking powder and salt together into bowl. Add milk, eggs and butter gradually, mixing well after each addition. Fold in blueberries.
- Spoon into 2 greased and floured 8-inch round baking pans.
- Bake at 350 degrees for 25 minutes or until light brown on top.
- Yield: 16 servings.

Approx Per Serving: Cal 162; Prot 3 g; Carbo 29 g; Fiber 1 g; T Fat 4 g;
23% Calories from Fat; Chol 36 mg; Sod 194 mg.

*Betty O'Halloran, **New England Region***
GFWC—Windham Women's Club, Salem NH

CORNMEAL BATTER BREAD

1 cup cornmeal
1 teaspoon salt
2 cups boiling water
1 cup milk

2 eggs
2 teaspoons baking powder
1½ tablespoons butter

- Combine cornmeal and salt in bowl; mix well. Add boiling water; stir until well mixed. Add milk, eggs and baking powder; mix well.
- Melt butter in 2-quart baking dish in 425-degree oven. Pour batter into hot butter.
- Bake at 425 degrees for 35 minutes.
- Yield: 6 servings.

Approx Per Serving: Cal 162; Prot 5 g; Carbo 20 g; Fiber 2 g; T Fat 6 g; 36% Calories from Fat; Chol 84 mg; Sod 529 mg.

*Beth Baskin, **Southeastern Region***
GFWC—Henry Clay Woman's Club, Ashland VA

BEST CORN BREAD EVER

1¼ cups self-rising cornmeal
8 ounces plain nonfat yogurt
2 eggs
1 8-ounce can cream-style corn

2 teaspoons baking powder
1 tablespoon sugar
¼ cup safflower or vegetable oil

- Combine all ingredients in bowl; mix well. Pour into greased 8x8-inch baking pan or into muffin cups.
- Bake at 425 degrees for 20 minutes or until golden brown.
- Yield: 12 servings.

Approx Per Serving: Cal 144; Prot 4 g; Carbo 19 g; Fiber <1 g; T Fat 6 g; 36% Calories from Fat; Chol 36 mg; Sod 372 mg.

*Julie E. Tolbert, **Southeastern Region***
GFWC—Waynesboro Juniors, Waynesboro VA

1972—*The Junior Woman's Club of Flint, Michigan, established a permanent recycling center for collection of glass, paper and aluminum. Proceeds from the recyclable were used to landscape the traffic triangle.*

BLACK-EYED PEA CORN BREAD

1 pound sausage
1 medium onion, chopped
1 cup white cornmeal
1/2 cup flour
1 teaspoon salt
1/2 teaspoon baking soda
2 eggs

1 cup buttermilk
1/2 cup oil
1   4-ounce can chopped green chilies
3/4 cup cream-style corn
8 ounces Cheddar cheese, shredded
1   15-ounce can black-eyed peas,
    drained

- Brown sausage with onion in skillet, stirring until crumbly; drain.
- Combine cornmeal, flour, salt and baking soda in bowl; mix well.
- Beat eggs, buttermilk and oil together in bowl. Add to dry ingredients, stirring just until mixed. Stir in sausage, chilies, corn, cheese and black-eyed peas. Pour into hot greased skillet.
- Bake at 350 degrees for 50 to 55 minutes or until bread tests done.
- Yield: 10 servings.

Approx Per Serving: Cal 420; Prot 16 g; Carbo 29 g; Fiber 5 g; T Fat 27 g;
58% Calories from Fat; Chol 85 mg; Sod 973 mg.

Alma St. John, **South Central Region**
GFWC—Amici Woman's Club, Stuttgart AR

SOUTHERN BROCCOLI CORN BREAD

1   7-ounce package corn muffin mix
8 ounces Cheddar cheese, shredded
4 eggs
1/2 cup melted margarine

1 medium onion, chopped
1   10-ounce package chopped
    broccoli, thawed

- Combine muffin mix, cheese, eggs, margarine, onion and broccoli in bowl; mix well. Pour into hot greased 9-inch cast-iron skillet.
- Bake at 350 degrees for 30 minutes or until brown.
- Yield: 6 servings.

Approx Per Serving: Cal 428; Prot 16 g; Carbo 17 g; Fiber 2 g; T Fat 33 g;
69% Calories from Fat; Chol 182 mg; Sod 618 mg.

Montae J. Cain, **Southern Region**
GFWC—Worthwhile Study Club, Jasper AL

1974—*GFWC started an alcohol and drug abuse education program for women and children.*

BROCCOLI CORN BREAD

3/4 cup margarine
12 ounces small curd cottage cheese
4 eggs
1/2 cup milk

1 10-ounce package frozen chopped broccoli, thawed
1/2 to 3/4 cup chopped onion
2 7-ounce packages corn bread mix

- Melt margarine in 9x13-inch baking pan in 350-degree oven.
- Combine cottage cheese, eggs and milk in bowl; mix well. Add broccoli, onion and corn bread mix; mix well. Pour into melted margarine.
- Bake at 350 degrees for 45 minutes.
- Yield: 12 servings.

Approx Per Serving: Cal 238; Prot 8 g; Carbo 15 g; Fiber 1 g; T Fat 16 g;
61% Calories from Fat; Chol 77 mg; Sod 447 mg.

Jeanne Coffield, **South Central Region**
GFWC—The Thursday Reading Club, Rockdale TX

CORN FINGERS

1/2 cup yellow cornmeal
1/2 cup flour
3 tablespoons sugar
1 1/4 teaspoons baking powder
1/2 teaspoon salt
1 teaspoon hot red pepper flakes

1/4 cup melted unsalted butter
1/3 cup whipping cream
1/3 cup milk
1 egg yolk
1 cup cooked corn kernels
1 egg white, stiffly beaten

- Preheat 2 greased cast-iron corn finger molds in 425-degree oven.
- Combine cornmeal, flour, sugar, baking powder, salt and red pepper flakes in bowl; mix well.
- Combine butter, cream, milk, egg yolk and corn in bowl; whisk lightly. Stir into dry ingredients just until moistened. Fold in egg white. Fill hot molds 3/4 full.
- Bake at 425 degrees for 15 minutes or until tops are golden brown. Invert onto wire rack. Serve warm or at room temperature.
- Yield: 12 servings.

Approx Per Serving: Cal 135; Prot 2 g; Carbo 16 g; Fiber 1 g; T Fat 7 g;
47% Calories from Fat; Chol 38 mg; Sod 138 mg.

Patricia B. Jordan, **Southeastern Region**
GFWC—Mocksville Woman's Club, Advance NC

CRAWFISH CORN BREAD

1 cup yellow cornmeal
1/2 teaspoon baking soda
1 teaspoon salt
1/3 cup olive oil
4 ounces egg substitute

1 16-ounce can cream-style corn
8 ounces Cheddar cheese, shredded
2 jalapeño peppers, chopped
1 cup chopped onion
1 pound crawfish tails

- Combine first 9 ingredients in bowl; mix just until moistened. Stir in crawfish tails. Pour into greased 9x13-inch baking pan.
- Bake at 375 degrees for 50 minutes or until golden brown.
- Cool in pan for 20 minutes before cutting into squares.
- May also be served as appetizer.
- Yield: 15 servings.

Approx Per Serving: Cal 197; Prot 12 g; Carbo 14 g; Fiber 2 g; T Fat 11 g; 48% Calories from Fat; Chol 58 mg; Sod 379 mg.

*Kitty Hensgens, **South Central Region***
GFWC—Attakapas Study Club, Crowley LA

CAJUN JALAPEÑO CORN BREAD

1 7-ounce package jalapeño corn
   bread mix
1 cup flour
1 cup cornmeal
2 teaspoons baking powder
1 teaspoon salt
1 tablespoon red pepper
1 teaspoon garlic powder
2 eggs, beaten

1 17-ounce can cream-style corn
1 16-ounce can whole kernel corn
1 cup shredded Cheddar cheese
1 cup water
1/4 cup vegetable oil
1/2 cup chopped green bell pepper
1 cup chopped onion
2 jalapeño peppers, chopped

- Combine first 7 ingredients in bowl; mix well.
- Combine eggs and remaining ingredients in bowl; mix well. Add to dry ingredients; mix well. Pour into greased 9x13-inch baking dish.
- Bake at 375 degrees for 40 minutes.
- May add 1 pound browned ground beef to batter for main dish.
- Yield: 24 servings.

Approx Per Serving: Cal 133; Prot 4 g; Carbo 19 g; Fiber 2 g; T Fat 5 g; 33% Calories from Fat; Chol 23 mg; Sod 298 mg.

*Gwen Frugé, **South Central Region***
GFWC—Unique Club, Opelousas LA

JALAPEÑO CORN BREAD

2¹/₂ cups cornmeal
1 cup flour
2 tablespoons sugar
1 tablespoon salt
4 teaspoons baking powder
2 cups buttermilk

3 eggs
1 16-ounce can cream-style corn
¹/₂ cup vegetable oil
1 large onion, finely chopped
7 jalapeño peppers, finely chopped
2 cups shredded Cheddar cheese

- Combine first 5 ingredients in bowl; mix well.
- Combine buttermilk and eggs in bowl; beat well. Add to dry ingredients, stirring just until moistened. Add corn, oil, onion, peppers and cheese; mix well. Pour into 2 greased 8x12-inch baking pans.
- Bake at 425 degrees for 35 minutes.
- May substitute cooked fresh or frozen corn for canned corn. May keep in refrigerator for several days before baking.
- Yield: 18 servings.

> *Approx Per Serving:* Cal 254; Prot 8 g; Carbo 29 g; Fiber 2 g; T Fat 12 g;
> 42% Calories from Fat; Chol 50 mg; Sod 619 mg.

> *Shirley C. Morgan,* **South Central Region**
> *GFWC—England Cosmopolitan Club, England AR*

CORN LIGHT BREAD

1¹/₂ cups self-rising cornmeal
¹/₂ cup flour
¹/₂ cup sugar

1¹/₂ cups buttermilk
¹/₄ cup melted shortening

- Combine all ingredients in bowl; mix well. Let stand at room temperature for 20 minutes. Stir lightly; pour into greased 5x9-inch loaf pan.
- Bake at 350 degrees for 1 hour or until bread tests done. Cool in pan for 10 minutes. Remove to wire rack to cool completely.
- Yield: 10 servings.

> *Approx Per Serving:* Cal 209; Prot 4 g; Carbo 35 g; Fiber <1 g; T Fat 6 g;
> 25% Calories from Fat; Chol 1 mg; Sod 381 mg.

> *Juanita R. Nash,* **Southeastern Region**
> *GFWC—Waverly Woman's Club, Waverly TN*

MEXICAN CORN BREAD

1 cup yellow cornmeal	1 cup cream-style corn
1 cup flour	¼ cup chopped onion
1 tablespoon baking powder	2 tablespoons chopped green chilies
1 teaspoon salt	2 tablespoons chopped pimento
1 egg	¼ cup butter
1 cup milk	½ cup shredded Cheddar cheese

- Combine first 4 ingredients in bowl; mix well.
- Combine egg, milk and corn in bowl; mix well.
- Sauté onion, green chilies and pimento in butter in skillet until onion is tender.
- Combine all mixtures. Add cheese, stirring just until mixed. Pour into buttered 8x8-inch baking pan.
- Bake at 400 degrees for 35 to 40 minutes or until bread tests done.
- Yield: 16 servings.

Approx Per Serving: Cal 128; Prot 4 g; Carbo 17 g; Fiber 1 g; T Fat 5 g; 36% Calories from Fat; Chol 27 mg; Sod 298 mg.

Kimberleigh G. Ploszaj, **South Central Region**
GFWC—Paradise Valley Junior Woman's Club, Phoenix AR

WEST VIRGINIA FRIED MUSH

3 cups water	1 cup cold water
1 cup yellow cornmeal	

- Pour 3 cups water into microwave-safe pitcher.
- Microwave on High until water comes to a boil.
- Mix cornmeal with remaining 1 cup cold water in bowl. Stir into boiling water with wooden spoon.
- Microwave on High for 10 minutes, stirring after 5 minutes.
- Pour into glass 10x13-inch dish. Place in microwave immediately.
- Microwave on High for 2 minutes.
- Cool, covered, in refrigerator overnight. Cut into squares.
- Fry in nonstick skillet on high heat until brown on both sides. Serve with margarine and syrup.
- Yield: 15 servings.

Approx Per Serving: Cal 34; Prot 1 g; Carbo 7 g; Fiber 1 g; T Fat <1 g; 3% Calories from Fat; Chol 0 mg; Sod <1 mg.

Barbara Hilling, **Southeastern Region**
GFWC—Mountaineer Woman's Club, Morgantown WV

ILLINOIS CORN SPOON BREAD

2 eggs, slightly beaten
1 7-ounce package corn muffin mix
1 8-ounce can cream-style corn
1 8-ounce can whole kernel corn
1 cup sour cream
1/2 cup melted butter

- Combine eggs, corn muffin mix, cream-style corn, whole kernel corn, sour cream and melted butter in bowl; mix well. Spread in buttered 7x11-inch baking dish.
- Bake at 350 degrees for 35 minutes.
- Yield: 12 servings.

Approx Per Serving: Cal 180; Prot 3 g; Carbo 13 g; Fiber 1 g; T Fat 14 g; 66% Calories from Fat; Chol 65 mg; Sod 262 mg.

Jacquelyn Pierce, **Great Lakes Region**
GFWC—Elgin Woman's Club, Elgin IL

KENTUCKY SPOON BREAD

1 cup boiling water
1/2 cup self-rising cornmeal
1 tablespoon margarine
1/2 cup milk
2 eggs, beaten

- Pour boiling water over cornmeal and margarine in bowl; mix well. Add milk; mix well. Beat in eggs. Pour into greased 1-quart baking dish.
- Bake at 400 degrees for 20 to 25 minutes or until set and sightly brown.
- Yield: 4 servings.

Approx Per Serving: Cal 157; Prot 6 g; Carbo 18 g; Fiber 0 g; T Fat 7 g; 40% Calories from Fat; Chol 111 mg; Sod 366 mg.

Sue D. Hamm, **Southeastern Region**
GFWC—Mt. Vernon Woman's Club, Mt. Vernon KY

1981—*Members of the Vermont Federation of Women's Clubs helped prepare living quarters for participants in the National Special Olympics.*

TWO-PEPPER CORN BREAD

1 cup buttermilk
1/2 cup egg substitute
1 tablespoon vegetable oil
1 tablespoon honey
1 red bell pepper, finely chopped
1 4-ounce can chopped green chilies,
   drained

1 cup flour
3/4 cup yellow cornmeal
2 teaspoons baking powder
1/2 teaspoon salt
1/2 teaspoon baking soda

- Spray 8x8-inch baking pan with nonstick cooking spray.
- Combine buttermilk, egg substitute, oil, honey, bell pepper and green chilies in bowl; mix well.
- Combine flour and remaining ingredients in bowl; mix well. Add buttermilk mixture, stirring just until moistened. Pour into prepared pan.
- Bake at 450 degrees for 25 minutes. Let cool in pan for 5 minutes. Cut into squares and serve.
- Yield: 4 servings.

Approx Per Serving: Cal 319; Prot 12 g; Carbo 55 g; Fiber 3 g; T Fat 6 g;
16% Calories from Fat; Chol 3 mg; Sod 856 mg.

*Beverley J. Scholl, **South Central Region**
GFWC—The Woman's Club of Colorado Springs, Colorado Springs CO*

EASY APPLESAUCE BREAD

3 1/2 cups flour
1 teaspoon salt
2 teaspoons baking soda
3 cups sugar
2/3 cup water

1 cup vegetable oil
4 eggs
2 cups unsweetened applesauce
1 cup chopped black walnuts

- Combine flour, salt and baking soda in mixer bowl; mix well. Add sugar, water, oil, eggs and applesauce. Beat for 3 minutes at medium speed. Stir in walnuts. Pour into 3 greased 5x9-inch loaf pans.
- Bake at 350 degrees for 1 hour.
- Yield: 24 servings.

Approx Per Serving: Cal 297; Prot 4 g; Carbo 42 g; Fiber 1 g; T Fat 13 g;
39% Calories from Fat; Chol 36 mg; Sod 170 mg.

*Alice S. Hopkins, **Southeastern Region**
GFWC—Pratt Woman's Club, Pratt WV*

APPLE AND CRANBERRY CHRISTMAS LOAVES

2/3 cup butter, softened
11/3 cups sugar
4 eggs
2 cups applesauce
1/2 cup milk
4 cups sifted flour

2 teaspoons baking powder
1 teaspoon baking soda
1 teaspoon salt
2 tablespoons grated lemon rind
1 cup cranberries, chopped

- Cream butter and sugar in mixer bowl until light and fluffy. Beat in eggs 1 at a time. Stir in applesauce and milk.
- Sift flour, baking powder, baking soda and salt together. Add to creamed mixture. Add lemon rind and cranberries; mix well. Pour into 2 greased 5x9-inch loaf pans.
- Bake at 350 degrees for 1 hour.
- Cool in pans for several minutes. Invert onto wire rack to cool completely.
- Yield: 24 servings.

Approx Per Serving: Cal 185; Prot 3 g; Carbo 29 g; Fiber 1 g; T Fat 6 g;
31% Calories from Fat; Chol 50 mg; Sod 208 mg.

*Alice T. Smith, **New England Region***
GFWC—Meriden Woman's Club, Meriden CT

APRICOT-PECAN TEA LOAF

2/3 cup milk
2 tablespoons lemon juice
1/3 cup butter, softened
1/2 cup sugar
1/4 cup packed light brown sugar
2 eggs
2 cups flour

11/2 teaspoons baking powder
3/4 teaspoon baking soda
1/4 teaspoon salt
1 cup chopped dried apricots
1 tablespoon grated lemon rind
1/2 cup chopped pecans

- Mix milk and lemon juice together.
- Cream butter, sugar and brown sugar in mixer bowl until light and fluffy. Beat in eggs 1 at a time.
- Mix flour, baking powder, baking soda and salt together. Add to creamed mixture alternately with milk mixture, beating well after each addition. Stir in apricots, lemon rind and pecans. Pour into greased 5x9-inch loaf pan.
- Bake at 350 degrees for 1 hour and 5 minutes or until bread tests done.
- Yield: 12 servings.

Approx Per Serving: Cal 282; Prot 5 g; Carbo 45 g; Fiber 3 g; T Fat 10 g;
31% Calories from Fat; Chol 51 mg; Sod 202 mg.

*Madeline Kirby, **Southeastern Region***
GFWC—Sebrell Club, Capron VA

KONA INN BANANA BREAD

1 cup butter, softened
2 cups sugar
6 ripe bananas, mashed
4 eggs, beaten

2¹/₂ cups cake flour
2 teaspoons baking soda
1 teaspoon salt

- Cream butter and sugar in mixer bowl until light and fluffy. Beat in mashed bananas and eggs.
- Sift flour, baking soda and salt together. Add to creamed mixture, stirring just until moistened. Pour into 2 greased 5x9-inch loaf pans.
- Bake at 350 degrees for 45 to 60 minutes or until bread tests done.
- Cool in pans for 10 minutes. Remove to wire rack to cool completely.
- Yield: 24 servings.

Approx Per Serving: Cal 213; Prot 2 g; Carbo 32 g; Fiber 1 g; T Fat 9 g; 37% Calories from Fat; Chol 56 mg; Sod 234 mg.

Marilyn Coy, **Western Region**
GFWC—St. Helena Junior Women's Club, St. Helena CA

BLUEBERRY-LEMON LOAF

1¹/₂ cups flour
1 teaspoon baking powder
¹/₄ teaspoon salt
6 tablespoons butter, softened
1 cup sugar
2 eggs

2 teaspoons grated lemon rind
¹/₂ cup milk
1¹/₂ cups blueberries
¹/₃ cup sugar
3 tablespoons lemon juice

- Mix flour, baking powder and salt together.
- Cream butter and 1 cup sugar in mixer bowl until light and fluffy. Beat in eggs 1 at a time. Add flour mixture and lemon rind alternately with milk. Fold in blueberries. Pour into greased 5x9-inch loaf pan.
- Bake at 325 degrees for 1 hour and 15 minutes or until bread tests done.
- Combine ¹/₃ cup sugar and lemon juice in saucepan. Bring to a boil, stirring frequently. Remove from heat.
- Pierce holes in top of bread with wooden pick. Pour glaze over bread. Cool in pan for 30 minutes. Remove to wire rack to cool completely.
- Yield: 12 servings.

Approx Per Serving: Cal 224; Prot 3 g; Carbo 38 g; Fiber 1 g; T Fat 7 g; 29% Calories from Fat; Chol 52 mg; Sod 138 mg.

Virginia Ditmars, **Middle Atlantic Region**
GFWC—Pennington Woman's Club, Pennington NJ

SOUR CREAM-BLUEBERRY BREAD

2 cups flour
1 teaspoon baking soda
1/2 teaspoon salt
1/2 teaspoon cinnamon
1 cup butter, softened
3/4 cup sugar

2 eggs
1 cup mashed bananas
1/2 cup sour cream
1 cup blueberries
1/2 cup chopped walnuts

- Sift flour, baking soda, salt and cinnamon together.
- Cream butter and sugar in mixer bowl until light and fluffy. Beat in eggs, bananas and sour cream. Fold in blueberries and walnuts. Pour into greased and floured 5x9-inch loaf pan.
- Bake at 350 degrees for 1 hour or until bread tests done.
- Cool completely in pan. Remove to serving plate.
- Yield: 12 servings.

Approx Per Serving: Cal 349; Prot 5 g; Carbo 36 g; Fiber 2 g; T Fat 22 g;
55% Calories from Fat; Chol 81 mg; Sod 305 mg.

*Doreen Duford, **New England Region***
GFWC—Manchester Juniors, Manchester NH

CRANBERRY-CHEESE BREAD

2 cups flour
1 cup sugar
1 1/2 teaspoons baking powder
1/2 teaspoon baking soda
1/2 teaspoon salt
2 teaspoons grated orange rind

2 tablespoons shortening
Juice of 1 orange
1 egg, beaten
1 1/2 cups shredded Cheddar cheese
1 cup cranberry halves
1/2 cup finely chopped walnuts

- Mix first 6 ingredients together in bowl. Cut in shortening until crumbly.
- Add enough water to orange juice to measure 3/4 cup. Beat orange juice and egg into dry ingredients. Stir in cheese, cranberries and walnuts. Pour into greased 5x9-inch loaf pan.
- Bake at 350 degrees for 60 minutes or until bread tests done. Cool in pan for several minutes. Remove to wire rack to cool completely.
- Yield: 12 servings.

Approx Per Serving: Cal 262; Prot 7 g; Carbo 36 g; Fiber 1 g; T Fat 11 g;
36% Calories from Fat; Chol 33 mg; Sod 259 mg.

*Gail LeShane, **New England Region***
GFWC—Nashua Jr. Women's Club, Hudson NH

DAKOTA HARVEST BREAD

3 eggs
1 cup sunflower oil
2 cups sugar
2 cups grated peeled zucchini
1 tablespoon molasses
1 tablespoon vanilla extract

3 cups sifted flour
1/4 teaspoon baking soda
1 tablespoon cinnamon
1 teaspoon salt
1/2 to 1 cup sunflower seed kernels

- Beat eggs in mixer bowl until thick and lemon-colored. Add oil gradually, beating constantly. Beat in sugar, zucchini, molasses and vanilla.
- Sift flour, baking soda, cinnamon and salt together. Add to batter; mix well. Stir in sunflower seed kernels. Spoon into 2 greased loaf pans.
- Bake at 350 degrees for 50 minutes.
- Cool in pans for 20 minutes. Remove to wire racks to cool completely. Serve with Dakota honey.
- Yield: 16 servings.

Approx Per Serving: Cal 371; Prot 6 g; Carbo 45 g; Fiber 2 g; T Fat 19 g; 46% Calories from Fat; Chol 40 mg; Sod 161 mg.

*Dolores Mutch, **Mississippi Valley Region***
GFWC—Larimore Tuesday Club, Larimore ND

FLORIDA ORANGE BREAD

1/2 cup sugar
1/4 cup water
1 tablespoon to 1/2 cup slivered orange rind
1 tablespoon butter
1 cup orange juice

1 egg, beaten
2 1/2 cups sifted flour
2 1/2 teaspoons baking powder
1/4 teaspoon baking soda
1/2 teaspoon salt

- Combine sugar, water and orange rind in saucepan.
- Cook over low heat until sugar dissolves, stirring constantly. Increase heat. Cook for 5 minutes or until liquid is reduced to 2/3 cup; remove from heat.
- Stir in butter until melted. Cool slightly. Add orange juice and egg; mix well.
- Sift remaining ingredients into bowl. Add orange juice mixture; mix just until moistened. Spoon into greased 5x9-inch loaf pan.
- Bake at 325 degrees for 45 minutes or until bread tests done.
- Cool in pan for several minutes. Remove to wire rack to cool completely.
- Yield: 8 servings.

Approx Per Serving: Cal 218; Prot 5 g; Carbo 44 g; Fiber 1 g; T Fat 3 g; 11% Calories from Fat; Chol 31 mg; Sod 284 mg.

*Nelle Myers, **Southern Region***
GFWC—Satellite Beach Woman's Club, Satellite Beach FL

PAPAYA BREAD

1/2 cup margarine, softened
1 cup sugar
2 eggs
1 cup mashed papaya
1/4 cup chopped walnuts
1/2 cup raisins

11/2 cups flour
1/4 teaspoon baking powder
1 teaspoon baking soda
1/2 teaspoon each cinnamon, allspice, ginger and salt

- Cream margarine and sugar in mixer bowl until light and fluffy. Beat in eggs. Stir in papaya, walnuts and raisins.
- Sift remaining ingredients together. Add to creamed mixture; mix well. Spoon into waxed paper-lined 5x9-inch loaf pan.
- Bake at 325 degrees for 11/4 hours or until wooden pick comes out clean.
- Cool in pan for several minutes. Remove to wire rack to cool completely.
- May spoon into 16 muffin cups and bake for 25 minutes if preferred.
- Yield: 8 servings.

Approx Per Serving: Cal 373; Prot 5 g; Carbo 55 g; Fiber 2 g; T Fat 15 g; 36% Calories from Fat; Chol 53 mg; Sod 402 mg.

Lois Topham, **Western Region**
GFWC—Tustin Area Woman's Club, Santa Ana CA

PINEAPPLE AND NUT BREAD

2 cups flour
1 cup sugar
2 teaspoons baking powder
1/2 teaspoon baking soda
1/2 teaspoon mace
3/4 teaspoon salt

1 cup chopped walnuts
1 egg
1 8-ounce can juice-pack crushed pineapple
1/2 cup milk
1/4 cup melted margarine

- Combine flour, sugar, baking powder, baking soda, mace, salt and walnuts in large bowl; mix well.
- Beat egg in mixer bowl. Add undrained pineapple, milk and margarine; mix well.
- Add pineapple mixture to dry ingredients; mix just until moistened. Spoon into greased 5x9-inch loaf pan.
- Bake at 350 degrees for 50 minutes or until wooden pick inserted in center comes out clean.
- Cool in pan for several minutes. Remove to wire rack to cool completely.
- Yield: 8 servings.

Approx Per Serving: Cal 395; Prot 7 g; Carbo 57 g; Fiber 2 g; T Fat 17 g; 37% Calories from Fat; Chol 29 mg; Sod 418 mg.

Phyllis Murrell, **Western Region**
GFWC—Rolando Woman's Club, San Diego CA

HUNGARIAN POPPY SEED BREAD

3 cups flour
2 cups sugar
1½ teaspoons baking soda
½ teaspoon salt
3 eggs

1½ cups oil
1 14-ounce can evaporated milk
1 teaspoon vanilla extract
1 12-ounce can poppy seed filling
1 cup chopped walnuts

- Sift first 4 dry ingredients into bowl. Add eggs, oil, evaporated milk and vanilla; mix well.
- Add poppy seed filling; beat for 2 minutes. Stir in walnuts. Spoon into oiled and floured 10-inch bundt pan.
- Bake at 350 degrees for 1 hour and 10 minutes or until bread tests done.
- Cool completely in pan. Remove to serving plate.
- May omit walnuts if preferred.
- Yield: 16 servings.

Approx Per Serving: Cal 542; Prot 7 g; Carbo 59 g; Fiber 3 g; T Fat 30 g; 50% Calories from Fat; Chol 51 mg; Sod 198 mg.

Cynthia Lucius, **Great Lakes Region**
GFWC—Women's Club of Flushing, Flushing MI

FANTASTIC PUMPKIN BREAD

4 eggs
3 cups sugar
1 cup oil
3⅓ cups sifted flour
½ teaspoon baking powder
2 teaspoons baking soda

1 tablespoon cinnamon
1 tablespoon nutmeg
1 teaspoon salt
½ 30-ounce can pumpkin pie filling
1 cup chopped walnuts
1 cup raisins

- Combine eggs and sugar in mixer bowl; beat until thick and lemon-colored. Beat in oil.
- Mix flour, baking powder, baking soda, cinnamon, nutmeg and salt together. Add to batter alternately with pumpkin pie filling, mixing well after each addition. Stir in walnuts and raisins.
- Fill 4 or 5 small coffee cans sprayed with nonstick cooking spray ½ full.
- Bake at 325 degrees for 1 hour or until bread tests done.
- Cool in coffee cans for several minutes. Remove to wire rack to cool completely.
- Yield: 24 servings.

Approx Per Serving: Cal 317; Prot 4 g; Carbo 48 g; Fiber 1 g; T Fat 13 g; 37% Calories from Fat; Chol 36 mg; Sod 183 mg.

Linda L. Vosko, **Middle Atlantic Region**
GFWC—Merchantville Area Junior Women's Club, Mt. Laurel NJ

RHUBARB BREAD

1½ cups packed brown sugar
⅔ cup oil
1 egg, beaten
1 teaspoon vanilla extract
2½ cups sifted flour
1 teaspoon baking soda

1 teaspoon salt
1 cup buttermilk
1½ cups finely chopped rhubarb
½ cup chopped walnuts
½ cup sugar
1 tablespoon butter

- Beat brown sugar, oil, egg and vanilla in mixer bowl until smooth.
- Sift dry ingredients together. Add to batter alternately with buttermilk, mixing well after each addition.
- Stir in rhubarb and walnuts. Spoon into greased and floured loaf pan. Sprinkle with mixture of sugar and butter.
- Bake at 350 degrees for 45 to 60 minutes or until bread tests done.
- Cool in pan for several minutes. Remove to wire rack to cool completely.
- Yield: 8 servings.

Approx Per Serving: Cal 620; Prot 7 g; Carbo 93 g; Fiber 2 g; T Fat 26 g; 37% Calories from Fat; Chol 32 mg; Sod 447 mg.

Olga Prothero, **Great Lakes Region**
GFWC—Baraboo Women's Club, Baraboo WI

COUNTY CORK SODA BREAD

4 cups flour
1 tablespoon baking powder
½ teaspoon baking soda
1 teaspoon salt

1 cup raisins
1 tablespoon caraway seed
1¾ cups buttermilk
¼ cup oil

- Mix flour, baking powder, baking soda, salt, raisins and caraway seed in bowl.
- Add buttermilk and oil; mix well. Shape into 2 loaves. Place on greased baking sheet. Cut cross in top of each loaf.
- Bake at 350 degrees for 50 minutes.
- According to Irish folklore, the cross will keep out the baking devils and assure a good loaf. Do not, however, praise the loaf until time to eat.
- Yield: 24 servings.

Approx Per Serving: Cal 125; Prot 3 g; Carbo 22 g; Fiber 1 g; T Fat 3 g; 19% Calories from Fat; Chol 1 mg; Sod 167 mg.

Thais Blatnik, **Southeastern Region**
GFWC—Weirton Woman's Club, Wheeling WV

1984—*GFWC opened the Women's History and Resource Center adjacent to its headquarters in Washington, D.C.*

SWEET POTATO BREAD

1¹/₂ cups sugar
¹/₂ cup canola oil
2 eggs
¹/₃ cup warm water
1³/₄ cups flour
1 teaspoon baking soda
¹/₂ teaspoon salt

1¹/₂ teaspoons cinnamon
1 teaspoon nutmeg
1 teaspoon ground cloves
1 cup mashed cooked sweet potatoes
¹/₂ cup chopped pecans
¹/₂ cup raisins

- Combine sugar, oil, eggs and water in mixer bowl; beat for 1 minute. Add mixture of flour, baking soda, salt and spices; mix until moistened.
- Stir in sweet potatoes, pecans and raisins. Spoon into two 4x8-inch foil loaf pans sprayed with nonstick cooking spray.
- Bake at 350 degrees for 1 hour or until loaves test done.
- Cool in pans for 1 minute. Remove to wire rack to cool completely. Serve with cream cheese.
- Yield: 16 servings.

Approx Per Serving: Cal 254; Prot 3 g; Carbo 39 g; Fiber 1 g; T Fat 10 g; 36% Calories from Fat; Chol 27 mg; Sod 131 mg.

Mary M. Smoot, **Southeastern Region**
GFWC—Henderson Woman's Club, Henderson NC

FROSTED SWEET POTATO BREAD

2 cups sugar
1 cup packed brown sugar
1 cup oil
1¹/₂ teaspoons salt
1 teaspoon each cinnamon, nutmeg
   and ground cloves
4 eggs
²/₃ cup water

1 cup mashed cooked sweet potatoes
3 cups sifted flour
2 teaspoons baking soda
³/₄ cup each raisins, pecans and coconut
¹/₄ cup margarine
¹/₂ cup packed brown sugar
3 tablespoons milk
¹/₂ teaspoon vanilla extract

- Combine sugar, 1 cup brown sugar, oil, salt and spices in mixer bowl. Beat until smooth. Beat in eggs.
- Beat water and sweet potatoes in small bowl. Add to batter; mix well. Sift in flour and baking soda; mix well.
- Stir in raisins, pecans and coconut. Spoon batter into 3 greased and floured 4x8-inch loaf pans.
- Bake at 350 degrees for 1 hour or until loaves test done.
- Bring margarine, ¹/₂ cup brown sugar and milk to a boil in saucepan. Cook for 1 minute. Stir in vanilla. Beat until slightly thickened. Spread on warm loaves.
- Yield: 24 servings.

Approx Per Serving: Cal 357; Prot 3 g; Carbo 53 g; Fiber 1 g; T Fat 16 g; 38% Calories from Fat; Chol 36 mg; Sod 247 mg.

Iris S. Brown, **Southeastern Region**
GFWC—Fuquay-Varina Woman's Club, Fuquay-Varina NC

ZUCCHINI BREAD

3 eggs
2¼ cups sugar
1 cup applesauce
1 tablespoon vanilla extract
2 cups grated zucchini
3 cups flour

1 tablespoon cinnamon
¼ teaspoon salt
1 cup chopped pecans
½ cup packed brown sugar
¼ cup sugar
2 tablespoons cinnamon

- Beat eggs in mixer bowl until light. Add 2¼ cups sugar, applesauce and vanilla; mix well. Stir in zucchini. Add flour, 1 tablespoon cinnamon and salt; mix well. Fold in pecans. Spoon into 2 greased and floured 5x9-inch loaf pans.
- Bake at 350 degrees for 1 hour.
- Sprinkle hot loaves with mixture of remaining ingredients. Cool on wire rack.
- May substitute 1 cup oil for applesauce.
- Yield: 16 servings.

Approx Per Serving: Cal 316; Prot 5 g; Carbo 62 g; Fiber 2 g; T Fat 6 g;
18% Calories from Fat; Chol 40 mg; Sod 52 mg.

*Vivian Dee Gearhart, **Middle Atlantic Region***
GFWC—Shenango Valley Women's Club, Greenville PA

POTICA

½ cup milk
¼ cup sugar
1 teaspoon salt
¼ cup shortening
2 envelopes dry yeast
⅓ cup warm water
2 eggs

3 to 3½ cups flour
¼ cup butter, softened
½ cup packed dark brown sugar
1 egg, beaten
2 cups ground walnuts
1 tablespoon grated orange rind

- Scald milk in saucepan. Stir in sugar, salt and shortening. Cool to lukewarm.
- Dissolve yeast in warm water in large bowl. Add cooled milk mixture, 2 eggs and half the flour; mix well. Add enough remaining flour to make a soft dough. Knead on floured surface until smooth and elastic. Place in greased bowl, turning to coat surface. Let rise, covered, in warm place for 1 hour or until doubled in bulk.
- Combine remaining ingredients in bowl; mix well.
- Punch dough down; divide into 2 portions. Roll each portion into 10x20-inch rectangle on floured surface.
- Spread evenly with walnut filling. Roll up rectangles from long sides to enclose fillings. Cut each roll into 3 equal portions. Place 3 portions seam side down into each of 2 greased 4x8-inch loaf pans. Let rise, covered, for 1 hour or to tops of pans.
- Bake at 350 degrees for 25 to 30 minutes or until golden brown. Cool on wire rack.
- Yield: 16 servings.

Approx Per Serving: Cal 316; Prot 7 g; Carbo 36 g; Fiber 2 g; T Fat 17 g;
47% Calories from Fat; Chol 49 mg; Sod 180 mg.

*Sue Huhn, **Great Lakes Region***
GFWC—Milwaukee-Suburban Woman's Club, Franklin WI

SWEDISH RYE BREAD

1 envelope or cake yeast
1 tablespoon sugar
1/2 cup warm water
1/4 cup molasses
1/2 cup packed brown sugar
1/2 cup sugar

2 tablespoons shortening
2 cups warm water
2 1/2 cups sifted rye flour
1 tablespoon fennel seed
2 teaspoons salt
4 1/2 to 5 cups all-purpose flour

- Dissolve yeast and 1 tablespoon sugar in 1/2 cup warm water in bowl. Add next 8 ingredients; mix well.
- Add enough all-purpose flour gradually to form a soft dough. Knead until smooth and elastic. Place in greased bowl, turning to coat surface.
- Let rise, covered, in warm place until doubled in bulk. Punch dough down and turn over. Let rise until 1 3/4 times bulk.
- Punch dough down. Let stand for 20 minutes. Shape into 3 loaves; place in greased loaf pans. Let rise until doubled in bulk.
- Bake at 300 to 350 degrees for 45 minutes. Remove to wire rack to cool.
- Yield: 24 servings.

Approx Per Serving: Cal 189; Prot 4 g; Carbo 40 g; Fiber 2 g; T Fat 2 g;
7% Calories from Fat; Chol 0 mg; Sod 182 mg.

Dorothy Crampton, **Great Lakes Region**
GFWC—Chesterton Woman's Club, Chesterton IN

ALABAMA THREE-GRAIN MUFFINS

3 eggs, slightly beaten
1 cup milk
1/2 cup cornmeal
1/3 cup self-rising flour

Nutmeg to taste
1 teaspoon salt
1 cup hot cooked rice
1 tablespoon butter

- Beat eggs with milk in large mixer bowl. Add cornmeal, flour, nutmeg and salt; mix well.
- Mix rice and butter in bowl. Add to egg mixture; mix well.
- Spoon into 12 muffin cups sprayed with nonstick cooking spray.
- Bake at 425 degrees for 25 minutes or until golden brown.
- May serve topped with creamed chicken or old-fashioned tomato gravy.
- Yield: 12 servings.

Approx Per Serving: Cal 92; Prot 3 g; Carbo 12 g; Fiber 1 g; T Fat 3 g;
31% Calories from Fat; Chol 59 mg; Sod 249 mg.

Sue Hamilton, **Southern Region**
GFWC—Valley Head Woman's Club, Mentone AL

1984–1994—*Mrs. George Bush serves as GFWC's Honorary Literacy Chairman.*

BEST BLUEBERRY MUFFINS

1/2 cup butter, softened
1 cup (or less) sugar
2 eggs
1 teaspoon vanilla extract
2 teaspoons baking powder
1/4 teaspoon salt

1/2 cup mashed blueberries
2 cups flour
1/2 cup milk
2 cups blueberries
1 tablespoon sugar
1/4 teaspoon nutmeg

- Cream butter in medium mixer bowl until light. Add 1 cup sugar gradually, beating until fluffy. Beat in eggs 1 at a time. Add vanilla, baking powder and salt; mix well.
- Stir in mashed blueberries. Fold in flour and milk 1/2 at a time with spatula. Stir in whole blueberries.
- Spoon into greased or foil-lined muffin cups. Sprinkle with mixture of 1 tablespoon sugar and nutmeg.
- Bake at 375 degrees for 25 to 30 minutes or until golden brown. Cool in pan for 30 minutes. Remove to wire rack to cool completely.
- Yield: 12 servings.

Approx Per Serving: Cal 257; Prot 4 g; Carbo 38 g; Fiber 1 g; T Fat 9 g;
32% Calories from Fat; Chol 58 mg; Sod 182 mg.

Madeleine Ciocco, **Middle Atlantic Region**
GFWC—Contemporary Woman's Club, Washington Township NJ

HEARTY BLUEBERRY MUFFINS

1 3/4 cups flour
1 1/4 cups sugar
1 teaspoon baking soda
1 teaspoon cinnamon
1/2 teaspoon salt

1 1/2 cups fresh blueberries
1/2 cup oil
2 eggs
1/2 cup chopped walnuts

- Mix flour, sugar, baking soda, cinnamon and salt in large bowl. Add blueberries; toss gently to coat well.
- Add oil and eggs; mix gently. Fold in walnuts; batter will be stiff. Spoon into paper-lined muffin cups.
- Bake at 325 degrees for 40 minutes or until muffins test done. Serve warm.
- May substitute 1 cup chopped peeled apples for blueberries and add 2/3 cup raisins, 1/2 teaspoon ground cloves and 1/8 teaspoon nutmeg.
- Yield: 12 servings.

Approx Per Serving: Cal 282; Prot 4 g; Carbo 38 g; Fiber 1 g; T Fat 13 g;
42% Calories from Fat; Chol 36 mg; Sod 171 mg.

Carole M. Lotito, **Middle Atlantic Region**
GFWC—Paskack Junior Woman's Club, River Vale NJ

MAINE WILD BLUEBERRY MUFFINS

1/3 cup shortening
3/4 cup sugar
1 egg, beaten
1 teaspoon vanilla extract
1 1/2 cups sifted flour
1 teaspoon baking soda

1 teaspoon cinnamon
1/2 cup sour milk
1 cup fresh Maine wild blueberries
1 tablespoon flour
2 tablespoons sugar
1 teaspoon cinnamon

- Cream shortening and 3/4 cup sugar in mixer bowl until light and fluffy. Beat in egg and vanilla.
- Sift 1 1/2 cups flour, baking soda and 1 teaspoon cinnamon together. Add to batter alternately with sour milk, mixing well after each addition. Toss blueberries with 1 tablespoon flour. Fold into batter.
- Spoon into 12 greased muffin cups. Sprinkle with mixture of 2 tablespoons sugar and 1 teaspoon cinnamon.
- Bake at 350 degrees for 30 minutes or until muffins test done.
- Yield: 12 servings.

Approx Per Serving: Cal 181; Prot 3 g; Carbo 28 g; Fiber 1 g; T Fat 7 g;
33% Calories from Fat; Chol 19 mg; Sod 80 mg.

*Nancy L. Blomquist, **New England Region***
GFWC—Castine Woman's Club, Castine ME

SOUTHERN BLUEBERRY MUFFINS

1/4 cup butter, softened
1/2 cup sugar
1 egg
3/4 cup low-fat milk
1/4 teaspoon vanilla extract

1 3/4 cups flour
2 1/2 teaspoons baking powder
1/2 teaspoon salt
1 cup fresh blueberries
1 tablespoon flour

- Cream butter and sugar in large mixer bowl until light and fluffy. Beat in egg, milk and vanilla.
- Mix 1 3/4 cups flour, baking powder and salt together. Add to batter; mix just until moistened.
- Toss blueberries with 1 tablespoon flour in bowl. Fold into batter. Spoon into 12 greased muffin cups.
- Bake at 425 degrees for 25 minutes or until golden brown. Serve warm.
- Yield: 12 servings.

Approx Per Serving: Cal 157; Prot 3 g; Carbo 25 g; Fiber 1 g; T Fat 5 g;
28% Calories from Fat; Chol 30 mg; Sod 204 mg.

*Susan S. Thompson, **Southern Region***
GFWC—Pavo Woman's Club, Pavo GA

EASTPORT FRUIT MUFFINS

2 cups flour
1 cup sugar
1 teaspoon (heaping) baking powder
1/2 teaspoon baking soda
1 cup plain yogurt

2 eggs
1/2 cup melted margarine
1 cup raspberries
Grated rind of 1/2 lemon

- Mix flour, sugar, baking powder and baking soda in bowl. Add yogurt, eggs and margarine; mix well.
- Fold in raspberries and lemon rind. Spoon into muffin tins which have been sprayed with nonstick cooking spray or lined with paper liners.
- Bake at 400 degrees for 15 minutes.
- May substitute blueberries, strawberries, pineapple or cranberries for blueberries and grated orange rind for lemon rind.
- Yield: 12 servings.

Approx Per Serving: Cal 238; Prot 4 g; Carbo 35 g; Fiber 1 g; T Fat 9 g; 35% Calories from Fat; Chol 38 mg; Sod 172 mg.

Constance Kotoski, **New England Region**
GFWC—Westminster Woman's Club, Westminster MA

MONTANA MOUNTAIN MUFFINS

4 cups flour
4 cups whole bran cereal
1 1/2 cups sugar
4 teaspoons baking powder
1 tablespoon baking soda
2 teaspoons salt

2 cups cold coffee
2 cups milk
6 eggs, beaten
1 1/2 cups oil
2 teaspoons vanilla extract
2 cups raisins

- Mix first 6 dry ingredients in bowl.
- Combine coffee, milk, eggs, oil and vanilla in bowl; mix well. Add to dry ingredients; mix just until moistened. Stir in raisins.
- Spoon into greased muffin cups, filling 2/3 full.
- Bake at 350 degrees for 20 minutes or until muffins test done.
- Yield: 60 servings.

Approx Per Serving: Cal 139; Prot 2 g; Carbo 19 g; Fiber 2 g; T Fat 7 g; 40% Calories from Fat; Chol 22 mg; Sod 176 mg.

Nan Boyer, **Western Region**
GFWC—Hamilton Women's Club, Hamilton MT

PUMPKIN AND APPLE STREUSEL MUFFINS

2½ cups flour
2 cups sugar
1 teaspoon baking soda
1 tablespoon pumpkin pie spice
½ teaspoon salt
2 eggs, slightly beaten
1 cup canned pumpkin

½ cup oil
2 cups finely chopped peeled apples
2 tablespoons flour
¼ cup sugar
½ teaspoon cinnamon
¼ cup butter

- Mix first 5 dry ingredients in bowl.
- Combine eggs, pumpkin and oil in bowl; mix well. Add to dry ingredients; mix just until moistened. Stir in apples.
- Spoon into greased muffin cups, filling ⅔ full.
- Mix 2 tablespoons flour, ¼ cup sugar and cinnamon in small bowl. Cut in butter until crumbly. Sprinkle over muffins.
- Bake at 350 degrees for 35 to 40 minutes or until muffins test done.
- Yield: 18 servings.

Approx Per Serving: Cal 261; Prot 3 g; Carbo 42 g; Fiber 1 g; T Fat 10 g;
32% Calories from Fat; Chol 31 mg; Sod 136 mg.

*Mrs. William A. Thompson, **Southeastern Region***
GFWC—Toano Woman's Club, Toano VA

RASPBERRY STREUSEL MUFFINS

½ cup butter, softened
½ cup sugar
1 egg
1 teaspoon vanilla extract
½ cup milk
½ cup sour cream
½ teaspoon each baking powder,
  baking soda and cinnamon

2 cups flour
1 cup raspberries
½ cup flour
½ cup quick-cooking oats
⅓ cup sugar
½ teaspoon cinnamon
⅛ teaspoon salt
6 tablespoons margarine

- Cream butter and ½ cup sugar in mixer bowl until light and fluffy. Beat in egg, vanilla, milk and sour cream.
- Mix baking powder, baking soda, ½ teaspoon cinnamon and 2 cups flour together. Add to batter; mix just until moistened. Fold in raspberries.
- Spoon into greased muffin cups, filling ⅔ full.
- Mix ½ cup flour, oats, ⅓ cup sugar, ½ teaspoon cinnamon and salt in small bowl. Cut in margarine until crumbly. Sprinkle over muffins.
- Bake at 375 degrees for 20 to 25 minutes or until muffins test done.
- Yield: 18 servings.

Approx Per Serving: Cal 212; Prot 3 g; Carbo 25 g; Fiber 1 g; T Fat 11 g;
47% Calories from Fat; Chol 29 mg; Sod 145 mg.

*Mary Ann Miller, **Mississippi Valley Region***
GFWC—El Carmin Club, Grand Junction IA

SQUASH MUFFINS

½ cup sugar
2 tablespoons oil
1 egg
½ cup milk

2 cups flour
2 teaspoons baking powder
1 teaspoon salt
1 cup squash purée

- Beat sugar and oil in mixer bowl until smooth. Add egg and milk; mix well.
- Sift dry ingredients together. Add to batter; mix just until moistened. Stir in squash purée.
- Spoon into 12 greased muffin cups.
- Bake at 375 degrees for 20 minutes or until muffins test done.
- May substitute pumpkin for squash.
- Yield: 12 servings.

Approx Per Serving: Cal 148; Prot 3 g; Carbo 26 g; Fiber 1 g; T Fat 3 g;
21% Calories from Fat; Chol 19 mg; Sod 243 mg.

*Joanne N. Wile, **New England Region***
GFWC—Rockport Woman's Club, Rockport MA

SWEET POTATO MUFFINS

3½ cups flour
2 teaspoons baking soda
1½ teaspoons cinnamon
1 teaspoon salt
3 cups sugar
1 cup oil

4 eggs, beaten
¾ cup buttermilk
1½ teaspoons vanilla extract
2 cups mashed cooked sweet potatoes
1 cup chopped pecans

- Sift flour, baking soda, cinnamon and salt into large mixer bowl. Add sugar, oil, eggs and buttermilk; mix well.
- Stir in vanilla, sweet potatoes and pecans. Spoon into greased muffin cups, filling ¾ full.
- Bake at 350 degrees for 20 to 25 minutes or until muffins test done. Serve muffins hot or cooled.
- Yield: 42 servings.

Approx Per Serving: Cal 183; Prot 2 g; Carbo 27 g; Fiber 1 g; T Fat 8 g;
38% Calories from Fat; Chol 20 mg; Sod 104 mg.

*Betty A. Price, **Southern Region***
GFWC—Woman's Club of Crescent City, Seville FL

1986—*Based on the result of a needs survey, the GFWC Brookings Club of South Dakota developed a program to channel community efforts on behalf ot 364 international students and other international visitors.*

PIZZA CRUSTS

1 envelope dry yeast
1 cup warm water
1 teaspoon sugar

1½ teaspoons salt
¼ cup oil
3 cups flour

- Dissolve yeast in warm water. Combine with sugar, salt and oil in bowl; mix well.
- Add 1½ cups flour; beat for 1 minute. Add remaining 1½ cups flour gradually, beating for 30 seconds after each addition.
- Knead on floured surface for 5 minutes or until smooth and elastic. Let rest in warm place for 10 minutes.
- Divide into 2 portions. Press into 2 pizza pans, stretching to fit pans. Add toppings as desired.
- Bake at 450 degrees for 15 minutes or until golden brown.
- Yield: 8 servings.

Approx Per Serving: Cal 235; Prot 5 g; Carbo 37 g; Fiber 2 g; T Fat 2 g;
7% Calories from Fat; Chol 0 mg; Sod 401 mg.
Nutritional information does not include toppings.

*Mary Anne Price, **Middle Atlantic Region***
GFWC—Civic League of Mechanicsburg, Enola PA

CORNMEAL ROLLS

⅓ cup cornmeal
½ cup sugar
1 teaspoon salt
½ cup shortening
2 cups milk

1 cake yeast or 1 envelope dry yeast
¼ cup lukewarm water
2 eggs, beaten
4 cups flour
2 tablespoons melted butter

- Combine cornmeal, sugar, salt, shortening and milk in double boiler.
- Cook until thickened, stirring frequently. Cool to lukewarm.
- Dissolve yeast in ¼ cup lukewarm water in bowl. Add to cornmeal mixture; mix well. Beat in eggs.
- Let rise, covered, in warm place for 2 hours.
- Add enough flour to make a soft dough. Knead until smooth and elastic. Place in greased bowl, turning to coat surface.
- Let rise for 1 hour. Punch dough down; place on floured surface. Roll out and cut with biscuit cutter. Brush with melted butter; fold into halves. Place on greased baking sheet.
- Let rise, covered, for 1 hour or until doubled in bulk.
- Bake at 375 degrees for 15 minutes or until golden brown.
- Yield: 30 servings.

Approx Per Serving: Cal 132; Prot 3 g; Carbo 18 g; Fiber 1 g; T Fat 5 g;
36% Calories from Fat; Chol 19 mg; Sod 90 mg.

*Linnie Copeland, **South Central Region***
GFWC—Borger Twentieth Century Club, Borger TX

DAKOTA DURUM OVERNIGHT BUNS

2 cups sugar
4 cups water
1 cup lard
1 tablespoon salt

1 envelope dry yeast
1/2 cup lukewarm water
4 eggs, beaten
16 cups flour

- Bring sugar and water to a boil in 2-quart saucepan. Simmer for 5 minutes. Pour over lard and salt in bowl; mix well. Cool to lukewarm.
- Dissolve yeast in lukewarm water in bowl. Add yeast and eggs to cooled mixture; mix well.
- Add flour 2 to 3 cups at a time, mixing well after each addition to form a dough. Knead for 5 minutes or until smooth and elastic.
- Let rise, covered, for 2 hours or until doubled in bulk. Punch dough down. Let rise again. Shape into buns. Place on greased baking sheet. Let rise overnight.
- Bake at 375 degrees for 13 to 15 minutes or until golden brown.
- Yield: 65 servings.

Approx Per Serving: Cal 169; Prot 3 g; Carbo 30 g; Fiber 1 g; T Fat 3 g;
16% Calories from Fat; Chol 20 mg; Sod 99 mg.

*Beverly Keller, **Mississippi Valley Region***
GFWC—North Dakota Vistarian Club, Bisbee ND

KOLACHES

1 tablespoon dry yeast
2 teaspoons sugar
1 cup lukewarm (110-degree) milk
1/2 cup melted margarine
2 teaspoons salt
1/2 cup sugar

1 cup lukewarm milk
2 egg yolks, beaten
1 egg, beaten
7 to 8 cups flour
1 cup melted lard
4   12-ounce cans Solo prune filling

- Dissolve yeast and 2 teaspoons sugar in lukewarm milk in bowl. Let stand for 10 minutes. Add next 4 ingredients; mix well. Let stand for 10 minutes.
- Beat in egg yolks and egg. Add 6 cups flour 1 to 2 cups at a time, mixing well after each addition. Knead in enough remaining flour to make a soft dough.
- Place in greased bowl, turning to coat surface. Let rise, covered, in warm place until light. Shape into 1-inch balls.
- Grease baking sheet with lard. Place balls 1 1/2 inches apart on baking sheet; brush with remaining lard. Let rise until light. Make indentation in each ball. Spoon prune filling into indentations.
- Bake at 450 degrees for 11 to 12 minutes or until golden brown.
- I baked this recipe on the Mall in Washington D.C. in 1991 when our family participated in the American Folklife Festival.
- Yield: 72 servings.

Approx Per Serving: Cal 165; Prot 5 g; Carbo 25 g; Fiber 2 g; T Fat 6 g;
33% Calories from Fat; Chol 12 mg; Sod 101 mg.

*Dorothy Simanek, **Mississippi Valley Region***
GFWC—R.A.R.E. Club, Walker IA

PUMPKIN ROLLS

1 cup milk, scalded
1/2 cup sugar
1/4 cup butter
1 1/2 cups mashed cooked pumpkin
1 1/2 teaspoons salt

1 cake yeast or 1 envelope dry yeast
1 teaspoon sugar
1/2 cup lukewarm water
1 egg, beaten
6 cups flour

- Combine milk, 1/2 cup sugar, butter, pumpkin and salt in large bowl; mix well. Cool to lukewarm.
- Dissolve yeast and 1 teaspoon sugar in lukewarm water in small bowl. Add yeast and egg to milk mixture; mix well.
- Add flour; mix to form dough. Knead on floured surface for 5 to 10 minutes or until smooth and elastic. Place in greased bowl, turning to coat surface.
- Let rise, covered, in warm place until doubled in bulk. Punch dough down. Let rise for 10 minutes longer.
- Shape into rolls; place in baking pan.
- Bake at 400 degrees for 15 minutes.
- May substitute squash for pumpkin.
- Yield: 36 servings.

Approx Per Serving: Cal 107; Prot 3 g; Carbo 20 g; Fiber 1 g; T Fat 2 g; 16% Calories from Fat; Chol 10 mg; Sod 105 mg.

Mary Lou Kelly, **New England Region**
GFWC—Woman's Club of Concord, Concord NH

SOPAIPILLAS

1 envelope dry yeast
1/4 cup warm water
1 1/4 cups milk, scalded, cooled to lukewarm
1 tablespoon sugar

4 cups (about) flour
1 teaspoon baking powder
1 teaspoon salt
2 tablespoons shortening
Oil for deep frying

- Dissolve yeast in water in bowl. Add milk.
- Combine 1 tablespoon sugar, flour, baking powder and salt in bowl. Cut in shortening until crumbly. Make well in center.
- Pour yeast mixture into well; mix to form smooth dough.
- Roll 1/3 at a time on floured surface. Cut into 4-inch squares.
- Deep-fry in hot oil until puffed and golden brown, spooning oil over tops and turning once; drain.
- My children call these Soapy Pillows.
- Yield: 48 servings.

Approx Per Serving: Cal 48; Prot 1 g; Carbo 9 g; Fiber <1 g; T Fat 1 g; 16% Calories from Fat; Chol 1 mg; Sod 54 mg.
Nutritional information does not include oil for deep frying.

Jill M. Hanson, **South Central Region**
GFWC—Santa Fe Junior Woman's Club, Los Alamos NM

NEVER-FAIL FLOUR TORTILLAS

4 cups flour
1 teaspoon salt

1 cup shortening
1 cup water, at room temperature

- Mix flour and salt in bowl. Add shortening; mix with hands until mixture resembles coarse cornmeal.
- Add water; mix lightly. Shape into ball. Let rest, covered, for 20 minutes.
- Knead lightly for 3 minutes. Shape into 25 balls. Roll each ball into 5 or 6-inch circle on floured surface.
- Bake on hot griddle for several seconds; turn tortillas over. Bake until light brown crust forms. Turn again. Cook until done to taste or slightly puffed.
- Yield: 25 servings.

Approx Per Serving: Cal 145; Prot 2 g; Carbo 15 g; Fiber 1 g; T Fat 8 g; 52% Calories from Fat; Chol 0 mg; Sod 86 mg.

Evangelina H. Ramirez, **South Central Region**
GFWC—Women's Club of Rio Grande City, Roma TX

GINGERBREAD WAFFLES

2 cups flour
1/2 cup sugar
1 1/2 teaspoons baking soda
2 teaspoons ginger
1 teaspoon cinnamon
1/4 teaspoon cloves
1/2 teaspoon salt
1/2 cup melted butter

2 eggs, beaten
3/4 cup molasses
1 cup boiling water
2 cups sugar
1/4 cup flour
2 cups cold water
2 teaspoons vanilla extract
1 tablespoon butter

- Mix 2 cups flour, 1/2 cup sugar, baking soda, spices and salt in bowl. Add 1/2 cup melted butter, eggs, molasses and boiling water; mix well.
- Spray preheated waffle iron with nonstick cooking spray. Spoon batter into waffle iron.
- Bake until golden brown.
- Combine 2 cups sugar and 1/4 cup flour in saucepan. Stir in 2 cups water.
- Cook until thickened, stirring constantly. Stir in vanilla and 1 tablespoon butter. Serve with waffles.
- Yield: 6 servings.

Approx Per Serving: Cal 761; Prot 7 g; Carbo 141 g; Fiber 1 g; T Fat 20 g; 23% Calories from Fat; Chol 118 mg; Sod 560 mg.

Dorothy Lawton, **Mississippi Valley Region**
GFWC—Franklin Culture Club, Cooper IA

DESSERTS

The pewter coffee service
(pictured here atop a
glass-topped coffee table in the
board room of GFWC's Women's
History and Resource Center,
adjacent to the original
Headquarters building) was a
gift of the Tennessee Federation
of Women's Clubs. The Civil
War-era empire sofa was a
bequest from the estate of
Michigan clubwoman
Jean McEntire Bruce.

APRICOT SHERBET

1 cup sugar
3 cups water
1 6-ounce can frozen orange juice
   concentrate
1 6-ounce can frozen lemonade
   concentrate

1 20-ounce can apricots, puréed
3 bananas, mashed
1 12-ounce can apricot nectar
1 cup whipping cream

▪ Combine sugar and water in saucepan. Bring to a boil. Simmer until thickened, stirring frequently. Cool slightly.
▪ Add orange juice and lemonade concentrates, apricots, bananas and apricot nectar; mix well. Pour into ice cream freezer container.
▪ Freeze according to manufacturer's instructions until mushy. Remove top carefully; add cream quickly.
▪ Freeze until firm. Let ripen, packed in ice, for 1 hour or longer before serving.
▪ May also store in freezer. Soften sherbet slightly and beat with electric mixer before serving.
▪ Yield: 12 servings.

Approx Per Serving: Cal 262; Prot 1 g; Carbo 50 g; Fiber 2 g; T Fat 8 g;
25% Calories from Fat; Chol 27 mg; Sod 12 mg.

*Ruth G. Congleton, **Southeastern Region***
GFWC—Woman's Club of Richmond, Richmond KY

FRESH PEACH ICE CREAM

4 cups mashed fresh peaches
2 cups sugar
5 eggs

2 13-ounce cans evaporated milk
2 cups milk
1 tablespoon vanilla extract

▪ Mix peaches and sugar in bowl.
▪ Beat eggs at medium speed in mixer bowl. Add evaporated milk, milk and vanilla. Stir in peach mixture. Pour into freezer container.
▪ Freeze according to manufacturer's instructions.
▪ Yield: 16 servings.

Approx Per Serving: Cal 241; Prot 7 g; Carbo 41 g; Fiber 1 g; T Fat 6 g;
23% Calories from Fat; Chol 84 mg; Sod 84 mg.

*Ethlene Tatham, **Southern Region***
GFWC—Toccoa Woman's Club, Toccoa GA

 GFWC **Volunteer**

1988—*GFWC instituted a youth suicide prevention program.*

AMARETTO CHEESECAKE

1½ cups graham cracker crumbs
2 tablespoons sugar
1 teaspoon cinnamon
6 tablespoons melted butter
24 ounces cream cheese, softened
1 cup sugar

4 eggs
⅓ cup amaretto
1 cup sour cream
4 teaspoons sugar
1 tablespoon amaretto

- Mix crumbs, 2 tablespoons sugar, cinnamon and butter in bowl. Press onto bottom and 1 inch up side of 10-inch springform pan.
- Beat cream cheese in mixer bowl until light and fluffy. Add 1 cup sugar gradually. Add eggs 1 at a time, beating well after each. Stir in ⅓ cup amaretto. Pour into prepared pan.
- Bake at 375 degrees for 45 to 50 minutes or until set.
- Spoon mixture of sour cream, 4 teaspoons sugar and 1 tablespoon amaretto over cake.
- Bake at 500 degrees for 5 minutes.
- Let stand to cool. Garnish with grated chocolate bar.
- Yield: 16 servings.

Approx Per Serving: Cal 368; Prot 6 g; Carbo 28 g; Fiber <1 g; T Fat 25 g;
62% Calories from Fat; Chol 118 mg; Sod 257 mg.

*Evalene H. Hawkins, **Southeastern Region***
GFWC—Fed. Womans Club of Petersburg, Petersburg VA

WHITE CHOCOLATE CHEESECAKE WITH HAZELNUT CRUST

¾ cup toasted hazelnuts
12 graham crackers, broken
¼ cup sugar
6 tablespoons melted butter
32 ounces cream cheese, softened

1¼ cups sugar
4 eggs
3 ounces white chocolate, melted
3 tablespoons hazelnut liqueur

- Wrap outside of greased 9-inch springform pan with foil.
- Chop hazelnuts in food processor. Add graham crackers and ¼ cup sugar. Process to fine crumbs. Add butter. Process until crumbs stick together. Press onto bottom and 1½ inches up side of pan.
- Bake at 325 degrees for 10 minutes.
- Cool on wire rack.
- Beat cream cheese in mixer bowl until light and fluffy. Add 1¼ cups sugar gradually. Add eggs 1 at a time, beating well after each addition. Add chocolate. Beat in liqueur. Pour into crust.
- Bake at 325 degrees for 1 hour and 20 minutes or until set.
- Cool completely. Chill, covered, for 24 hours.
- Yield: 14 servings.

Approx Per Serving: Cal 490; Prot 8 g; Carbo 34 g; Fiber 1 g; T Fat 36 g;
66% Calories from Fat; Chol 146 mg; Sod 296 mg.

*Mary Wartenbarg, **Middle Atlantic Region***
GFWC—Huntington Township Women's Club, Huntington NY

ITALIAN CHEESECAKE

1³/₄ cups amaretto cookie or vanilla
    wafer crumbs
6 tablespoons melted butter
3 pounds ricotta cheese
1 cup sugar
¹/₂ cup whipping cream

4 eggs
2 teaspoons vanilla extract
1 tablespoon grated orange rind
¹/₂ cup flour
1 cup miniature chocolate chips
³/₄ cup golden raisins

- Mix cookie crumbs and butter in bowl. Press onto bottom and side of 10-inch springform pan.
- Beat cheese at low speed in mixer bowl. Add sugar, whipping cream, eggs, vanilla, orange rind and flour 1 ingredient at a time, beating continuously. Beat at medium speed for 3 minutes after last addition.
- Fold in chocolate chips and raisins. Pour into prepared pan.
- Bake at 325 degrees for 1 hour or until set.
- Turn off oven. Let stand in oven for 1 hour.
- Yield: 16 servings.

Approx Per Serving: Cal 418; Prot 13 g; Carbo 38 g; Fiber 1 g; T Fat 25 g;
53% Calories from Fat; Chol 124 mg; Sod 167 mg.

Annette R. Falk, **Middle Atlantic Region**
GFWC—Middlesex Area Jr. Woman's Club, Middlesex NJ

THE GREAT PUMPKIN CHEESECAKE

5 tablespoons melted margarine
3 tablespoons sugar
1 cup graham cracker crumbs
16 ounces low-fat cream cheese,
    softened
1 cup sugar

3 eggs
¹/₂ cup whipping cream
1 cup solid-pack pumpkin
1 teaspoon vanilla extract
1 teaspoon pumpkin pie spice
8 ounces whipped topping

- Mix margarine, 3 tablespoons sugar and crumbs in bowl. Press into 9-inch springform pan.
- Beat cream cheese and 1 cup sugar in mixer bowl until smooth. Add eggs 1 at a time, beating well after each. Add whipping cream and pumpkin. Stir in vanilla and pie spice. Pour into prepared pan.
- Bake at 300 degrees for 1 hour.
- Let stand for 45 minutes.
- Chill for 2 hours.
- Spread with whipped topping.
- Yield: 12 servings.

Approx Per Serving: Cal 368; Prot 7 g; Carbo 37 g; Fiber 1 g; T Fat 22 g;
53% Calories from Fat; Chol 88 mg; Sod 360 mg.

Shirley J. Parks, **Great Lakes Region**
GFWC—Edmore Woman's Club, Edmore MI

CHARLOTTE AU CHOCOLAT

48 ladyfingers, split
2 cups semisweet chocolate pieces
6 eggs, separated

2 tablespoons sugar
2 cups whipping cream, whipped

- Line bottom and side of 9-inch springform pan with ladyfingers.
- Melt chocolate in double boiler. Cool completely. Add egg yolks 1 at a time, beating well after each addition.
- Beat egg whites in mixer bowl until frothy. Add sugar gradually, beating constantly until stiff peaks form. Beat 1/4 egg whites into chocolate mixture. Fold in remaining egg whites and whipped cream.
- Alternate layers of chocolate mixture and ladyfingers until all ingredients are used, ending with chocolate.
- Chill for 4 hours.
- Garnish with whipped cream and chocolate wafers.
- Yield: 16 servings.

Approx Per Serving: Cal 364; Prot 6 g; Carbo 36 g; Fiber 1 g; T Fat 23 g; 55% Calories from Fat; Chol 121 mg; Sod 63 mg.

Margaret E. Spurgat, **Middle Atlantic Region**
GFWC—Village Improvement Association, Lewes DE

DEATH BY CHOCOLATE

1   22-ounce package Jiffy brownie mix
2 tablespoons coffee
1   4-ounce package chocolate mousse
    mix

4 Heath candy bars, chopped
1/2 cup chopped pecans
8 ounces whipped topping

- Bake brownies using package directions. Pierce holes in hot brownies; drizzle with coffee. Cut into small pieces.
- Prepare chocolate mousse using package directions.
- Layer brownies, mousse, candy bars, pecans and whipped topping 1/2 at a time in glass serving bowl.
- Chill in refrigerator overnight.
- Spoon into sherbet glasses.
- May substitute chocolate liqueur for coffee.
- Yield: 15 servings.

Approx Per Serving: Cal 394; Prot 5 g; Carbo 32 g; Fiber <1 g; T Fat 29 g; 63% Calories from Fat; Chol 93 mg; Sod 119 mg.

Gladys O. Smith, **Mississippi Valley Region**
GFWC—Woman's Literary Club, Winthrop Iowa

COTTAGE CHEESE SOUFFLÉ WITH FRUIT

1 16-ounce can pitted sour cherries,
    drained
Juice of 1 lemon
²/₃ cup sugar
2 cups cottage cheese
3 egg yolks

2 teaspoons baking powder
¹/₂ cup farina
3 egg whites, stiffly beaten
¹/₄ cup dry bread crumbs
2 tablespoons butter

- Mix cherries, lemon juice and a small amount of sugar in bowl.
- Process cottage cheese in blender until smooth.
- Mix with egg yolks, remaining sugar, baking powder and farina in bowl. Add cherries and egg whites; mix well. Pour into greased soufflé dish.
- Sprinkle with mixture of bread crumbs and butter.
- Bake at 375 degrees for 1 hour.
- Serve hot.
- Yield: 8 servings.

Approx Per Serving: Cal 242; Prot 11 g; Carbo 33 g; Fiber 1 g; T Fat 8 g;
28% Calories from Fat; Chol 96 mg; Sod 369 mg.

Phyllis J. Lovitz, **Middle Atlantic Region**
GFWC—Woman's Club of Hellertown, Hellertown PA

IT'S A DEEP DARK SECRET DESSERT

1 pound dates, chopped
1 cup sugar
1 cup coarsely chopped walnuts
4 egg yolks, beaten
¹/₂ cup sifted flour
1 teaspoon baking powder
¹/₄ teaspoon salt
2 teaspoons vanilla extract
4 egg whites, stiffly beaten

4 bananas, coarsely chopped
2 11-ounce cans mandarin oranges,
    drained
1 20-ounce can pineapple chunks,
    drained
1 20-ounce can fruit cocktail, drained
15 Tokay grapes
8 ounces whipped topping
¹/₂ cup red and green maraschino cherries

- Combine dates, sugar and walnuts in bowl; mix well. Add eggs; mix well.
- Sift flour, baking powder and salt together. Add to date mixture. Add vanilla; mix well. Fold in stiffly beaten egg whites. Pour into greased 9x13-inch baking dish.
- Bake at 350 degrees for 55 minutes or until cake tests done. Cool in pan for several minutes. Remove onto wire rack to cool completely.
- Crumble cake into bowl. Add next 5 ingredients; mix well. Shape into mound on serving plate. Frost with whipped topping.
- Garnish with red maraschino cherries for berries and green maraschino cherries cut to resemble leaves.
- Yield: 15 servings.

Approx Per Serving: Cal 378; Prot 5 g; Carbo 72 g; Fiber 4 g; T Fat 11 g;
24% Calories from Fat; Chol 57 mg; Sod 85 mg.

Verna D. Birkeland, **Mississippi Valley Region**
GFWC—Octavo Woman's Club, Bristol SD

MUTTER'S BRATZELI

1¹/₂ cups butter, softened
1 cup packed brown sugar
1 cup sugar
4 eggs
1 teaspoon vanilla extract

1¹/₂ teaspoons cinnamon
¹/₂ teaspoon salt
Grated rind of 1 lemon
1 tablespoon lemon juice
4 cups flour

- Cream butter in mixer bowl. Add sugars; beat well. Add eggs 1 at a time, beating well after each. Add remaining ingredients; mix well.
- Cover dough. Chill for 3 hours or overnight.
- Shape into 1-inch balls.
- Place 4 balls at a time on hot Bratzeli iron. Press down.
- Cook for 1 to 2 minutes or until browned.
- Yield: 80 servings.

Approx Per Serving: Cal 80; Prot 1 g; Carbo 11 g; Fiber <1 g; T Fat 4 g;
42% Calories from Fat; Chol 20 mg; Sod 48 mg.

Dina Speich, **Great Lakes Region**
GFWC—Monroe Club, Monroe WI

PERSIMMON PUDDING

1¹/₄ cups packed brown sugar
1¹/₂ cups warm water
2 tablespoons melted butter
1 cup flour
1 teaspoon baking powder
¹/₂ teaspoon baking soda

¹/₂ teaspoon salt
1 cup sugar
1 cup milk
¹/₂ teaspoon vanilla extract
1 cup persimmon purée
¹/₂ cup chopped pecans

- Combine first 3 ingredients in bowl; mix well. Pour into 10-inch square baking pan. Mix flour, baking powder, baking soda, salt and sugar together in mixer bowl. Beat in milk and vanilla until smooth. Stir in persimmon purée and pecans. Pour over brown sugar mixture in pan. Do not stir.
- Bake at 375 degrees for 45 minutes. Spoon into stemmed glasses. Garnish with whipped cream.
- May substitute ¹/₂ cup chopped dates and omit baking soda to make Date Nut Pudding.
- Yield: 6 servings.

Approx Per Serving: Cal 573; Prot 5 g; Carbo 115 g; Fiber 2 g; T Fat 12 g;
19% Calories from Fat; Chol 16 mg; Sod 377 mg.

Peggy O'Neal, **South Central Region**
GFWC—Antlers 20th Century Club, Hugo OK

GRAPE NUT PUDDING

4 cups milk
1 cup Grape Nuts
4 eggs, beaten
1 cup sugar

⅛ teaspoon salt
1 teaspoon vanilla extract
Nutmeg to taste

- Pour milk over Grape Nuts in bowl. Add eggs, sugar, salt and vanilla; mix well.
- Pour into 9x13-inch baking pan. Sprinkle with nutmeg.
- Place baking pan in larger pan filled with 1 to 2 inches of hot water.
- Bake at 350 degrees for 1 hour or until knife inserted near center comes out clean.
- Do not use Grape Nut flakes in this recipe.
- Yield: 15 servings.

Approx Per Serving: Cal 140; Prot 5 g; Carbo 23 g; Fiber <1 g; T Fat 4 g;
23% Calories from Fat; Chol 66 mg; Sod 116 mg.

Mary-Pat Marcello, **New England Region**
GFWC—Matawan Jr. Woman's Club, Middletown NJ

MAPLE SYRUP MOUSSE

¾ cup maple syrup
4 egg yolks, beaten
6 egg whites, stiffly beaten

1 cup whipping cream, whipped
2 cups chopped pecans or walnuts

- Bring maple syrup to a boil in saucepan. Cook until maple syrup is reduced by ¼. Pour over egg yolks in mixer bowl in thin, steady stream, beating continuously until mixture cools.
- Fold in egg whites and whipped cream.
- Spoon into bowl or individual glasses.
- Chill until slightly set.
- Sprinkle with pecans.
- Yield: 8 servings.

Approx Per Serving: Cal 420; Prot 7 g; Carbo 26 g; Fiber 2 g; T Fat 34 g;
70% Calories from Fat; Chol 147 mg; Sod 57 mg.

Mary Castorani, **New England Region**
GFWC—Salem Women's Club, Salem NH

1990—*GFWC is featured in Smithsonian Institution exhibit on women in the Progressive Era, "From Parlor to Politics."*

Indian Pudding with Maple Syrup

1¹/₂ cups raisins
3 cups scalded milk
1 cup cornmeal
1¹/₂ cups cold milk
¹/₂ cup molasses
¹/₃ cup maple syrup

1 teaspoon salt
¹/₂ teaspoon ginger
¹/₂ teaspoon cinnamon
¹/₄ teaspoon allspice
¹/₄ teaspoon nutmeg
¹/₄ cup butter

- Mix raisins and scalded milk in saucepan. Add mixture of cornmeal and cold milk.
- Cook for 8 to 10 minutes or until thickened, stirring constantly.
- Add remaining ingredients; mix well. Pour into 2-quart baking dish.
- Set dish in larger pan filled with 1 inch cold water.
- Bake at 300 degrees for 2¹/₂ hours.
- Let stand for 2 hours.
- Garnish with whipped cream or ice cream.
- Yield: 8 servings.

Approx Per Serving: Cal 367; Prot 7 g; Carbo 64 g; Fiber 3 g; T Fat 11 g;
25% Calories from Fat; Chol 34 mg; Sod 381 mg.

Martha E. Brown, **New England Region**
GFWC—Antrim Woman's Club, Antrim NH

Fruit and Nut Bread Pudding

16 slices bread, torn into pieces
2 cups sugar
4 eggs
3 cups milk
2 teaspoons cinnamon
¹/₂ teaspoon salt

2 teaspoons vanilla extract
1 21-ounce can apple pie filling,
    slices cut into halves
2 cups coarsely chopped pecans
1 cup golden raisins
³/₄ cup melted butter

- Combine bread and sugar in large bowl.
- Beat eggs, milk, cinnamon, salt and vanilla in mixer bowl until foamy. Pour over bread; mix well.
- Chill, covered, for 2 hours.
- Add remaining ingredients to chilled mixture. Spoon into greased 9x13-inch baking pan.
- Bake at 350 degrees for 45 to 50 minutes or until firm.
- Serve warm or cold.
- Garnish with whipped cream.
- Yield: 15 servings.

Approx Per Serving: Cal 494; Prot 8 g; Carbo 65 g; Fiber 3 g; T Fat 24 g;
43% Calories from Fat; Chol 88 mg; Sod 355 mg.

A. Marie Wright, **New England Region**
GFWC—Houlton Women's Club, Houlton ME

TIPSY PUDDING

4 eggs, beaten
1/2 cup sugar
1 quart milk, scalded
1 teaspoon vanilla extract
Nutmeg to taste

1   12-ounce stale sponge cake
2 cups souppernong wine
8 ounces almonds, slivered
1 cup whipped cream, whipped
1/4 cup current jelly

- Combine eggs and sugar in saucepan; mix well. Add hot milk, mixing well. Cook over low heat until thickened and mixture coats a spoon, stirring constantly. Add vanilla and nutmeg.
- Cut sides and bottom of sponge cake to fit glass serving bowl. Pierce deep holes in cake; drizzle with wine. Let stand until wine is absorbed.
- Press almonds into surface of cake. Pour custard over all.
- Top with whipped cream and currant jelly.
- Chill until serving time.
- Yield: 10 servings.

Approx Per Serving: Cal 501; Prot 13 g; Carbo 45 g; Fiber 3 g; T Fat 28 g; 52% Calories from Fat; Chol 202 mg; Sod 192 mg.

*Frances Butler, **Southeastern Region**
GFWC—Amherst Woman's Club, Amherst VA*

WOODFORD PUDDING

1/2 cup butter, softened
1 cup sugar
3 eggs, slightly beaten
1 teaspoon baking soda
1/2 cup buttermilk
1 cup flour
1 teaspoon cinnamon

1 cup blackberry jam
1 1/4 cups milk
2 tablespoons cornstarch
1/4 cup light corn syrup
1 cup packed brown sugar
2 tablespoons butter

- Cream 1/2 cup butter and sugar in mixer bowl until light and fluffy. Beat in eggs.
- Dissolve baking soda in buttermilk. Add buttermilk mixture and mixture of flour and cinnamon to creamed mixture alternately, beating well after each addition. Stir in jam. Spoon into 7x11-inch glass baking dish.
- Bake at 325 degrees for 40 minutes.
- Combine milk and cornstarch in saucepan.
- Cook over medium heat until thickened and bubbly, stirring constantly.
- Cook for 2 minutes longer, stirring occasionally. Remove from heat.
- Stir in brown sugar and butter.
- Pour over warm cake.
- Yield: 8 servings.

Approx Per Serving: Cal 611; Prot 6 g; Carbo 110 g; Fiber 1 g; T Fat 18 g; 26% Calories from Fat; Chol 124 mg; Sod 306 mg.

*Pat Cummins, **Southeastern Region**
GFWC—Florence Woman's Club, Burlington KY*

NORTH DAKOTA RHUBARB CRISP

3 cups 1/2-inch pieces red strawberry
  rhubarb
3/4 cup sugar
1 tablespoon flour
1/2 teaspoon nutmeg
11/4 cups flour

1 cup packed brown sugar
1 cup oats
1/4 teaspoon salt
1/2 cup melted margarine
1/3 cup melted shortening

- Combine rhubarb pieces and mixture of next 3 ingredients in bowl, tossing to mix. Spread into greased 8x8-inch baking dish.
- Combine 11/4 cups flour and remaining ingredients in bowl; mix well. Sprinkle over rhubarb.
- Bake at 350 degrees for 30 minutes or until light brown. Serve warm or cold garnished with whipped cream or ice cream.
- May substitute 1 cup chopped crab apples and 1 tablespoon frozen orange juice concentrate for 1 cup rhubarb for variation.
- Yield: 9 servings.

Approx Per Serving: Cal 445; Prot 4 g; Carbo 68 g; Fiber 3 g; T Fat 19 g;
37% Calories from Fat; Chol 0 mg; Sod 194 mg.

*Harriet Q. Heilman, **Mississippi Valley Region***
GFWC—Rugby Literary Club, Rugby ND

ZUCCHINI CRISP

8 cups thinly sliced peeled zucchini
2/3 cup lemon juice
1 cup sugar
1 teaspoon cinnamon
1/4 teaspoon nutmeg

4 cups flour
11/2 cups margarine
2 cups sugar
1/8 teaspoon salt
1 teaspoon cinnamon

- Mix zucchini and lemon juice in saucepan.
- Cook for 20 to 35 minutes. Add 1 cup sugar, 1 teaspoon cinnamon and nutmeg. Cook for 10 minutes or until tender.
- Mix flour, margarine, 2 cups sugar and salt in bowl. Add 1/2 cup flour mixture to saucepan.
- Pat 1/2 remaining flour mixture into 9x13-inch baking pan.
- Bake at 375 degrees for 10 minutes.
- Spread with zucchini mixture. Top with remaining flour mixture. Sprinkle with 1 teaspoon cinnamon.
- Bake for 30 minutes.
- Yield: 15 servings.

Approx Per Serving: Cal 451; Prot 5 g; Carbo 68 g; Fiber 2 g; T Fat 19 g;
37% Calories from Fat; Chol 0 mg; Sod 235 mg.

*Rosemarie Glaser, **Middle Atlantic Region***
GFWC—Westwood Women's Club, Pittsburgh, PA

ZWIEBACK TORTE

³/₄ 12-ounce package zwieback,
    finely crushed
¹/₂ cup melted butter
³/₄ cup sugar
¹/₄ teaspoon cinnamon
3 egg yolks, beaten
Salt to taste

¹/₂ cup sugar
1 tablespoon (heaping) cornstarch
1 teaspoon vanilla extract
2 cups milk, scalded
3 egg whites
3 tablespoons sugar

- Combine zwieback crumbs and next 3 ingredients in bowl, tossing to mix. Reserve ³/₄ cup mixture. Press remaining mixture into greased springform pan.
- Combine egg yolks, salt, ¹/₂ cup sugar and cornstarch in double boiler; mix well. Add vanilla and scalded milk, mixing well. Cook over hot water until thickened, stirring constantly. Pour over crumb crust.
- Beat egg whites until soft peaks form. Add 3 tablespoons sugar gradually, beating until stiff. Spread over custard; sprinkle with reserved crumb mixture.
- Bake at 350 degrees for 30 minutes.
- Yield: 8 servings.

Approx Per Serving: Cal 449; Prot 8 g; Carbo 64 g; Fiber <1 g; T Fat 18 g;
37% Calories from Fat; Chol 119 mg; Sod 227 mg.

Louise Barce, **Great Lakes Region**
GFWC—PPC of Former 2nd District Presidents, Park Forest IL

COUNTRY APPLE AND PRUNE CAKE

2 cups sugar
1¹/₂ cups oil
3 eggs
2 cups shredded peeled apples
3 cups flour
2 teaspoons baking powder

1 teaspoon salt
1 teaspoon cinnamon
¹/₂ teaspoon ground cloves
2 cups chopped dried prunes
1 cup chopped pecans
¹/₄ cup confectioners' sugar

- Combine sugar, oil and eggs in mixer bowl. Beat at medium speed for 2 minutes. Fold in apples.
- Add mixture of flour, baking powder, salt and spices gradually, beating well after each addition. Stir in prunes and pecans.
- Pour into greased and floured 10-inch tube pan.
- Bake at 325 degrees for 1 hour and 20 minutes or until cake tests done.
- Cool in pan for 15 minutes. Invert onto wire rack to cool completely. Dust with confectioners' sugar just before serving.
- Yield: 14 servings.

Approx Per Serving: Cal 672; Prot 7 g; Carbo 99 g; Fiber 8 g; T Fat 31 g;
40% Calories from Fat; Chol 46 mg; Sod 218 mg.

Barbara Kerr, **Southeastern Region**
GFWC—Clinton Woman's Club, Clinton NC

FRESH APPLE CAKE

3 cups finely chopped, peeled, hard,
    juicy apples
1 cup chopped black walnuts
1¹/₃ cups oil
2 cups sugar
3 eggs
3 tablespoons vanilla extract
3 cups flour, sifted

1 teaspoon salt
1 teaspoon apple pie spice
1 teaspoon baking soda
1 cup packed light brown sugar
¹/₄ cup evaporated milk
Pinch of salt
¹/₂ cup margarine
1 teaspoon vanilla extract

- Combine apples and walnuts in bowl; mix well. Set aside.
- Combine oil, sugar, eggs and 3 tablespoons vanilla in mixer bowl. Beat until smooth.
- Sift next 4 ingredients together 3 times. Add to batter alternately with apple mixture, mixing well after each addition. Pour into greased 10-inch tube pan.
- Bake at 300 degrees for 1¹/₂ hours or until cake tests done. Cool in pan for 10 minutes. Remove to wire rack to cool until slightly warm.
- Combine brown sugar, evaporated milk, a pinch of salt and margarine in saucepan.
- Bring to a boil over low heat; remove from heat. Stir in 1 teaspoon vanilla.
- Let stand until cool. Spread over warm cake. Let stand until glaze is set.
- Yield: 24 servings.

Approx Per Serving: Cal 364; Prot 4 g; Carbo 43 g; Fiber 1 g; T Fat 20 g;
49% Calories from Fat; Chol 27 mg; Sod 185 mg.

Alice T. Baldwin, **Southeastern Region**
GFWC—Woman's Club of Sandston, Highland Springs VA

NORWEGIAN APPLE-WALNUT BUNDT CAKE

1¹/₂ cups sugar
¹/₂ cup packed brown sugar
¹/₂ cup oil
2 eggs, slightly beaten
2 tablespoons rum or vanilla extract
4 cups chopped, peeled Granny Smith
    apples

2 cups sifted flour
2 teaspoons baking soda
1 teaspoon cinnamon
1 teaspoon salt
1 cup chopped walnuts
2 cups prepared fondant

- Combine sugar, brown sugar and oil in mixer bowl. Beat until creamy. Add eggs, rum and apples; mix well.
- Sift flour, baking soda, cinnamon and salt together. Add to batter; mix well. Stir in walnuts. Pour into greased and floured bundt pan.
- Bake at 325 degrees for 1 hour or until cake tests done. Cool in pan for 15 minutes. Invert onto wire rack to cool completely.
- Roll fondant on confectioners' sugar-coated surface. Cover cake with fondant.
- Yield: 12 servings.

Approx Per Serving: Cal 500; Prot 5 g; Carbo 84 g; Fiber 2 g; T Fat 17 g;
30% Calories from Fat; Chol 38 mg; Sod 343 mg.

Bonnie Claycomb, **Great Lakes Region**
GFWC—Lake Orion Women's Club, Lake Orion MI

BLUEBERRY-MAPLE SYRUP CAKE

1/3 cup butter, softened
1/2 cup sugar
3 eggs
3/4 cup maple syrup
21/4 cups flour

1 tablespoon baking powder
1/2 cup milk
2 cups fresh or frozen blueberries
1/4 cup confectioners' sugar

- Cream butter and sugar in mixer bowl until light and fluffy. Beat in eggs 1 at a time. Blend in maple syrup.
- Sift flour and baking powder together. Add to creamed mixture alternately with milk, beginning and ending with flour and beating well after each addition.
- Fold in blueberries gently. Pour into greased and floured small (11/2-quart) bundt pan.
- Bake at 350 degrees for 45 to 50 minutes or until cake is brown and tests done. Invert onto wire rack to cool completely. Dust with confectioners' sugar.
- Yield: 12 servings.

Approx Per Serving: Cal 273; Prot 5 g; Carbo 48 g; Fiber 1 g; T Fat 7 g;
24% Calories from Fat; Chol 68 mg; Sod 152 mg.

*Doreen Duford, **New England Region***
GFWC—Manchester Juniors, Manchester NH

BLUEBERRY-SOUR CREAM CAKE

1/2 cup butter, softened
1 cup sugar
3 eggs
1 cup sour cream
1 teaspoon vanilla extract
2 cups sifted flour

1 teaspoon baking soda
1/2 teaspoon salt
2 cups blueberries
1/2 cup packed brown sugar
1/2 teaspoon cinnamon
1/2 cup chopped pecans

- Cream butter and sugar in mixer bowl until light and fluffy. Add eggs 1 at a time, beating well after each addition. Blend in sour cream and vanilla.
- Sift flour, baking soda and salt together. Add blueberries gently, tossing lightly to coat berries.
- Fold flour and blueberries gently into batter. Spread half the batter in greased 9x13-inch cake pan.
- Sprinkle mixture of brown sugar, cinnamon and pecans over batter. Spread remaining batter over top.
- Bake at 350 degrees for 40 to 45 minutes or until cake tests done. Cool in pan on wire rack. Cut into squares.
- Yield: 12 servings.

Approx Per Serving: Cal 352; Prot 5 g; Carbo 48 g; Fiber 1 g; T Fat 17 g;
42% Calories from Fat; Chol 83 mg; Sod 257 mg.

*Dorothy S. Sudrabin, **Middle Atlantic Region***
GFWC—Woman's Club of Berkeley Heights, Inc., Berkeley Heights NJ

MAINE BLUEBERRY CAKE

3/4 cup sugar
1/2 cup butter, softened
1 egg
1/2 cup milk
2 cups flour
1/2 teaspoon salt

2 teaspoons baking powder
2 cups blueberries
1/2 cup sugar
1/3 cup flour
1 teaspoon cinnamon
1/4 cup butter, softened

- Cream 3/4 cup sugar and 1/2 cup butter in mixer bowl until light and fluffy.
- Mix egg and milk in small bowl. Sift 2 cups flour, salt and baking powder together.
- Add to creamed mixture alternately with milk mixture, mixing well after each addition. Fold in blueberries gently. Spread batter in greased 9x9-inch cake pan.
- Sift remaining 1/2 cup sugar, 1/3 cup flour and cinnamon together into bowl. Cut in remaining 1/4 cup butter until crumbly. Sprinkle over batter.
- Bake at 375 degrees for 30 to 40 minutes or until cake tests done. Cool in pan.
- Yield: 9 servings.

Approx Per Serving: Cal 397; Prot 5 g; Carbo 58 g; Fiber 2 g; T Fat 17 g;
38% Calories from Fat; Chol 67 mg; Sod 337 mg.

Gloria Tewhey, **New England Region**
GFWC—Maine Federation of Women's Clubs, Gorham ME

TOASTED BUTTER PECAN CAKE

1 1/3 cups chopped pecans
1/4 cup melted butter
2 cups sugar
1 1/4 cups butter, softened
4 eggs
3 cups sifted flour
2 teaspoons baking powder

1/2 teaspoon salt
1 cup milk
2 teaspoons vanilla extract
4 cups confectioners' sugar
1 teaspoon vanilla extract
2 tablespoons (about) whipping cream
2/3 cup pecans

- Combine 1 1/3 cups pecans and melted butter in shallow baking pan. Bake at 350 degrees for 20 to 25 minutes or until toasted; set aside.
- Cream sugar and 1 cup butter in mixer bowl until light and fluffy. Beat in eggs 1 at a time. Sift flour, baking powder and salt together. Add to creamed mixture alternately with milk, beating well after each addition. Fold in 2 teaspoons vanilla and toasted pecans. Pour into 3 greased and floured 8 or 9-inch round cake pans.
- Bake at 350 degrees for 20 to 30 minutes or until layers test done. Cool in pans for 5 minutes. Remove to wire rack to cool completely.
- Cream remaining 1/4 cup butter, confectioners' sugar and 1 teaspoon vanilla in mixer bowl until light and fluffy. Add cream; mix well. Stir in pecans. Frost cake.
- Yield: 12 servings.

Approx Per Serving: Cal 757; Prot 8 g; Carbo 105 g; Fiber 2 g; T Fat 36 g;
43% Calories from Fat; Chol 125 mg; Sod 373 mg.

Nettie Grace Herring, **Southeastern Region**
GFWC—Rose Hill Woman's Club, Rose Hill NC

CAKE THAT CAN'T LAST

3 cups flour, sifted
2 cups sugar
1 teaspoon baking soda
1 tablespoon cinnamon
1 teaspoon salt
1½ cups oil
3 eggs
2 cups mashed bananas
1 8-ounce can juice-pack crushed pineapple
1½ teaspoons vanilla extract
1 cup chopped pecans
8 ounces cream cheese, softened
½ cup margarine, softened
1 tablespoon hot chocolate mix
4 cups confectioners' sugar

- Mix first 11 ingredients in bowl until moistened; do not beat.
- Spoon into oiled bundt pan. Bake at 350 degrees for 1 hour and 20 minutes or until cake tests done. Cool in pan on wire rack overnight. Remove to serving plate.
- Beat remaining ingredients in mixer bowl until smooth. Frost cake.
- Yield: 16 servings.

Approx Per Serving: Cal 704; Prot 6 g; Carbo 90 g; Fiber 2 g; T Fat 38 g;
47% Calories from Fat; Chol 55 mg; Sod 323 mg.

*Elouise Ware, **Southeastern Region***
GFWC—Sparta Woman's Club, Sparta TN

CALIFORNIA CHRISTMAS CAKE

1 cup butter, softened
1½ cups sugar
2 eggs
2 tablespoons grated orange rind
2 teaspoons grated lemon rind
2¾ cups flour
2 teaspoons baking powder
1 teaspoon baking soda
½ teaspoon salt
1 cup chopped slivered almonds
1 cup buttermilk
¾ cup golden raisins
½ cup finely chopped candied pineapple
½ cup finely chopped candied red cherries
¾ cup sugar
½ cup orange juice
3 tablespoons lemon juice
4 to 5 tablespoons rum

- Cream butter and 1½ cups sugar in mixer bowl until light and fluffy. Beat in eggs and grated fruit rinds.
- Mix flour, baking powder, baking soda, salt and almonds together. Add to batter alternately with buttermilk, mixing well after each addition. Stir in raisins and candied fruit. Spoon into greased and floured 3-quart molded cake pan.
- Bake at 350 degrees for 1 to 1¼ hours. Heat next 3 ingredients in saucepan until sugar dissolves; remove from heat. Stir in rum.
- Pierce hot cake. Pour rum sauce over cake. Let stand in pan until cool. Remove cake and store, tightly covered or wrapped, for 1 or 2 days before serving.
- Yield: 16 servings.

Approx Per Serving: Cal 441; Prot 6 g; Carbo 67 g; Fiber 2 g; T Fat 17 g;
35% Calories from Fat; Chol 58 mg; Sod 283 mg.

*Virginia K. Crain, **Western Region***
GFWC—Alpha Literary & Improvement Club, Lompoc CA

CHOCOLATE CARROT CAKE

2 cups flour	1 teaspoon salt
1¹/₂ cups sugar	1 teaspoon cinnamon
1 cup oil	1 teaspoon vanilla extract
¹/₂ cup orange juice	4 eggs
¹/₄ cup baking cocoa	2 cups shredded carrots
2 teaspoons baking soda	1 3¹/₂-ounce can flaked coconut

- Combine first 10 ingredients in large mixer bowl; beat at low speed just until mixed, scraping bowl with spatula. Beat at high speed for 2 minutes.
- Stir in carrots and coconut. Spoon into greased and floured 10-inch bundt pan.
- Bake at 350 degrees for 50 to 55 minutes or until wooden pick comes out clean. Cool in pan for 10 to 15 minutes. Remove to wire rack to cool completely.
- Yield: 16 servings.

Approx Per Serving: Cal 310; Prot 4 g; Carbo 36 g; Fiber 2 g; T Fat 17 g; 50% Calories from Fat; Chol 53 mg; Sod 260 mg.

*Sarah Arnold Gose, **Southeastern Region***
GFWC—Somo Sala Circle, Morristown TN

UPSIDE-DOWN GERMAN CHOCOLATE CAKE

¹/₄ cup margarine	2¹/₂ cups flour
1¹/₄ cups water	1¹/₂ cups sugar
1 cup packed brown sugar	1 teaspoon baking soda
1 cup coconut	¹/₂ teaspoon salt
2 cups miniature marshmallows	1 cup sour cream
1 cup chopped pecans	¹/₂ cup margarine, softened
4 ounces German's sweet chocolate	3 eggs
¹/₂ cup water	1 teaspoon vanilla extract

- Melt ¹/₄ cup margarine in 1¹/₄ cups water in small saucepan over medium heat. Pour into 9x13-inch cake pan. Stir in brown sugar and coconut; spread evenly in pan. Sprinkle with marshmallows and pecans.
- Melt chocolate in ¹/₂ cup water in saucepan over low heat. Combine with remaining ingredients in mixer bowl. Beat at low speed for 3 minutes.
- Spoon evenly in prepared dish. Place on baking sheet.
- Bake at 325 degrees for 40 to 50 minutes or until wooden pick comes out clean. Cool on wire rack. Invert servings onto serving plates.
- Yield: 15 servings.

Approx Per Serving: Cal 489; Prot 5 g; Carbo 69 g; Fiber 2 g; T Fat 23 g; 41% Calories from Fat; Chol 49 mg; Sod 272 mg.

*Joyce Long, **Great Lakes Region***
GFWC—Bloomdale Research Club, Bloomdale OH

EASTERN SHORE OLD-FASHIONED COCONUT CAKE

2 cups sugar
1 cup oil
5 eggs
2 cups flour
1¹/₂ teaspoons baking powder
¹/₂ teaspoon salt
¹/₂ cup milk

1 teaspoon vanilla extract
1 teaspoon coconut extract
1 7-ounce can flaked coconut
1 cup sugar
¹/₂ cup water
1 teaspoon coconut extract

- Beat 2 cups sugar and oil in mixer bowl until smooth. Beat in eggs 1 at a time.
- Combine flour, baking powder and salt in bowl. Add to batter alternately with milk, vanilla and 1 teaspoon coconut extract, mixing well after each addition.
- Stir in coconut. Spoon into greased and floured tube pan.
- Bake at 350 degrees for 1 hour.
- Boil remaining ingredients in saucepan for 1 minute. Pierce holes in hot cake with long fork. Pour hot sauce over cake.
- Cool cake in pan. Remove to serving plate.
- Yield: 16 servings.

Approx Per Serving: Cal 406; Prot 4 g; Carbo 55 g; Fiber 2 g; T Fat 20 g; 43% Calories from Fat; Chol 68 mg; Sod 126 mg.

*Hilda O. Micari, **Southeastern Region***
President of Baltimore District GFWC, Baltimore MD

BEE'S KNEES CREAM CHEESE CAKE

1¹/₂ cups margarine, softened
3 cups sugar
8 ounces cream cheese, softened
6 eggs
3 cups flour
Salt to taste

1 teaspoon vanilla extract
6 tablespoons margarine, softened
8 ounces cream cheese, softened
1 1-pound package confectioners'
   sugar
¹/₂ teaspoon vanilla extract

- Cream 1¹/₂ cups margarine, sugar and 8 ounces cream cheese in mixer bowl until light and fluffy. Beat in eggs 1 at a time.
- Add flour, salt and 1 teaspoon vanilla; mix well. Spoon into greased and floured tube pan.
- Bake at 325 degrees for 1¹/₄ hours or until cake tests done. Cool in pan for several minutes. Remove to wire rack to cool completely.
- Cream 6 tablespoons margarine and 8 ounces cream cheese in mixer bowl until smooth. Add confectioners' sugar and ¹/₂ teaspoon vanilla; mix well. Spread on cooled cake.
- Yield: 16 servings.

Approx Per Serving: Cal 680; Prot 7 g; Carbo 90 g; Fiber 1 g; T Fat 34 g; 44% Calories from Fat; Chol 111 mg; Sod 362 mg.

*Tammy Hayes, **Southeastern Region***
GFWC—Hendersonville Woman's Club, Hendersonville TN

DOVER CAKE

1 cup butter, softened
2 cups sugar
6 egg yolks
1 cup milk
4 cups flour

1 tablespoon baking powder
1/8 teaspoon salt
6 egg whites, stiffly beaten
1/2 teaspoon each almond, vanilla, rum and rose extracts

- Cream butter and sugar in mixer bowl until light and fluffy. Beat in egg yolks and milk. Sift in flour, baking powder and salt; mix well.
- Fold in egg whites and flavorings. Spoon into greased and floured tube pan.
- Place in preheated 350-degree oven. Reduce oven temperature to 250 degrees.
- Bake for 1 1/4 hours or until cake tests done. Cool in pan for several minutes. Remove to wire rack to cool completely.
- The rose extract can be purchased at a drug store.
- Yield: 16 servings.

Approx Per Serving: Cal 352; Prot 6 g; Carbo 50 g; Fiber 1 g; T Fat 14 g; 37% Calories from Fat; Chol 113 mg; Sod 254 mg.

Beverly Page, **Southeastern Region**
GFWC—South Arundel Club, Inc., North Beach MD

STEAMED LIGHT FRUITCAKES À LA TANNER

2 cups flour
1 pound dates, chopped
8 ounces candied cherries, chopped
8 ounces dried apricots, chopped
1 pound golden raisins
4 ounces pineapple, finely chopped
8 ounces candied orange peel, chopped
8 ounces candied lemon peel, chopped
8 ounces citron, chopped

1 pound almonds
2 cups butter, softened
2 cups sugar
10 eggs
1/2 cup strawberry preserves
2 cups flour
8 teaspoons baking powder
1 cup pineapple juice
1 cup brandy

- Sift 2 cups flour over mixture of fruit and nuts in large bowl.
- Cream butter and sugar in mixer bowl until light and fluffy. Beat in eggs 1 at a time.
- Add preserves and mixture of 2 cups flour and baking powder 1/3 at a time, alternating with pineapple juice and brandy and mixing well after each addition. Fold in fruit mixture.
- Spoon into greased molds, filling 2/3 full. Tie a piece of moistened baking parchment over the top of the molds. Place on rack in pressure cooker.
- Cook without pressure for 15 minutes. Cook at 15 pounds pressure for an additional 40 minutes using manufacturer's instructions.
- Cool fruitcakes in molds on wire rack. Remove from molds and wrap in foil.
- Yield: 60 servings.

Approx Per Serving: Cal 290; Prot 4 g; Carbo 45 g; Fiber 3 g; T Fat 11 g; 34% Calories from Fat; Chol 52 mg; Sod 121 mg.

Muriel T. Ives, **Western Region**
GFWC—Lake Arrowhead Woman's Club, Lake Arrowhead CA

SOUTHERN SPICY GINGERBREAD

3/4 cup melted shortening
3/4 cup packed brown sugar
2 eggs
3/4 cup molasses
2 teaspoons baking soda
1 cup boiling water
2 1/3 cups flour
1/2 teaspoon baking powder
2 teaspoons ginger

1 1/2 teaspoons cinnamon
1/2 teaspoon each cloves and nutmeg
1/2 cup milk
1/2 cup water
1 cup packed brown sugar
1 1/2 tablespoons flour
1/8 teaspoon nutmeg
2 tablespoons butter
1/2 teaspoon vanilla extract

- Combine shortening and 3/4 cup brown sugar in mixer bowl; mix well. Beat in eggs and molasses. Add mixture of baking soda and boiling water.
- Mix 2 1/3 cups flour with next 5 ingredients in bowl. Add to batter gradually, mixing well after each addition. Spoon into greased 9x13-inch cake pan.
- Bake at 350 degrees for 40 to 45 minutes or until gingerbread tests done.
- Bring next 5 ingredients to a boil in saucepan. Cook until slightly thickened; remove from heat. Stir in butter and vanilla. Serve with warm gingerbread.
- Yield: 15 servings.

Approx Per Serving: Cal 347; Prot 3 g; Carbo 56 g; Fiber 1 g; T Fat 13 g; 33% Calories from Fat; Chol 34 mg; Sod 163 mg.

*Ruby Carlton, **Southeastern Region***
GFWC—Woman's Club of Bluefield, Bluefield VA

KENTUCKY JAM CAKE

1 cup sugar
1 cup packed brown sugar
3/4 cup butter, softened
3 eggs
2 1/2 cups flour
2 tablespoons baking cocoa
1 teaspoon baking powder
1/2 teaspoon baking soda

2 teaspoons cinnamon
1/2 teaspoon each cloves, allspice and nutmeg
1/2 cup each cold coffee and buttermilk
1 1/2 cups blackberry jam
1 cup chopped walnuts
1 cup raisins
1 teaspoon vanilla extract

- Cream sugar, brown sugar and butter in mixer bowl until light and fluffy. Beat in eggs.
- Sift dry ingredients together. Add to batter alternately with coffee and buttermilk, mixing well after each addition.
- Stir in jam, walnuts, raisins and vanilla. Spoon into greased and floured bundt pan.
- Bake at 375 degrees for 1 hour. Cool in pan for several minutes; remove to wire rack to cool completely.
- Yield: 16 servings.

Approx Per Serving: Cal 440; Prot 5 g; Carbo 75 g; Fiber 2 g; T Fat 15 g; 29% Calories from Fat; Chol 64 mg; Sod 153 mg.

*Mary Crompton, **Southeastern Region***
GFWC—Valley Woman's Club, Louisville KY

ORANGE AND DATE-NUT CAKE

1 cup milk
2 tablespoons vinegar
1 cup shortening
1 cup sugar
2 eggs
1 teaspoon vanilla extract
2¼ cups flour

1 teaspoon baking soda
1 cup chopped pecans
1 cup chopped dates
Grated rind of 2 oranges
Juice of 2 oranges
¾ cup sugar

- Mix milk and vinegar in bowl. Let stand until soured. Cream shortening and 1 cup sugar in mixer bowl until light and fluffy. Beat in eggs and vanilla.
- Add mixture of flour and baking soda alternately with soured milk, mixing well after each addition. Stir in pecans, dates and orange rind.
- Spoon into greased and floured tube pan.
- Bake at 300 degrees for 1 hour.
- Cook orange juice and ¾ cup sugar in saucepan for 5 minutes. Pour over hot cake in pan. Let stand overnight. Remove cake to serving plate.
- Yield: 16 servings.

Approx Per Serving: Cal 367; Prot 4 g; Carbo 47 g; Fiber 2 g; T Fat 19 g;
46% Calories from Fat; Chol 29 mg; Sod 68 mg.

Lynn Ball, **Southern Region**
GFWC—St. Petersburg Junior Woman's Club, St. Petersburg FL

PECAN PRALINE CAKE

½ cup butter
1 cup buttermilk
2 cups packed light brown sugar
2 eggs
2 cups flour
1 teaspoon baking soda
1 tablespoon baking cocoa

1 tablespoon vanilla extract
½ cup butter
1 cup packed light brown sugar
⅓ cup evaporated milk
1 cup chopped pecans
1   6-ounce can coconut

- Melt ½ cup butter in small saucepan over low heat. Stir in buttermilk. Combine with 2 cups brown sugar and eggs in large mixer bowl; mix well.
- Sift in flour, baking soda and cocoa; mix well. Stir in vanilla. Spoon into greased and floured 9x13-inch cake pan.
- Bake at 350 degrees for 35 minutes.
- Combine remaining ingredients in saucepan.
- Cook over low heat until butter melts, mixing well. Spread over warm cake.
- Broil 4 inches from heat source for 1 to 2 minutes or until golden brown.
- Serve warm with whipped cream flavored with cinnamon.
- Yield: 15 servings.

Approx Per Serving: Cal 503; Prot 5 g; Carbo 73 g; Fiber 2 g; T Fat 23 g;
40% Calories from Fat; Chol 64 mg; Sod 217 mg.

Priscilla Killens, **Southern Region**
GFWC—Newton Culture Club, Newton MS

AMISH HALF-A-POUND CAKE

2 cups sifted flour
1¹/₂ cups sugar
4 eggs, at room temperature
1 cup butter, softened
¹/₂ cup milk

2 teaspoons baking powder
¹/₂ teaspoon mace
¹/₂ teaspoon salt
2 teaspoons vanilla extract

- Combine all ingredients in mixer bowl. Beat at medium speed for 20 minutes.
- Spoon into greased and floured 10-inch tube pan. Place in cold oven. Set oven temperature at 350 degrees.
- Bake for 1 hour. Invert cake pan on wire rack to cool. Remove cake from pan.
- Dust with confectioners' sugar or frost with chocolate buttercream frosting.
- Yield: 16 servings.

Approx Per Serving: Cal 251; Prot 3 g; Carbo 30 g; Fiber <1 g; T Fat 13 g;
47% Calories from Fat; Chol 85 mg; Sod 226 mg.

*Mildred Young, **Middle Atlantic Region***
GFWC—Woman's Club of Maple Shade, Maple Shade NJ

GEORGIA PEACHY POUND CAKE

1 cup margarine, softened
3 cups sugar
6 eggs
3 cups flour
¹/₄ teaspoon baking soda

¹/₄ teaspoon salt
¹/₂ cup sour cream
2 cups chopped peeled fresh peaches
1 teaspoon vanilla extract
1 teaspoon almond extract

- Cream margarine and sugar in mixer bowl until light and fluffy. Beat in eggs 1 at a time.
- Combine dry ingredients. Add to creamed mixture alternately with sour cream, beginning and ending with dry ingredients and mixing well after each addition.
- Fold in peaches and flavorings. Spoon into greased 10-inch tube pan.
- Bake at 350 degrees for 1 hour and 15 minutes to 1 hour and 20 minutes or until cake tests done. Cool in pan for several minutes. Remove cake to wire rack to cool completely.
- Yield: 16 servings.

Approx Per Serving: Cal 390; Prot 5 g; Carbo 59 g; Fiber 1 g; T Fat 15 g;
35% Calories from Fat; Chol 83 mg; Sod 211 mg.

*Ann Story, **Southern Region***
GFWC—Warner Robins Woman's Club, Warner Robins GA

POTATO CAKE

3/4 cup shortening
2 cups sugar
4 eggs, beaten
2 cups flour
1/2 cup baking cocoa
2 teaspoons baking powder
2 teaspoons nutmeg

2 teaspoons cinnamon
1 teaspoon allspice
1/2 teaspoon salt
1 cup milk
1 teaspoon vanilla extract
1 cup mashed cooked potatoes
1 cup chopped walnuts

- Cream shortening and sugar in mixer bowl until light and fluffy. Beat in eggs.
- Sift dry ingredients together. Add to batter alternately with milk, mixing well after each addition.
- Stir in vanilla, potatoes and walnuts. Spoon into 2 greased and floured 9-inch cake pans.
- Bake at 350 degrees for 40 minutes. Cool in pans for several minutes. Remove to wire rack to cool completely. Frost with chocolate buttercream frosting.
- Yield: 16 servings.

Approx Per Serving: Cal 333; Prot 5 g; Carbo 43 g; Fiber 2 g; T Fat 17 g; 44% Calories from Fat; Chol 56 mg; Sod 173 mg.

Nita Carey, **Western Region**
GFWC—SGVD Board Alumnae, Duarte CA

HOOSIER PUMPKIN CAKE ROLL

3 eggs
1 cup sugar
1 cup canned pumpkin
1 teaspoon lemon juice
3/4 cup flour
1 teaspoon baking powder
2 teaspoons pumpkin pie spice

1/2 teaspoon salt
3/4 cup finely chopped pecans
1/2 cup confectioners' sugar
8 ounces cream cheese, softened
1/4 cup margarine, softened
1 cup confectioners' sugar
1/2 teaspoon vanilla extract

- Beat eggs at high speed in mixer bowl for 5 minutes. Beat in sugar gradually. Stir in pumpkin and lemon juice.
- Sift flour, baking powder, pumpkin pie spice and salt together. Fold into batter.
- Spoon into waxed paper-lined 10x15-inch cake pan. Sprinkle with pecans.
- Bake at 350 degrees for 15 minutes. Invert onto thin kitchen towel sprinkled with 1/2 cup confectioners' sugar; remove waxed paper. Roll cake up in towel from narrow side. Let stand until cool.
- Combine remaining ingredients in mixer bowl; beat until smooth.
- Unroll cake. Spread with cream cheese mixture. Roll to enclose filling. Chill until serving time.
- Yield: 12 servings.

Approx Per Serving: Cal 327; Prot 5 g; Carbo 41 g; Fiber 1 g; T Fat 17 g; 45% Calories from Fat; Chol 74 mg; Sod 236 mg.

Jean Webb, **Great Lakes Region**
GFWC—Tercera Club, Poseyville IN

SHOE BOX CAKE

1 1-pound package graham crackers,
   finely crushed
2 cups sugar
1 cup melted butter
2 teaspoons baking powder

2 cups milk
1 cup coarsely chopped black walnuts
2 cups coarsely chopped pecans
8 ounces shredded coconut
6 eggs, beaten

- Combine first 8 ingredients in mixer bowl; mix until smooth. Add eggs; mix well.
- Pour into shoe box lined with waxed paper.
- Bake at 250 degrees for 3½ hours. Cool in box for several minutes. Remove to wire rack to cool completely.
- This works because of the lower baking temperature. May substitute English walnuts for black walnuts.
- Yield: 24 servings.

Approx Per Serving: Cal 391; Prot 6 g; Carbo 39 g; Fiber 2 g; T Fat 25 g;
55% Calories from Fat; Chol 77 mg; Sod 259 mg.

*Shelby P. Hamlett, **Southeastern Region***
GFWC Recording Secretary, 1992–94, Roanoke VA

SHOO-FLY CAKE

4 cups flour
¾ cup shortening
2 cups packed dark brown sugar

1 cup dark molasses
1 tablespoon baking soda
2 cups hot water

- Combine flour, shortening and brown sugar in bowl; mix with pastry blender until crumbly. Reserve 1 cup crumb mixture.
- Combine remaining crumb mixture with next 3 ingredients in bowl; mix well.
- Spoon into greased 9x13-inch cake pan; sprinkle with reserved crumbs.
- Bake at 350 degrees for 45 to 50 minutes or until cake tests done. Remove to wire rack to cool completely.
- Yield: 15 servings.

Approx Per Serving: Cal 394; Prot 3 g; Carbo 72 g; Fiber 1 g; T Fat 11 g;
24% Calories from Fat; Chol 0 mg; Sod 201 mg.

*Marcia L. Wilson, **Middle Atlantic Region***
GFWC—Women's Community Club of Littlestown, Hanover PA

1990—*GFWC celebrated its Centennial.*

SWEDISH NUT CAKE

2 eggs
2 cups sugar
2 cups flour
2 teaspoons baking soda
1 teaspoon vanilla extract
1 20-ounce can crushed pineapple

1/2 cup chopped walnuts
8 ounces cream cheese, softened
1/2 cup margarine, softened
1 3/4 cups confectioners' sugar
1 teaspoon vanilla extract
1/2 cup finely chopped walnuts

- Combine eggs, sugar, flour, baking soda, vanilla, undrained pineapple and 1/2 cup walnuts in bowl; mix by hand until moistened.
- Spoon into greased and floured 9x13-inch cake pan.
- Bake at 350 degrees for 40 minutes. Cool in pan for 10 minutes.
- Combine remaining ingredients in mixer bowl; mix well. Spread on warm cake. Cool to room temperature. Cut into squares.
- Yield: 15 servings.

Approx Per Serving: Cal 416; Prot 5 g; Carbo 63 g; Fiber 1 g; T Fat 17 g; 36% Calories from Fat; Chol 45 mg; Sod 237 mg.

*Mrs Albert Orne, **Great Lakes Region***
GFWC—Roseland Woman's Club, Crete IL

GRATED SWEET POTATO CAKE

2 cups sugar
1 1/2 cups oil
4 eggs
2 1/2 cups self-rising flour
2 teaspoons cinnamon
3 cups grated sweet potatoes
1 cup chopped pecans

1 cup grated coconut
1/2 cup margarine, softened
8 ounces cream cheese, softened
1 teaspoon vanilla extract
1 1-pound package confectioners' sugar, sifted
2 tablespoons hot water

- Beat sugar and oil in mixer bowl until smooth. Beat in eggs 1 at a time.
- Sift flour and cinnamon together. Add 1/3 at a time to batter, mixing well after each addition.
- Fold in sweet potatoes, pecans and coconut. Spoon into greased and floured 10-inch tube pan.
- Bake at 300 degrees for 1 hour or until cake tests done. Cool in pan for several minutes. Remove to wire rack to cool completely.
- Cream margarine and cream cheese in mixer bowl until light and fluffy. Add vanilla and confectioners' sugar gradually, mixing well. Add enough hot water to make of spreading consistency.
- Spread frosting on cake.
- May bake cake in two 9-inch cake pans for 40 minutes if preferred.
- Yield: 16 servings.

Approx Per Serving: Cal 724; Prot 6 g; Carbo 90 g; Fiber 3 g; T Fat 40 g; 48% Calories from Fat; Chol 69 mg; Sod 346 mg.

*Marian Cotney, **Southern Region***
GFWC—Inter Se Club of Wadley, Wadley AL

1915 TENT CITY TOSS-IN

2 cups sugar
2 cups strong coffee
2 cups raisins
1 medium apple, peeled, grated
2 cups flour

1 teaspoon each baking powder,
    baking soda, cinnamon, allspice,
    nutmeg and ground cloves
1 cup chopped walnuts

- Simmer sugar, coffee, raisins and apple in large saucepan for 10 minutes. Cool for 10 minutes.
- Combine remaining ingredients in bowl. Add to cooled coffee mixture; mix well.
- Spoon into greased 9x13-inch cake pan.
- Bake at 350 degrees for 25 minutes. Cool on wire rack.
- May frost if desired. This moist cake contains no eggs or shortening.
- Yield: 15 servings.

Approx Per Serving: Cal 286; Prot 4 g; Carbo 60 g; Fiber 2 g; T Fat 5 g;
16% Calories from Fat; Chol 0 mg; Sod 82 mg.

*Kay Linton, **Western Region***
GFWC—Anchorage Woman's Club, Anchorage AK

MARSHMALLOW MARBLE-TOP FUDGE

3 cups semisweet chocolate chips
2 tablespoons butter
1 14-ounce can sweetened condensed
    milk
1½ teaspoons vanilla extract

⅛ teaspoon salt
1 cup chopped walnuts
2 cups miniature marshmallows
2 tablespoons butter

- Combine chocolate chips, 2 tablespoons butter, condensed milk, vanilla and salt in heavy saucepan.
- Cook over low heat until chocolate melts; remove from heat. Stir in walnuts. Spread evenly in foil-lined 8-inch square dish.
- Combine marshmallows and remaining 2 tablespoons butter in medium saucepan.
- Cook over low heat until melted. Spread over fudge; swirl with knife.
- Chill for 2 hours or until firm. Remove from dish; peel off foil. Cut into squares.
- Store, loosely covered, at room temperature.
- Yield: 60 servings.

Approx Per Serving: Cal 90; Prot 1 g; Carbo 10 g; Fiber <1 g; T Fat 6 g;
52% Calories from Fat; Chol 4 mg; Sod 22 mg.

*Doris A. Botsch, **Middle Atlantic Region***
GFWC—Twentieth Century Club of Smyrna, Smyrna DE

MACKINAC ISLAND VANILLA FUDGE

1/2 cup milk
1/2 cup butter
1/2 cup packed brown sugar
1/2 cup sugar

1/8 teaspoon salt
2 1/2 cups unsifted confectioners' sugar
1 teaspoon vanilla extract
1/4 cup chopped pecans

- Combine milk, butter, brown sugar, sugar and salt in 2-quart glass mix-and-pour bowl.
- Microwave, uncovered, on High for 3 minutes. Stir mixture, scraping side of bowl to dissolve sugar crystals. Insert microwave candy thermometer.
- Microwave, uncovered, on High for 6 to 7 minutes or to 235 degrees on candy thermometer, soft-ball stage, stirring once or twice.
- Add confectioners' sugar and vanilla. Beat at medium speed of electric mixer for about 8 minutes or until thickened. Stir in pecans.
- Spread in buttered 5x9-inch dish. Let stand until set. Cut into squares.
- Yield: 30 servings.

Approx Per Serving: Cal 105; Prot <1 g; Carbo 18 g; Fiber <1 g; T Fat 4 g;
32% Calories from Fat; Chol 9 mg; Sod 39 mg.

Elma Lou Davis, **Great Lakes Region**
GFWC—Macomb Woman's Club, Macomb IL

KENTUCKY COLONELS

1/2 cup butter, softened
3 tablespoons sweetened condensed milk
1/3 cup plus 2 teaspoons bourbon
7 1/2 cups confectioners' sugar

1/2 cup finely chopped pecans
1 cup semisweet chocolate chips
1 tablespoon melted paraffin
36 pecan halves

- Combine butter, condensed milk and bourbon in large mixer bowl; mix well.
- Add confectioners' sugar. Knead until smooth. Knead in chopped pecans. Shape into 1-inch balls.
- Combine chocolate and paraffin in double boiler.
- Cook over hot water until chocolate melts, stirring constantly.
- Dip each candy ball into chocolate mixture with wooden pick. Place on waxed paper-lined surface. Remove wooden pick.
- Press pecan half into each candy. Let stand until firm.
- May substitute 1 tablespoon melted shortening for paraffin in chocolate mixture. Chocolate coating may be soft to the touch.
- Yield: 36 servings.

Approx Per Serving: Cal 176; Prot 1 g; Carbo 29 g; Fiber <1 g; T Fat 7 g;
34% Calories from Fat; Chol 7 mg; Sod 24 mg.

Janice K. Geise, **Southeastern Region**
GFWC—Florence Woman's Club, Union KY

MEXICAN ORANGE CANDY

1 cup sugar
1/4 cup water
2 cups sugar
1 cup evaporated milk

1/8 teaspoon salt
2 teaspoons freshly grated orange rind
1 cup chopped walnuts

- Heat 1 cup sugar in heavy saucepan over medium heat until sugar melts and is caramelized or golden brown, stirring constantly.
- Add water. Stir until caramelized sugar dissolves completely. Add remaining 2 cups sugar, evaporated milk and salt; mix well.
- Bring to a boil over low heat, stirring constantly. Cook to 236 degrees on candy thermometer, soft-ball stage, stirring frequently; remove from heat.
- Let stand until cooled to lukewarm; do not stir. Add orange rind and walnuts.
- Beat until candy loses its gloss and holds shape when dropped from spoon. Pour into lightly buttered 8-inch square dish.
- Let stand until set. Cut into squares while warm.
- Yield: 64 servings.

Approx Per Serving: Cal 54; Prot 1 g; Carbo 10 g; Fiber <1 g; T Fat 1 g; 24% Calories from Fat; Chol 1 mg; Sod 9 mg.

Shirley Basel, **South Central Region**
GFWC—Tucson ESO, Tucson Arizona

SOUR CREAM PRALINES

1   16-ounce package dark brown sugar
1 cup sugar
1 cup sour cream

1/2 cup marshmallow creme
3 cups pecan halves

- Combine brown sugar, sugar and sour cream in saucepan; mix well.
- Cook mixture over low heat to 240 degrees on candy thermometer, soft-ball stage, stirring frequently.
- Add marshmallow creme. Let stand until creme melts.
- Beat until mixture is thickened and holds its shape. Stir in pecans.
- Drop by spoonfuls onto waxed paper-lined surface. Let stand until firm. Store in airtight container.
- May substitute 1 cup miniature marshmallows for marshmallow creme.
- Yield: 36 servings.

Approx Per Serving: Cal 154; Prot 1 g; Carbo 23 g; Fiber 1 g; T Fat 7 g; 42% Calories from Fat; Chol 3 mg; Sod 11 mg.

Erlene Thomas, **South Central Region**
GFWC—McCamey Woman's Study Club, McCamey TX

BLACK WALNUT TAFFY

3 cups sugar
2 cups whipping cream
2 cups light corn syrup
¼ cup butter
3 tablespoons shaved paraffin

1 teaspoon (heaping) unflavored
  gelatin
¼ cup water
1 cup finely chopped black walnuts
1 teaspoon vanilla extract

- Combine sugar, cream, corn syrup, butter and paraffin in saucepan; mix well.
- Cook over low heat to 236 degrees on candy thermometer, soft-ball stage. Add gelatin dissolved in ¼ cup water.
- Cook to 260 degrees on candy thermometer, hard-ball stage. Pour into platter or shallow dish. Let stand until cool.
- Add walnuts and vanilla. Pull until taffy is creamy and smooth. Cut into desired lengths. Wrap individual pieces in plastic wrap.
- Yield: 60 servings.

Approx Per Serving: Cal 116; Prot <1 g; Carbo 19 g; Fiber <1 g; T Fat 5 g;
37% Calories from Fat; Chol 13 mg; Sod 15 mg.

Mrs. Dana Johnson, **Mississippi Valley Region**
GFWC—Ladies' Library Club, Republic KS

HOMESTEADER "ANYTHING GOES" COOKIES

¾ cup Grape Nuts
¾ cup finely crushed graham crackers
¾ cup finely snipped dried apricots
½ cup finely chopped pecans

½ cup sifted confectioners' sugar
¼ cup light corn syrup
1 tablespoon orange juice
¼ cup sifted confectioners' sugar

- Combine cereal, graham cracker crumbs, apricots, pecans and ½ cup confectioners' sugar in bowl; mix well. Stir in corn syrup and orange juice.
- Shape into ¾-inch balls with buttered hands. Coat with remaining ¼ cup confectioners' sugar.
- This is an Alaskan homesteader recipe. Out in the wilderness, where you have to pack all your supplies on your back, you use whatever you have at the time to make cookies. You don't have to use precious fuel to cook these either!
- Yield: 36 servings.

Approx Per Serving: Cal 58; Prot 1 g; Carbo 11 g; Fiber 1 g; T Fat 1 g;
21% Calories from Fat; Chol 0 mg; Sod 33 mg.

R. J. Linton, **Western Region**
GFWC—Kenai Keys Kountry Klub, Anchorage AL

1992—*GFWC co-sponsored national student poster contest in honor of the 50th anniversary of U.S. Savings Bonds.*

APPLESAUCE BROWNIES

1½ cups sugar
½ cup shortening
2 eggs, beaten
2 cups flour
½ teaspoon salt
1 teaspoon baking soda

2 tablespoons baking cocoa
½ teaspoon cinnamon
2 cups chunky applesauce
1 cup chocolate chips
½ cup chopped pecans
2 tablespoons sugar

- Cream 1½ cups sugar and shortening in mixer bowl until light and fluffy. Add eggs; mix well.
- Sift flour, salt, baking soda, baking cocoa and cinnamon together. Add to creamed mixture alternately with applesauce, mixing well after each addition.
- Spread in nonstick 10x15-inch baking pan. Sprinkle chocolate chips, pecans and remaining 2 tablespoons sugar over batter.
- Bake at 350 degrees for about 20 minutes or until edges pull away from sides of pan; do not overbake. Let stand until cool. Cut into bars.
- Yield: 24 servings.

Approx Per Serving: Cal 204; Prot 2 g; Carbo 30 g; Fiber 1 g; T Fat 9 g; 39% Calories from Fat; Chol 18 mg; Sod 87 mg.

Marjorie Tribby, **Mississippi Valley Region**
GFWC—TRR Club, La Cygne KS

DANISH PASTRY APPLE BARS

2½ cups flour
1 teaspoon salt
1 cup margarine
1 egg yolk
½ cup (about) milk
1 cup crushed cornflakes

10 tart apples, peeled, thinly sliced
¾ cup sugar
1 teaspoon cinnamon
1 egg white, beaten
2 cups favorite confectioners' sugar
    frosting

- Combine flour and salt in bowl. Cut in margarine until crumbly.
- Beat egg yolk in measuring cup. Add enough milk to egg yolk to measure ⅔ cup liquid; mix well. Stir into flour mixture.
- Divide dough into 2 portions, 1 slightly larger than the other. Roll larger portion on floured surface to fit over bottom and up sides of nonstick 10x15-inch baking pan. Place in pan.
- Sprinkle cornflakes, apples, sugar and cinnamon over pastry.
- Top with remaining pastry; seal edges and cut slits in top. Brush with egg white.
- Bake at 325 degrees for 50 minutes or until golden brown.
- Frost with confectioners' sugar frosting while warm. Cool. Cut into bars.
- Yield: 24 servings.

Approx Per Serving: Cal 241; Prot 2 g; Carbo 37 g; Fiber 2 g; T Fat 10 g; 37% Calories from Fat; Chol 14 mg; Sod 233 mg.

Pat Beauchamp, **Great Lakes Region**
GFWC—Escanaba Women's Club, Escanaba MI

BUTTER RICHES

3/4 cup butter, softened
1/2 cup packed brown sugar
1 tablespoon sugar
1 egg yolk
1 teaspoon vanilla extract
2 cups (about) sifted flour

1/4 cup sugar
1/4 cup butter
2 1/2 cups sifted confectioners' sugar
1 teaspoon vanilla extract
1/4 cup (about) whipping cream
168 almond slivers

- Cream 3/4 cup butter in mixer bowl until fluffy. Add brown sugar and 1 tablespoon sugar. Beat until light.
- Beat in egg yolk and 1 teaspoon vanilla. Add enough flour to make stiff dough; mix well.
- Shape into marble-sized balls. Place on greased cookie sheet. Flatten with glass dipped in remaining 1/4 cup sugar.
- Bake at 350 degrees for 7 to 9 minutes or until light golden brown. Remove to wire rack to cool.
- Brown remaining 1/4 cup butter in saucepan over low heat; remove from heat. Stir in confectioners' sugar and remaining 1 teaspoon vanilla.
- Add cream 1 tablespoon at a time until of spreading consistency, mixing well after each addition. Spread over cookies. Arrange 2 slivered almonds in "V" shape on each cookie.
- Yield: 84 servings.

Approx Per Serving: Cal 57; Prot <1 g; Carbo 8 g; Fiber <1 g; T Fat 3 g;
45% Calories from Fat; Chol 9 mg; Sod 20 mg.

*Alice H. Aishton, **Southeastern Region***
GFWC—Woman's Club of Manassas, Manassas VA

GROWN-UP CHOCOLATE CHIP COOKIES

3/4 cup butter, softened
3/4 cup sugar
1/2 teaspoon vanilla extract
1 1/2 cups flour

1/4 cup dark rum
1 1/2 cups ground hazelnuts
2/3 cup miniature chocolate chips

- Cream butter and sugar at medium speed in mixer bowl until light and fluffy. Add vanilla; mix well.
- Add flour and rum alternately, beating constantly at low speed. Stir in hazelnuts and chocolate chips.
- Drop by teaspoonfuls 2 inches apart on greased cookie sheet.
- Bake on middle rack at 350 degrees for 12 to 15 minutes or until browned. Cool on cookie sheet for 1 minute. Remove to wire rack to cool completely.
- Yield: 30 servings.

Approx Per Serving: Cal 179; Prot 2 g; Carbo 14 g; Fiber 1 g; T Fat 13 g;
65% Calories from Fat; Chol 12 mg; Sod 40 mg.

*Marie K. Knoeller, **Middle Atlantic Region***
GFWC—Village Improvement Association, Cranford NJ

CHOCOLATE-CARAMEL COOKIES

2¹/₂ cups flour
³/₄ cup baking cocoa
1 teaspoon baking soda
1 cup sugar
1 cup packed brown sugar
1 cup margarine, softened
2 teaspoons vanilla extract
2 eggs

¹/₂ cup chopped pecans
1   9-ounce package Rolo chewy
    caramels
¹/₂ cup chopped pecans
1 tablespoon sugar
4 ounces white vanilla-flavored candy
    coating, melted

▪ Combine flour, baking cocoa and baking soda in bowl; mix well. Set aside.
▪ Cream sugars and margarine in mixer bowl until light and fluffy. Add vanilla and eggs; mix well. Add flour mixture; mix well. Stir in ¹/₂ cup pecans.
▪ Shape into balls around each caramel, covering completely. Coat 1 side of each ball with mixture of remaining ¹/₂ cup pecans and 1 tablespoon sugar.
▪ Place uncoated side down on ungreased cookie sheet.
▪ Bake at 375 degrees for 8 minutes or until cookies start to crack on top; do not overbake. Remove to wire rack to cool completely.
▪ Drizzle melted candy coating over cookies. Let stand until coating is firm.
▪ Yield: 48 servings.

Approx Per Serving: Cal 158; Prot 2 g; Carbo 22 g; Fiber 1 g; T Fat 8 g;
43% Calories from Fat; Chol 9 mg; Sod 79 mg.

Elsie Williams, **Mississippi Valley Region**
GFWC—Lowell Get-Together Club, New London IA

MAPLE BARS

¹/₂ cup sugar
¹/₂ cup shortening
¹/₂ cup maple syrup
1 egg
²/₃ cup sifted flour

1 cup chopped pecans
1 cup oats
¹/₂ teaspoon baking powder
1 teaspoon vanilla extract

▪ Combine sugar, shortening, maple syrup and egg in bowl; mix well.
▪ Add mixture of flour, pecans, oats and baking powder; mix well Blend in vanilla.
▪ Spread in greased 8x8-inch baking pan.
▪ Bake at 350 degrees for 30 minutes. Cut into bars while warm.
▪ Yield: 16 servings.

Approx Per Serving: Cal 198; Prot 2 g; Carbo 21 g; Fiber 1 g; T Fat 12 g;
54% Calories from Fat; Chol 13 mg; Sod 17 mg.

Maydene Bone, **New England Region**
GFWC—South Ryegate Women's Club, South Ryegate VT

PIKE'S PEAK PEANUT BUTTER BARS

1/2 cup peanut butter
1/3 cup butter, softened
3/4 cup packed brown sugar
3/4 cup sugar
2 eggs

2 teaspoons vanilla extract
1 cup flour
1 teaspoon baking powder
1/4 teaspoon salt
2 cups chocolate chips

- Cream peanut butter, butter, brown sugar and sugar in mixer bowl until blended. Add eggs 1 at a time, beating well after each addition. Blend in vanilla. Add mixture of flour, baking powder and salt; mix well. Stir in 1 cup chocolate chips.
- Spread batter in greased 9x13-inch baking pan. Sprinkle remaining 1 cup chocolate chips over top.
- Bake at 350 degrees for 3 minutes or until chocolate chips melt. Swirl batter with knife to marbleize.
- Bake for 25 minutes longer or until edges pull from sides of pan; do not overbake.
- Let stand until cool. Cut into bars.
- Yield: 24 servings.

Approx Per Serving: Cal 209; Prot 3 g; Carbo 28 g; Fiber 1 g; T Fat 11 g; 44% Calories from Fat; Chol 25 mg; Sod 91 mg.

Kris Hauck, **Western Region**
GFWC—Madison Valley Woman's Club, Ennis MT

COWBOY SOUR CREAM-APPLE PIE

3/4 cup sugar
2 tablespoons flour
1 egg
1 cup sour cream
1 teaspoon vanilla extract
1/4 teaspoon nutmeg

1   21-ounce can apple pie filling
1 unbaked 9-inch pie shell
1/3 cup sugar
1/3 cup flour
1 teaspoon cinnamon
1/4 cup butter

- Sift 3/4 cup sugar and 2 tablespoons flour into bowl. Add egg, sour cream, vanilla and nutmeg; mix until smooth.
- Stir in pie filling. Pour into pie shell.
- Bake at 400 degrees for 30 minutes.
- Combine 1/3 cup sugar, 1/3 cup flour, cinnamon and butter in small bowl; mix until crumbly. Sprinkle over pie.
- Bake for 10 minutes longer.
- Yield: 8 servings.

Approx Per Serving: Cal 436; Prot 4 g; Carbo 62 g; Fiber 2 g; T Fat 20 g; 40% Calories from Fat; Chol 55 mg; Sod 233 mg.

Jerry Wade, **South Central Region**
GFWC—Kachina Woman's Club, Phoenix AZ

MICHIGAN APPLE STREUDEL PIE

5 to 7 apples, peeled, cored
1/2 cup sugar
1 teaspoon cinnamon
1 unbaked 9-inch pie shell

1/2 cup sugar
3/4 cup flour
1/3 cup margarine

- Cut each peeled apple into eighths. Combine with 1/2 cup sugar and cinnamon in bowl; toss to coat. Place in pie shell.
- Mix 1/2 cup sugar, flour and margarine in small bowl until crumbly. Sprinkle mixture over apples.
- Bake at 400 degrees for 40 to 45 minutes or until golden brown.
- Yield: 8 servings.

Approx Per Serving: Cal 382; Prot 3 g; Carbo 60 g; Fiber 3 g; T Fat 16 g; 36% Calories from Fat; Chol 0 mg; Sod 227 mg.

Gloria Downhour, **Great Lakes Region**
GFWC-MI President, Mt. Pleasant MI

AVOCADO-LIME PIE

16 graham crackers, crushed
1/2 cup melted butter
1 9-ounce can crushed pineapple
3 tablespoons lime juice
1 3-ounce package lime gelatin

1 large ripe avocado, mashed
6 ounces cream cheese, softened
1/4 teaspoon salt
1 cup whipping cream, whipped

- Mix graham cracker crumbs and melted butter in bowl. Press over bottom and side of pie plate.
- Bake at 375 degrees for 10 minutes.
- Drain pineapple, reserving syrup. Combine reserved syrup, lime juice and enough boiling water to measure 2 cups. Dissolve gelatin in hot liquid in large bowl. Chill until syrupy, stirring occasionally.
- Beat avocado, cream cheese and salt in mixer bowl until smooth. Stir in drained pineapple. Add to gelatin; mix well. Fold in 1/2 cup whipped cream. Pour into prepared pie plate.
- Chill until firm. Garnish with remaining whipped cream.
- Yield: 8 servings.

Approx Per Serving: Cal 445; Prot 5 g; Carbo 30 g; Fiber 3 g; T Fat 35 g; 69% Calories from Fat; Chol 95 mg; Sod 360 mg.

Grace J. Johnston, **Southern Region**
GFWC—Lake Wales Woman's Club, Inc., Lake Wales FL

1991—GFWC led international letter-writing campaign for women and children seeking peaceful resolution to the crisis in the Persian Gulf.

EASY BUTTERMILK PIE

3 eggs, beaten
1 tablespoon flour
1 teaspoon vanilla extract
1¹/₂ cups sugar

¹/₂ cup buttermilk
6 tablespoons melted margarine
1 unbaked 9-inch pie shell

- Combine eggs, flour, vanilla, sugar, buttermilk and margarine in bowl; mix well. Pour into pie shell.
- Bake at 415 degrees for 20 minutes. Reduce oven temperature to 350 degrees. Bake until knife inserted in center comes out clean.
- Yield: 8 servings.

Approx Per Serving: Cal 373; Prot 4 g; Carbo 49 g; Fiber <1 g; T Fat 18 g;
44% Calories from Fat; Chol 80 mg; Sod 281 mg.

*Tempa G. Endicott, **Southeastern Region***
GFWC—Midway Woman's Club, Midway KY

CHESS PIE

¹/₂ cup melted butter
1 tablespoon cornmeal
1 cup sugar
1¹/₂ tablespoons flour
¹/₂ teaspoon (or more) nutmeg
3 egg yolks
¹/₂ cup milk

1 teaspoon vanilla extract
1 unbaked 9-inch pie shell
3 egg whites
¹/₄ teaspoon cream of tartar
¹/₈ teaspoon salt
9 tablespoons sugar
¹/₂ teaspoon vanilla extract

- Combine first 5 ingredients in bowl; mix well. Blend in egg yolks 1 at a time. Add milk and 1 teaspoon vanilla; blend well. Pour into pie shell.
- Bake at 450 degrees for 5 minutes or until crust sets. Reduce oven temperature setting to 325 degrees, opening oven door to cool down. Bake for 30 to 45 minutes or until top is brown. Cool slightly.
- Beat egg whites in mixer bowl until foamy. Add cream of tartar and salt. Beat until soft peaks form. Add 9 tablespoons sugar 1 tablespoon at a time, beating until stiff peaks form. Beat in ¹/₂ teaspoon vanilla. Spread over pie, sealing to edge.
- Bake at 375 degrees for 10 minutes or until brown.
- Let pie stand in oven with door ajar until completely cool. This will keep meringue from falling or beading.
- Yield: 8 servings.

Approx Per Serving: Cal 413; Prot 5 g; Carbo 52 g; Fiber 1 g; T Fat 22 g;
46% Calories from Fat; Chol 113 mg; Sod 297 mg.

*Joyce R. Ware, **Southeastern Region***
GFWC—Sparta Woman's Club, Sparta TN

CHOCOLATE MARBLED RUM PIE

1/2 cup sugar
1 tablespoon unflavored gelatin
Salt to taste
1 cup milk
2 egg yolks
1 cup semisweet chocolate chips

5 tablespoons rum
2 egg whites
1 cup whipping cream
1 teaspoon vanilla extract
1 baked 9-inch pie shell

- Combine sugar, gelatin and salt in medium saucepan. Add milk and egg yolks; mix well. Cook over low heat until thickened, stirring constantly. Remove from heat.
- Add chocolate chips; stir until melted. Blend in rum. Chill until partially set.
- Beat egg whites until soft peaks form. Fold into chocolate mixture gently.
- Whip cream with vanilla. Alternate layers of whipped cream and chocolate mixture in pie shell, ending with whipped cream. Swirl through layers with knife to marbleize. Chill until firm.
- Yield: 8 servings.

Approx Per Serving: Cal 432; Prot 6 g; Carbo 37 g; Fiber 1 g; T Fat 29 g;
60% Calories from Fat; Chol 98 mg; Sod 180 mg.

*Christiane Engler, **Mississippi Valley Region***
GFWC—Federated Women's Club, Farmington MO

TIN-ROOF FUDGE PIE

1 unbaked 9-inch pie shell
2 ounces milk chocolate
1 tablespoon margarine
20 caramels
1/3 cup whipping cream
1 1/2 cups Spanish peanuts
8 ounces dark chocolate

2 tablespoons margarine
1 cup whipping cream
2 teaspoons vanilla extract
5 caramels
3 tablespoons whipping cream
1 teaspoon margarine

- Bake pie shell at 450 degrees for 9 to 11 minutes or until golden brown. Cool.
- Melt milk chocolate with 1 tablespoon margarine in small saucepan over low heat, stirring until smooth. Spread over crust. Chill until firm. Melt 20 caramels with 1/3 cup whipping cream in saucepan over low heat, stirring constantly until smooth. Stir in peanuts. Spoon over chocolate-lined pie crust. Cool.
- Melt dark chocolate with 2 tablespoons margarine in saucepan over low heat, stirring until smooth. Let stand for 10 minutes.
- Whip 1 cup whipping cream with vanilla until soft peaks form. Fold into chocolate mixture. Spread over peanut layer.
- Chill for 2 hours. Melt remaining 5 caramels with 3 tablespoons whipping cream and 1 teaspoon margarine in small saucepan, stirring until smooth. Drizzle over pie.
- Yield: 8 servings.

Approx Per Serving: Cal 745; Prot 12 g; Carbo 53 g; Fiber 4 g; T Fat 57 g;
66% Calories from Fat; Chol 64 mg; Sod 277 mg.

*Kim Potter, **Middle Atlantic Region***
GFWC—Century Club, Wilkins Township PA

SURPRISE PIE

1 cup cranberries
1 apple, peeled, cored
4 ounces crushed pineapple, drained
1/2 cup packed brown sugar
1/2 cup sugar

1 teaspoon grated orange rind
1/4 teaspoon nutmeg
1/2 teaspoon cinnamon
1 2-crust package All Ready pie crusts
5 cups sliced peeled apples

- Combine first 8 ingredients in food processor. Process until well mixed.
- Spread half the mixture evenly over bottom of pastry-lined 9-inch pie plate. Arrange apple slices in prepared pie plate. Spread remaining cranberry mixture over apples.
- Top with remaining pie pastry, sealing edge and cutting vents.
- Bake at 400 degrees for 15 minutes. Cover edge with foil to prevent excessive browning. Bake for 35 to 40 minutes longer or until brown.
- Yield: 8 servings.

Approx Per Serving: Cal 400; Prot 3 g; Carbo 65 g; Fiber 3 g; T Fat 15 g;
34% Calories from Fat; Chol 0 mg; Sod 284 mg.

*Christine Curtis, **New England Region***
GFWC—Bethel Women's Club, Bethel CT

GRAPE PIE

3 cups Concord grapes
1 cup sugar
3 tablespoons flour
1 tablespoon butter
1 tablespoon lemon juice

1 unbaked 9-inch pie shell
1 cup flour
1/2 cup sugar
1/4 cup melted butter

- Rinse, drain and stem grapes. Squeeze pulp from skins into saucepan; reserve skins. Simmer pulp for 5 minutes; do not add water. Press hot pulp through sieve to remove seed.
- Combine strained pulp with reserved skins in bowl. Stir in mixture of 1 cup sugar and 3 tablespoons flour. Blend 1 tablespoon butter with lemon juice. Stir into grape mixture.
- Pour into pie shell. Combine 1 cup flour, 1/2 cup sugar and 1/4 melted butter in small bowl; mix until crumbly. Sprinkle over grape mixture.
- Bake at 350 degrees for 40 minutes.
- Yield: 8 servings.

Approx Per Serving: Cal 431; Prot 4 g; Carbo 72 g; Fiber 2 g; T Fat 15 g;
31% Calories from Fat; Chol 19 mg; Sod 200 mg.

*Dorothy Hughes, **Southeastern Region***
GFWC—Harpers Ferry Woman's Club, Harpers Ferry WV

GREEN TOMATO AND APPLE PIE

2 cups chopped apples
1½ cups chopped green tomatoes
1 teaspoon cinnamon
¼ teaspoon cloves
¼ teaspoon allspice
¼ teaspoon nutmeg

½ cup raisins, cooked
1 tablespoon vinegar
1 cup sugar
1 recipe 2-crust pie pastry
1 tablespoon butter

- Combine apples, green tomatoes, spices, raisins, vinegar and sugar in large bowl; mix well.
- Pour into pastry-lined 9-inch pie plate. Dot with butter. Top with remaining pie pastry, sealing edge and cutting vents.
- Bake at 450 degrees for 15 minutes. Reduce oven temperature to 375 degrees. Bake for 35 minutes longer.
- This pie tastes similar to mincemeat pie.
- Yield: 6 servings.

Approx Per Serving: Cal 492; Prot 4 g; Carbo 76 g; Fiber 3 g; T Fat 20 g; 36% Calories from Fat; Chol 5 mg; Sod 391 mg.

Betty Garman, Mississippi Valley Region
GFWC—Estudie Club, Kiowa KS

SLICED GREEN TOMATO PIE

6 to 8 green tomatoes
1½ cups sugar
3 tablespoons flour
1 tablespoon cinnamon

1 recipe 2-crust pie pastry
1 tablespoon butter
1 tablespoon sugar

- Slice green tomatoes to yield about 4 cups very thin slices. Combine with 1½ cups sugar, flour and cinnamon in bowl; mix gently.
- Arrange slices in pastry-lined 9-inch pie plate. Dot with butter. Top with remaining pastry, sealing edge and cutting vents. Sprinkle remaining 1 tablespoon sugar over top.
- Bake at 425 degrees for 35 to 45 minutes or until golden brown.
- This will taste like apple pie and really fool your family.
- Yield: 8 servings.

Approx Per Serving: Cal 408; Prot 4 g; Carbo 66 g; Fiber 1 g; T Fat 15 g; 33% Calories from Fat; Chol 4 mg; Sod 305 mg.

Barbara Gripp, Mississippi Valley Region
GFWC—Stratford Woman's Club, Lehigh IA

1991—*GFWC Headquarters designated a National Historic Landmark by the National Park Service. The building's notable features include murals painted by Albert Herter.*

MONTANA HUCKLEBERRY PIE

3 eggs, separated
1 teaspoon lemon juice
1 recipe Classic Flaky Pie Pastry
1 cup sugar
1/2 cup flour

3 cups Montana huckleberries
1 1/2 cups low-fat buttermilk
4 tablespoons lemon juice
10 tablespoons sugar

- Mix egg whites with 1 teaspoon lemon juice and set aside. Beat egg yolks and set aside.
- Line pie plate with Classic Flaky Pie Pastry, shaping and fluting 1/2-inch edge. Brush with beaten egg yolks. Mix 1 cup sugar and 1/2 cup flour in bowl. Sprinkle about 2 tablespoons mixture over bottom of prepared pie plate. Add 2 3/4 cups huckleberries.
- Combine remaining flour mixture with remaining egg yolks, buttermilk and 3 tablespoons lemon juice in bowl; mix well. Pour over huckleberries.
- Bake at 425 degrees for 45 minutes.
- Bring remaining 1/4 cup huckleberries, 1 tablespoon lemon juice and 4 tablespoons sugar to a boil in saucepan; reduce heat. Simmer for 10 minutes. Let stand until cool.
- Beat egg whites mixture in mixer bowl until foamy. Add 6 tablespoons sugar gradually, beating constantly until stiff peaks form. Spread meringue over hot pie, sealing to edge. Drizzle huckleberry sauce over meringue; swirl slightly.
- Reduce oven temperature to 350 degrees. Bake pie for 15 minutes longer or until meringue is lightly browned.
- Cool on wire rack away from drafts.
- Yield: 6 servings.

Approx Per Serving: Cal 602; Prot 10 g; Carbo 95 g; Fiber 3 g; T Fat 21 g;
31% Calories from Fat; Chol 106 mg; Sod 295 mg.
Nutritional information includes pastry.

CLASSIC FLAKY PIE PASTRY

1 1/3 cups flour
1/2 teaspoon salt
1/2 cup shortening

3 tablespoons plus 1 teaspoon cold water

- Mix flour with salt in bowl. Cut in shortening until crumbly.
- Sprinkle with water 1 spoonful at a time, tossing with fork until mixture clings together. Shape into 5 or 6-inch disc.
- Roll on floured surface into circle 1 inch larger than inverted pie plate. Fold into fourths; fit into pie plate.
- Yield: 6 servings.

Helen Kleffner, **Western Region**
GFWC—Canton Woman's Club, Townsend MT

PONTE VEDRA GUAVA CREME DE FRUIT PIE

1 14-ounce can sweetened condensed
   milk
1 cup low-fat plain yogurt
2/3 cup guava paste (Iberia)
1/3 cup lemon juice
2 cups crumbled coconut macaroons
1/4 cup margarine, softened
8 ounces whipped topping

- Combine condensed milk, yogurt, guava paste and lemon juice in food processor. Process until smooth.
- Mix macaroon crumbs with margarine in bowl. Press over bottom and side of 9-inch pie plate. Pour in guava mixture.
- Freeze until firm.
- Top with whipped topping.
- May substitute gingersnap crumbs for macaroon crumbs.
- Yield: 8 servings.

Approx Per Serving: Cal 826; Prot 11 g; Carbo 107 g; Fiber <1 g; T Fat 42 g;
44% Calories from Fat; Chol 19 mg; Sod 194 mg.

Gwen Holborn, ***Southern Region***
GFWC—The Ponte Vedra Woman's Club, Ponte Vedra Beach FL

KEY LIME CHIFFON PIE

1 3-ounce package lime gelatin
1 cup boiling water
1/2 cup fresh lime juice
1 teaspoon grated lime rind
2 egg yolks
1 14-ounce can sweetened condensed
   milk
2 egg whites, stiffly beaten
8 ounces whipped topping
1 10-ounce graham cracker pie shell

- Dissolve gelatin in boiling water in small bowl. Add lime juice and grated lime rind. Cool to lukewarm.
- Beat egg yolks in mixer bowl. Blend in gelatin and condensed milk gradually. Chill until thickened.
- Fold in stiffly beaten egg whites and half the whipped topping. Pour into pie shell. Chill until firm.
- Spread remaining whipped topping over top. Garnish with sprinkle of additional lime rind.
- Yield: 8 servings.

Approx Per Serving: Cal 540; Prot 9 g; Carbo 73 g; Fiber 1 g; T Fat 25 g;
41% Calories from Fat; Chol 70 mg; Sod 384 mg.

Mrs. Douglas McNealy, ***South Central Region***
GFWC—Rocksprings Woman's Club, Rocksprings TX

GFWC
Volunteer

1992—*In response to Hurricane Andrew, the DeQuincy Study Club of Louisiana launched "Operation School Tools" in which children from unharmed schools donated supplies to those schools devastated by the storm.*

CREAM CHEESE-KEY LIME PIE

8 ounces cream cheese, softened
1   14-ounce can sweetened condensed
      milk
12 ounces whipped topping

1 cup lime juice
Green food coloring to taste
1 baked 9-inch pie shell

- Blend cream cheese and condensed milk in bowl until smooth. Add whipped topping; mix well.
- Add lime juice and food coloring; mix quickly before mixture thickens. Pour into pie shell.
- Chill for several hours.
- Yield: 8 servings.

Approx Per Serving: Cal 514; Prot 8 g; Carbo 50 g; Fiber 1 g; T Fat 33 g;
56% Calories from Fat; Chol 48 mg; Sod 295 mg.

Treva Kintner, **Southern Region**
GFWC—Kissimmee Woman's Club, Kissimmee FL

SOUTHERN BUTTERMILK-LEMON PIE

2 cups buttermilk
2 cups sugar
3 egg yolks, beaten
1/2 cup fresh lemon juice
1 tablespoon grated lemon rind

3 tablespoons (heaping) cornstarch
1 baked 9-inch pie shell
3 egg whites
1/2 teaspoon cream of tartar
3 tablespoons sugar

- Combine first 6 ingredients in glass bowl; mix well.
- Microwave on High for 10 to 12 minutes or until thickened, stirring occasionally. Pour into pie shell.
- Beat egg whites with cream of tartar in mixer bowl until soft peaks form. Add 3 tablespoons sugar gradually, beating constantly until stiff peaks form. Spread over top, sealing to edge.
- Bake at 400 degrees until meringue is lightly browned.
- Chill for 3 hours or longer.
- May omit meringue and top with whipped topping.
- Yield: 8 servings.

Approx Per Serving: Cal 393; Prot 6 g; Carbo 72 g; Fiber 1 g; T Fat 10 g;
23% Calories from Fat; Chol 82 mg; Sod 225 mg.

Jody Zakany, **Southern Region**
GFWC—Frostproof Woman's Club, Frostproof FL

1993—GFWC assisted UNICEF with Somalia Famine Relief fund-raising effort.

SISTER JENNY'S SHAKER LEMON PIE

1¹/₂ cups sugar
¹/₄ teaspoon salt
³/₄ cup flour
2 cups boiling water
4 egg yolks, at room temperature
Juice and grated rind of 2 lemons
1 tablespoon butter

1 baked 9-inch pie shell
4 egg whites
¹/₄ teaspoon salt
¹/₄ teaspoon cream of tartar
²/₃ cup sugar
2 lemons, thinly sliced
¹/₄ cup sugar

- Combine first 3 ingredients in double boiler over hot water or in saucepan over low heat. Stir in boiling water gradually. Cook until thickened, stirring constantly.
- Pour hot mixture in fine stream into beaten egg yolks, stirring vigorously constantly. Add lemon juice, lemon rind and butter. Pour into double boiler. Cook over hot water for 5 to 8 minutes or until thickened, stirring constantly.
- Pour into pie shell. Chill in refrigerator.
- Beat egg whites with salt and cream of tartar in mixer bowl until soft peaks form. Add ²/₃ cup sugar gradually, beating until stiff peaks form. Spread over pie, sealing to edge.
- Sprinkle lemon slices with ¹/₄ cup sugar. Arrange lemon slices slightly overlapping over meringue.
- Bake at 425 degrees for 3 to 5 minutes or until meringue is lightly browned.
- Yield: 8 servings.

Approx Per Serving: Cal 449; Prot 6 g; Carbo 82 g; Fiber 1 g; T Fat 12 g;
23% Calories from Fat; Chol 110 mg; Sod 314 mg.

Margaret Geibel, **Middle Atlantic Region**
GFWC—Lebanon Valley Women's Club, Lebanon Springs NY

PLANTATION MACAROON PIE

6 tablespoons melted margarine
1¹/₃ cups sugar
2 tablespoons flour
3 eggs

1 12-ounce can evaporated milk
1 3¹/₂-ounce can coconut
1 teaspoon vanilla extract

- Combine margarine, sugar and flour in bowl; mix well.
- Add eggs, evaporated milk, coconut and vanilla; mix well.
- Pour into greased and floured deep-dish pie plate.
- Bake at 350 degrees for 35 to 40 minutes or until firm.
- May use egg substitute, evaporated skim milk and diet margarine for a low-fat tasty version of this pie.
- Yield: 8 servings.

Approx Per Serving: Cal 354; Prot 6 g; Carbo 44 g; Fiber 2 g; T Fat 18 g;
45% Calories from Fat; Chol 92 mg; Sod 175 mg.

Yolanda P. Payne, **Southern Region**
GFWC—Eliza Lucas Woman's Club, Mt. Pleasant SC

AUNT ELEANOR'S MAPLE-NUT PIE

3 eggs
3/4 cup sugar
3/4 cup Vermont maple syrup
2 tablespoons melted butter

1/8 teaspoon salt
1 tablespoon vinegar
1 cup pecans
1 unbaked 9-inch pie shell

- Beat eggs in large bowl. Stir in sugar gradually. Blend in maple syrup, butter, salt and vinegar.
- Stir in pecans. Pour into pie shell.
- Bake at 450 degrees for 10 minutes.
- Reduce oven temperature to 350 degrees; do not open oven door.
- Bake for 30 to 35 minutes longer or until set.
- Cool completely before serving.
- Yield: 8 servings.

Approx Per Serving: Cal 414; Prot 5 g; Carbo 51 g; Fiber 1 g; T Fat 23 g;
48% Calories from Fat; Chol 88 mg; Sod 226 mg.

Barbara Jean Barker, **New England Region**
GFWC—Poultney Woman's Club, Poultney VT

OLD-FASHIONED MOCK MINCEMEAT PIE

1 cup chopped peeled apples
2 cups sugar
1 cup bread cubes
1 tablespoon (or more) vinegar
1 cup hot water
1 cup raisins

1 egg, beaten
1/4 cup butter, softened
2 teaspoons cinnamon
1/2 teaspoon nutmeg
1 recipe 2-crust pie pastry

- Combine apples, sugar and bread in bowl. Pour desired amount of vinegar into 1-cup measure. Add enough cold water to measure 1 cup. Add to apple mixture.
- Add 1 cup hot water, raisins, egg, butter and spices; mix well.
- Pour into pastry-lined deep-dish pie plate. Top with remaining pastry, sealing edge and cutting vents.
- Bake at 450 degrees for 15 minutes. Reduce oven temperature to 350 degrees.
- Bake for 45 minutes longer or until brown.
- Yield: 8 servings.

Approx Per Serving: Cal 739; Prot 7 g; Carbo 106 g; Fiber 3 g; T Fat 34 g;
40% Calories from Fat; Chol 42 mg; Sod 630 mg.

Mary L. Sirbu, **Great Lakes Region**
GFWC—The Marion B. Roth Club, Poland OH

AMAZING PEANUT PIE

24 butter crackers, finely crushed
1/2 cup sugar
3/4 cup chopped roasted peanuts
3 egg whites
1/4 teaspoon cream of tartar

1/2 cup sugar
1 teaspoon vanilla extract
1 cup whipping cream, whipped
1/4 cup chopped roasted peanuts

- Combine first 3 ingredients in bowl; mix well and set aside.
- Beat egg whites with cream of tartar in mixer bowl until soft peaks form. Add 1/2 cup sugar gradually, beating constantly until stiff peaks form. Beat in vanilla.
- Fold in crumb mixture gently. Spread in greased pie plate.
- Bake at 350 degrees for 20 to 25 minutes or until light brown. Let stand until cool.
- Top with whipped cream; sprinkle with remaining 1/4 cup peanuts.
- Chill for 3 to 4 hours.
- Yield: 8 servings.

Approx Per Serving: Cal 336; Prot 6 g; Carbo 35 g; Fiber 1 g; T Fat 21 g; 53% Calories from Fat; Chol 41 mg; Sod 123 mg.

Harriett E. Downs, **Southern Region**
GFWC—Williston Woman's Club, Williston FL

ALABAMA PECAN PIE

1/2 cup semisweet chocolate chips
1 unbaked 9-inch pie shell
2 eggs
1/2 cup sugar
3/4 cup dark corn syrup
1/4 teaspoon salt

1/4 cup melted margarine
2 tablespoons bourbon
1 cup pecan halves
1 cup whipping cream
2 tablespoons confectioners' sugar
1/4 cup chopped pecans

- Sprinkle chocolate chips evenly over bottom of unbaked pie shell. Place in freezer for 10 minutes.
- Beat eggs in mixer bowl. Add sugar, corn syrup, salt, margarine and bourbon; beat until blended. Pour over chocolate chips. Arrange pecan halves over filling.
- Bake at 350 degrees for 50 to 55 minutes or just until set. Cool on wire rack.
- Whip cream with confectioners' sugar. Swirl over pie. Top with chopped pecans.
- Yield: 8 servings.

Approx Per Serving: Cal 606; Prot 5 g; Carbo 58 g; Fiber 2 g; T Fat 41 g; 60% Calories from Fat; Chol 94 mg; Sod 322 mg.

Betty B. Edwards, **Southern Region**
GFWC—Athenian Study Club—Piedmont, Jacksonville AL

NEW ORLEANS PECAN PIE

3 egg yolks, beaten
1 cup sour cream
1 cup sugar
¼ cup cornstarch
¼ teaspoon grated lemon rind

Salt to taste
1 baked 9-inch pie shell
3 egg whites
1 cup packed brown sugar
1 cup chopped pecans

- Combine first 6 ingredients in top of double boiler over boiling water; mix well.
- Cook until thickened, stirring constantly. Pour into pie shell.
- Beat egg whites in mixer bowl until soft peaks form. Add brown sugar gradually, beating constantly until stiff peaks form.
- Fold in pecans gently. Spread over filling, sealing to edge.
- Bake at 425 degrees until light brown.
- Chill for several hours before serving.
- May substitute ¼ teaspoon lemon extract for lemon rind.
- Yield: 8 servings.

Approx Per Serving: Cal 542; Prot 6 g; Carbo 76 g; Fiber 1 g; T Fat 26 g;
42% Calories from Fat; Chol 93 mg; Sod 191 mg.

*Laura Cook, **Southeastern Region***
GFWC—Clinton Woman's Club, Clinton NC

PLUM PIE

1 cup (about) cut up plums
1 unbaked 9-inch pie shell
1 cup sugar

3 tablespoons flour
1 cup whipping cream
Cinnamon-sugar to taste

- Place enough plums in pie shell to cover bottom of shell.
- Mix sugar and flour in bowl. Add whipping cream; mix well. Pour over plums. Sprinkle with cinnamon-sugar.
- Bake at 350 degrees for 40 minutes or until set.
- Wild plums are especially good for this pie but any kind will work. May also use peaches.
- Yield: 8 servings.

Approx Per Serving: Cal 333; Prot 2 g; Carbo 41 g; Fiber 1 g; T Fat 19 g;
49% Calories from Fat; Chol 41 mg; Sod 149 mg.

*Helen Kill, **Mississippi Valley Region***
GFWC—The Students Club of Morris, Morris MN

PRALINE-RAISIN PIE

1/2 cup sugar
1/8 teaspoon salt
1 tablespoon flour
1 tablespoon lemon juice
1 egg, beaten
2 cups raisins

2/3 cup buttermilk
1 unbaked 9-inch pie shell
1/2 cup packed brown sugar
1/4 cup butter, softened
1/3 cup flour
1/2 cup finely chopped pecans

- Combine first 7 ingredients in bowl; mix well. Pour into pie shell.
- Combine brown sugar, butter, 1/3 cup flour and pecans in bowl; mix until crumbly. Sprinkle over raisin mixture.
- Bake at 425 degrees for 15 minutes. Reduce oven temperature to 350 degrees.
- Bake for 25 to 30 minutes longer.
- Yield: 8 servings.

Approx Per Serving: Cal 490; Prot 5 g; Carbo 79 g; Fiber 4 g; T Fat 19 g; 34% Calories from Fat; Chol 43 mg; Sod 262 mg.

Joy A. Roberts, **South Central Region**
GFWC—Amity Club, Moran TX

PRALINE PIE

3 egg whites
1/2 teaspoon baking powder
1 cup sugar
1 teaspoon vanilla extract

20 butter crackers, crushed
3/4 cup chopped pecans
8 ounces whipped topping

- Beat egg whites with baking powder in mixer bowl until stiff. Add sugar gradually, beating until very stiff. Beat in vanilla.
- Fold in cracker crumbs and pecans gently. Pour into well greased 9-inch pie plate.
- Bake at 350 degrees for 30 minutes.
- Serve with whipped topping.
- Yield: 10 servings.

Approx Per Serving: Cal 244; Prot 2 g; Carbo 31 g; Fiber 1 g; T Fat 14 g; 48% Calories from Fat; Chol 0 mg; Sod 98 mg.

Pam Stracener, **South Central Region**
GFWC—Bluebonnet Literary Club, Gilmer TX

FRESH STRAWBERRY PIE

1¹/₄ cups flour
¹/₂ teaspoon salt
¹/₃ cup shortening
3 to 4 tablespoons cold water
6 cups fresh strawberries

1 cup water
¹/₂ cup sugar
3 tablespoons cornstarch
1 3-ounce package wild strawberry gelatin

- Mix flour and salt in bowl. Cut in shortening until crumbly. Sprinkle with cold water, tossing until mixture clings together. Roll and fit into pie shell, fluting edge.
- Bake at 450 degrees for 10 to 12 minutes or until golden brown. Cool.
- Crush 1 cup of the small strawberries. Cut remaining strawberries into halves.
- Combine crushed strawberries and 1 cup water in small saucepan. Bring to a boil. Simmer for 2 minutes. Press through sieve.
- Blend sieved strawberries, sugar, cornstarch and gelatin in saucepan. Cook over medium heat until thickened and clear, stirring constantly.
- Spread about ¹/₄ cup mixture over bottom and side of pie shell. Alternate layers of strawberries and sauce in pie shell ending with sauce. Chill for 3 to 4 hours.
- Garnish with whipped topping.
- Yield: 6 servings.

Approx Per Serving: Cal 372; Prot 5 g; Carbo 63 g; Fiber 5 g; T Fat 12 g;
29% Calories from Fat; Chol 0 mg; Sod 226 mg.

*Gloria J. G. Gardner, **Great Lakes Region***
GFWC—Intermediate Study Club, Belleville MI

SWEET POTATO DELIGHT PIE

20 butter crackers, crushed
1 cup chopped pecans
2 egg whites
¹/₄ teaspoon cream of tartar
³/₄ cup sugar
2 cups mashed sweet potatoes

1 egg, slightly beaten
¹/₃ cup packed brown sugar
¹/₃ cup butter
¹/₈ teaspoon orange extract
¹/₈ teaspoon nutmeg

- Mix cracker crumbs and pecans in bowl. Set aside.
- Beat egg whites with cream of tartar in mixer bowl until soft peaks form. Add sugar gradually, beating constantly until stiff peaks form. Fold in pecan mixture gently. Pat over bottom and side of buttered 9-inch pie plate.
- Bake at 300 degrees for 30 minutes. Turn off oven. Let stand in oven with door ajar for 15 minutes longer.
- Combine sweet potatoes and remaining ingredients in top of double boiler over hot water. Cook until thickened, stirring frequently. Let stand until cool. Pour into cooled meringue shell. Garnish with whipped topping and cherries.
- Yield: 8 servings.

Approx Per Serving: Cal 412; Prot 4 g; Carbo 57 g; Fiber 3 g; T Fat 21 g;
44% Calories from Fat; Chol 47 mg; Sod 172 mg.

*Shirley Meche, **South Central Region***
GFWC—Unique Club, Opelousas LA

NUTRITIONAL GUIDELINES,

INDEX

&

ORDER INFORMATION

NUTRITIONAL GUIDELINES

The editors have attempted to present these family recipes in a form that allows approximate nutritional values to be computed. Persons with dietary or health problems or whose diets require close monitoring should not rely solely on the nutritional information provided. They should consult their physicians or a registered dietitian for specific information.

Abbreviations for Nutritional Profile

Cal — Calories
Prot — Protein
Carbo — Carbohydrates

Dietary Fiber — Fiber
T Fat — Total Fat
Chol — Cholesterol

Sod — Sodium
gr — gram
mg — milligrams

Nutritional information for these recipes is computed from information derived from many sources, including materials supplied by the United States Department of Agriculture, computer databanks and journals in which the information is assumed to be in the public domain. However, many specialty items, new products and processed foods may not be available from these sources or may vary from the average values used in these profiles. More information on new and/or specific products may be obtained by reading the nutrient labels. Unless otherwise specified, the nutritional profile of these recipes is based on all measurements being level.

- **Artificial sweeteners** vary in use and strength so should be used "to taste," using the recipe ingredients as a guideline. Sweeteners using aspartame (NutraSweet and Equal) should not be used as a sweetener in recipes involving prolonged heating which reduces the sweet taste. For further information, refer to package information.
- **Alcoholic ingredients** have been analyzed for the basic ingredients, although cooking causes the evaporation of alcohol thus decreasing caloric content.
- **Buttermilk**, **sour cream** and **yogurt** are the types available commercially.
- **Cake mixes** which are prepared using package directions include 3 eggs and ½ cup oil.
- **Chicken**, cooked for boning and chopping, has been roasted; this method yields the lowest caloric values.
- **Cottage cheese** is cream-style with 4.2% creaming mixture. Dry-curd cottage cheese has no creaming mixture.
- **Eggs** are all large. To avoid raw eggs that may carry salmonella as in eggnog or 6-week muffin batter, use an equivalent amount of commercial egg substitute.
- **Flour** is unsifted all-purpose flour.
- **Garnishes**, serving suggestions and other optional additions and variations are not included in the profile.
- **Margarine** and **butter** are regular, not whipped or presoftened.
- **Milk** is whole milk, 3.5% butterfat. Lowfat milk is 1% butterfat. Evaporated milk is whole milk with 60% of the water removed.
- **Oil** is any type of vegetable cooking oil. Shortening is hydrogenated vegetable shortening.
- **Salt** and other ingredients to taste as noted in the ingredients have not been included in the nutritional profile.
- If a choice of ingredients has been given, the nutritional profile information reflects the first option. If a choice of amounts has been given, the nutritional profile reflects the greater amount.

Index

AMERICAN BUFFET

You may order additional copies of *American Buffet* for the price of
$14.95 each plus $2.00 postage and handling per book ordered.
Mail to:

General Federation of Women's Clubs
1734 N Street, N.W.
Washington, D.C. 20036-2990

Make checks payable to:
General Federation of Women's Clubs

Please send me _____ copies of **American Buffet**.   @ $14.95 each $ _____
Postage and Handling   @ $ 2.00 each $ _____
                                              Total $ _____

Please Print:

Name_____

Address_____

City/State/Zip _____

Telephone No. _____

(in case we have questions)

General Federation of Women's Clubs
1734 N Street, N.W.
Washington, D.C. 20036-2990

Make checks payable to:
General Federation of Women's Clubs

Please send me _____ copies of **American Buffet**.   @ $14.95 each $ _____
Postage and Handling   @ $ 2.00 each $ _____
                                              Total $ _____

Please Print:

Name_____

Address_____

City/State/Zip _____

Telephone No. _____

(in case we have questions)

ACKNOWLEDGEMENTS

GFWC gratefully acknowledges the contribution of the following to the publication of this cookbook:

GFWC Executive Committee, 1992–94

Ann L. Holland, International President
Jeannine C. Faubion, President-elect
Faye Z. Dissinger, First Vice President
Maxine S. Scarbro, Second Vice President
Shelby P. Hamlett, Recording Secretary
Carol Estes Smith, Treasurer
Roberta A. Dyrsten, Director of Junior Clubs

Marianne Maynard, GFWC Fund Raising Chairman, 1992–94
Judith Walter Maggrett, GFWC Executive Director
Laurie Cooper, Program Coordinator
Deborah Koehle, Director of Publications
Sally Kranz, Public Relations Director
Cynthia Swanson, GFWC Women's History and Resource Center Director
Barbara Engelhardt, Proofreader

Members of the General Federation of Women's Clubs
who generously contributed recipes and support.